Sweet Tooth

Also by Kate Hopkins

99 Drams of Whiskey

Sweet Tooth

The Bittersweet History of Candy

Kate Hopkins

St. Martin's Press

New York

www.stmartins.com

Library of Congress Cataloging-in-Publication Data

Hopkins, Kate.
   Sweet tooth : the bittersweet history of candy / Kate Hopkins.—1st ed.
      p. cm.
   Includes bibliographical references.
   ISBN 978-0-312-66810-5 (hbk.)
   ISBN 978-1-250-01119-0 (e-book)
  1. Candy—History.   2. Candy industry—History.   I. Title.
  TX784.H67 2012
  641.85'3—dc23

                                    2012009741

First Edition: May 2012

10 9 8 7 6 5 4 3 2 1

Contents

Sweet Tooth

Chapter 1

The Innocence of Candy

• • • • • • • • • • • •

It's odd, the memories that stay with you. I can recall being about four years old, and my parents had taken the family to a diner that was tucked back in a strip mall in the blue-collar town of Butler, Pennsylvania. I can remember one of my four siblings creating a bit of a fuss over the lack of hot dogs on the menu. I can remember the cup of coffee that my dad ordered, and the plain ceramic mug in which it was served. I can even remember the pattern of the Formica that surfaced the table.

But the event that makes the day most memorable was that this was the day I first spit out a piece of candy.

The candy itself was a Brach's jelly nougat, a smallish piece of candy that the waitress gave to each of us children while our parents drank coffee and checked the validity of the bill.

The candy perplexed me. The texture of the nougat was soft and gritty, and the jelly pieces stuck in the candy felt oddly out of place. The colors were new to me as well, with the pieces retaining either a matted pink or a dull orange after surviving whatever process the folks at Brach's had inflicted upon them. What fruits they were supposed to represent is likely unknown to all except the people who made these candies.

It was not as if I disliked the piece of candy. It was chock-full of sugar, and thus had an appeal that would raise the eyebrows of most preschoolers and test the patience of the majority of parents out there. But it wasn't chocolate. Nor was it a Life Saver, a marshmallow, or even a candy cane. It was something else.

I spat it out into my hand and looked at it. I reflected for a moment on whether it tasted good, setting aside for the time being the fact that it tasted weird. It did pass the sweetness test, so how bad could it be?

My father, of course, solved the situation, demanding that I stop "playing with my food," not recognizing the moment for what it was. I was tasting nougat for the first time, and I was determining whether it was worth the effort.

It was.

What makes this scene so important in my development was that it was the first time I can remember having a surprising moment with a piece of candy. This was the first time that candy had left me intrigued.

This is what makes that moment so memorable. It wasn't that I mindlessly liked candy. It was the first time that I had formed an educated opinion about food, based on experience and introspection. Not only did I like the nougat, I liked the process that allowed me to reach that conclusion. I vowed right then and there to repeat it as often as possible. I have since had ample opportunity to accomplish this goal.

For the first dozen or so years of my life, candy was the panacea for every trial and tribulation that came my way. If I scraped my knee, my mom would be there with a Tootsie Pop. When I learned I needed glasses, my dad stopped to buy me some Bub's Daddy bubble gum.* After the first day of kindergarten, Mom marked the occasion with Smarties. (These would be the compressed sugar Smarties known in the United States, not the candy-covered chocolates known to Canadians and Brits, which were closer in design to M&M's.) Candy was something that lessened pain and made life a little more tolerable.

But it was more than just that. Candy also made appearances when life was to be celebrated. Easter, Christmas, and Halloween all came with copious amounts of sugary treats. Birthday parties held in the neighborhood ensured that each young guest received a bag of goodies. Trips to the grandparents on my mother's side promised, at the very least, rock candy, but usually something more. My paternal grandmother was *not* a fan of candy, and trips to her house meant little chance of a candy high, though she did have a way with cakes, cookies, and pies, so those of us who equated sugar with love were able to welcome visits to her house without fear.

In short, candy was available in good times and bad. It was the initial mixed message that was fed to my siblings and me. This environment set the table for the first few years of my life. Candy was our ambrosia. We tolerated the healthy meals of fish sticks and broccoli but counted the days to the next holiday or birthday party. Mrs. Paul could take a flying leap for all we cared, but Peter Paul was looked upon with an admiration that left him just behind Jesus and Santa Claus. Along with Dolly Madison, Peter Paul sponsored the several Charlie Brown cartoon specials that were shown throughout the year. Only later

---

* For those who don't remember, Bub's Daddy bubble gum was *the* bubble gum to have before Bubble Yum hit the market a few years later. Coming in flavors that included grape, apple, as well as the classic bubble gum, it was sold in a twelve-inch long tubular shape that was not only delicious but the perfect shape to whip trouble-seeking brothers and sisters who wanted to swipe the gum when they thought you weren't looking.

did I learn that Peter Paul was not a person, but a company, and that the wife of President James Madison had precious little to do with Zingers and Donut Gems.

Then, when I was seven, an amazing thing happened. My father instituted a practice that changed my candy life forever. He offered every one of his children an allowance. Into our greedy, grimy little hands, he placed money, with a promise of more each week. In theory, I'm sure he felt he was teaching us fiscal responsibility. In practice, what we learned was thrift shopping. Why buy a twenty-five-cent Milky Way bar, when for the same price we could buy Lemonheads, Boston Baked Beans, and a three-pack of Lik-m-Aid? Making a big purchase such as a Snickers bar was deemed financially irresponsible.

Economics seemed to filter throughout our family's candy universe. At Halloween, each of us children would go off with our circle of friends, the older children dressed in costumes of their own creations, while we younger kids wore those prepackaged costumes that smelled of polyvinyl and included cheap plastic masks that chafed the face. Not that the masks mattered, because they would fall off when the cheap rubber band broke fifteen minutes after we set off on our routes. After all five of us had completed our neighborhood rounds, we would compare stashes while a parent looked on.

A currency system was soon created, and trades occurred in great haste. Our living room looked like an elementary school version of the New York Stock Exchange as our entire evening's haul littered the floor. Soon, a hierarchy of candy developed. In the middle of the value range sat the York Peppermint Pattie. Those above the York Peppermint Pattie were highly valued: Snickers and Reese's Peanut Butter Cups at the top, with 3 Musketeers and $100,000 bars close behind. Those below the pattie line were trade bait, valued more for the quantity one could collect than for the short-term indulgence of the "quality" candy

Kate's Candy Bag

YORK PEPPERMINT PATTIE

A mint fondant that's encased in dark chocolate, the York Peppermint Pattie was created in York, Pennsylvania (hence, its name), where it was purchased by the Peter Paul company in 1972, which became the property of Cadbury in 1978, which sold the confection and recipe to Hershey in 1988. The York Peppermint Pattie was known primarily for two things: coincidentally having the same name as a character in Charles Schulz's comic strip Peanuts; *and commercials that compared the sensation of eating a York Peppermint Pattie to skiing in the alps or being trapped on a glacier. This I thought strange, for when I bit into a York Peppermint Pattie, I got the sensation of eating chocolate right after brushing my teeth.*

Candy Exchange Rate:
1 York Peppermint Pattie = 1 York Peppermint Pattie

bars that one experienced. These included Chuckles, Good & Plenty, and the worst thing one could get during the Halloween excursions—the dreaded popcorn ball.

We were sure it was no coincidence that those who gave away these lame treats were childless. When popcorn ball givers walked the streets of our neighborhood, children would look upon them as if they were extras from *Village of the Damned*. These miscreants wouldn't escape our suspicion until the next

Halloween, when inevitably they changed from popcorn balls to chocolates or their porch lights were no longer lit.

But really, it was the trading for candy that I remember most. With four siblings in the house, I had to develop strategies in trading. Those of us who traded quickly for Milky Ways and Clark bars often found ourselves without candy a mere three days later. Those of us who traded for the multitudes of Bazooka Joes, Sugar Babies, and the odd bags of candy corn soon found ourselves holding a monopoly over the family candy supply by election day.

Easter was the second most anticipated candy holiday on the calendar. Various Sunday school lessons instructed us that Easter Sunday was the day we celebrated Jesus Christ's resurrection. What my pack of friends and I believed was that Easter was the day that Jesus, in the form of a bunny, showed up at our houses in the middle of the night, tossed hard-boiled eggs all over the place, and then apologized for the mess we'd have to clean up by leaving a basket full of candy. We started the morning by recovering all the eggs that Jesus had haphazardly thrown around the house. By the end of the day, we were stuffed full of marshmallow Peeps, jelly beans, and loads of chocolate.

It was the chocolate that resulted in the first upgrade in the quality of the candy we were given. When we were younger we received chocolate rabbits, which we thought a tad cruel, and we questioned whether we would go to hell for biting off the rabbit ears first. Over the course of the next few years, this evolved into us children imitating the rabbits as their horrible child overlords chomped into their chocolate flesh. The last year we had chocolate rabbits, our father noticed us screaming in sadistic glee while doing our best bunny impersonations of these confections, pleading, "Oh my god, no! No! No! Don't eat my . . . !" and then immediately devouring the rabbit's head. The next year, each of us received a softball-sized chocolate cream–filled egg, with fondant decorations. While he clearly paid more money for these treats, the cost was likely offset by enabling him to survive Easter Sunday without once thinking we would end up being a family of serial killers. In that light, it seems like money well spent.

When I was a kid, my favorite days of the year could be ranked this way:

1. Christmas
2. Halloween
3. My birthday
4. Any day that I was able to receive/discover/consume candy
5. Easter

Two of those days are up there because of the abundance of gifts. Four of them involved candy or sweets. When I was a child, life was merely the time that happened in between these days. The truly memorable moments were the ones when candy and presents abounded. When you're a child, nothing is better than a day when people give you stuff and you are allowed to eat as much candy as you want.

Thirty-odd years later, those types of days seem long gone. I now see Christmas as a cynical marketing enterprise that uses religion as a rationalization for maxing out one's credit card. Halloween has evolved from a night when I dressed in costume in order to beg for candy from neighbors, to a night when I dressed in costume in order to share whiskey, vodka, and kegs of beer with like-minded college friends, to a night I have to remind myself that the holiday still exists. Nowadays, I end up forgetting about Halloween until the last possible moment, at which point my only options are to either make a dash to the drugstore to buy a bag or two of Hershey's Miniatures or make sure I leave my porch light off. I'm not sure there's anything more pathetic than a woman in her forties trying to avoid seven-year-olds dressed as hobos and princesses.

As for my birthday, the less said about it the better.

And Easter? Easter went by the wayside when I could not find anything in the Bible about chocolate rabbits and jelly beans. If Christianity wanted to retain my interest in the day celebrating the resurrection of Christ, it could have at least explained how marshmallow Peeps entered into the equation. If they had found a stain mark on the shroud of Turin that came from the filling of a Cadbury Creme Egg, it's possible that I would still be celebrating Christ's ascension with ham and spiced gumdrops.

In other words, I grew up into a cynical adult. No longer does bliss seem like an attainable goal. Instead I have settled for "comfort." I've compromised the joys of my childhood in order to have a better understanding of the world around me.

Candy falls squarely into this worldview. No longer is it representative of the happiness that life can bring you. Now it represents the unhealthy, the immature, and the gluttonous. So I have set candy aside in order to pursue the American dream—a two-and-a-half-bedroom house with a white picket fence, a thirty-year mortgage, and ready access to the local grocery store.

But in middle age, with the brute force of a watermelon dropped from a fifth-floor balcony to the sidewalk below, I had a startling revelation: I was miserable chasing that dream. I didn't want my life to be defined by a house that was smack in the middle of suburbia. I didn't want to have political discussions based on whether I could get a better tax rate on my mortgage. I didn't want to be associated with people who defended wars that allowed us to have cheaper gas.

Every day, the media presents me with things that are going wrong. My country is fighting two wars. Several banks nearly brought down the world's economy. Institutional religions are either advocating hate or covering up the sins of their priests.

This is adulthood? The joys of our childhood never prepared us for this. I didn't want any of this. Ever. What I wanted was to enjoy life, not to feel constricted by it.

One night, at a coffee shop, I told my partner Tara about these feelings that my midlife crisis had unleashed.

"So?" she replied. "Nothing is stopping you from acting like a child."

"Nothing except social etiquette. No one wants to see a forty-three-year-old skip down the street in a jumper emblazoned with a Sesame Street logo."

"No, no. You misunderstand," she said. "Take the best aspects of both worlds. Take the best aspect of your childhood and combine it with the best aspect of adulthood."

I mulled her statement over a bit. I looked around the room and watched other customers of the coffee shop. I watched them drink their lattes. I watched them take advantage of the free wi-fi. And I watched them eat the cupcakes that had become the recent trend here in Seattle—a little piece of childhood that was now being sold to adults for a mere two dollars.

A thought hit me. I needed a cure for this midlife crisis. And I knew exactly what I needed to do.

"Candy!" I said to Tara.

"Bweh?" she countered, confused by my non sequitur.

"What's the one thing that defines adulthood?" I asked.

"I don't know. . . . Responsibility?" she said, reaching for the first idea that entered her mind.

"Exactly! With that comes the need to make money in order to fulfill those responsibilities. It pays for the roof over your head, the food in your stomach, the car that allows you to commute to your job. Now, what defines childhood?"

Tara blinked.

"Candy?" she said.

"Yes! And adulthood is the stage in your life when you can afford all the candy you want, but you don't. Instead you use money to buy a car, pay the rent, go to the doctor."

Tara looked at me, clearly unsure on what I was about to propose.

"So what if I spent my money on all the candy I wanted? On all the candy I could? And not just the stuff I can get at the Rite Aid, or out of vending machines. What if I went out and searched for weird candy?"

Tara put her latte down. "So, your idea for a cure for a midlife crisis is to binge on candy?"

I paused and thought about it more. "What if I used this 'bingeing' as a means to another end? If I were in academia, I could say I was studying the history of candy."

"So you're going to travel the world, claiming you're studying the history of candy, but instead you're using it as an excuse to do a yearlong Halloween? All to solve your midlife crisis?"

I mulled her last statement for a bit before realizing she had crystallized the idea perfectly.

This was how I found myself, a few months later, thousands of miles away, chasing down the meaning of life and the history of candy and indulging in the ultimate childhood fantasy. That I was doing it at the age of forty-three was unfortunate but necessary. After all, adulthood does afford some measure of luxury over childhood, with financial resources being chief among them.

My cure for my midlife crisis? I was going to do what I had to. I was going to Italy.

Chapter 2

Onward … to Italy?

● ● ● ● ● ● ● ● ●

*T*here is a parallel between wanderlust and the delight we felt as children when we acquired candy. There's this bliss that some of us feel when we uncover the unknown. When we experience things for the first time, a joy overcomes us as we get the experience of the new. When we travel, we admit to ourselves that we aren't as knowledgeable as we sometimes believe ourselves to be. It's a similar experience that we had as children as we bit into out first chocolate bar or licked our first lollipop. For every new travel adventure, and all subsequent consumption of candy, there is a part of us that simply wants to recreate that initial, joyous feeling. That feeling fills some of us with pure, unadulterated awe.

For the record, it's difficult for me to find awe and wonder while jet-lagged. In fact, in such a state, it's difficult for me to find my passport, debit card, notebook, guide, or general sense of optimism. What is easy for me to find is coffee, regardless of where I am. And where I am is in Palermo, Sicily, still groggy after the previous day's nineteen hours of travel.

I'd like to say that I picked Sicily out of the blue, that it just happened to have its own unique candy history, much like any other region on the planet. But the truth is that the history of Sicily plays an integral role in the development of Western candy culture, mostly because it plays an integral role in the history of sugar. Without ready access to sugar, candy as you and I know it would be far different.

This is an oversimplification. It also gives the impression that before sugar, the Western world knew no sweets. This is flat-out wrong, what with everything from honey to date syrup being used in the various cradles of Western civilization. So where should I start? Where does one turn when searching for that moment in time without which Hershey would not exist? What event had to occur in order for Jolly Rancher to make their Blue Raspberry? What is the first question one should ask to find the answers to these nonrhetorical questions?

The best question I could come up with is, why do we even like sweets?

There are several hypotheses out there, each making what sounds like a valid point. Some make a biological argument: we desire sweets because they helped our *Homo sapiens* ancestors to discern between "safe" and "unsafe" foods. Others make a physiological argument: as children, we need the calories that accompany sweets in order to help provide energy for our developing bodies. But neither of these positions explains why we still pursue sweets long after we, as a culture, have settled into domestication or we, as individuals, have grown into adulthood.

Ah, yes. Adulthood again. The period of time when we are under the impression that we have outgrown candy. It's easy for us to rationalize that we have put candy aside as we have grown older. Marshmallows, bubble gum, and lollipops are for children. Candy is a product for the immature.

Except that it isn't. Yes, many of us may have put away the bubble gum and lollipops and continue to turn up our noses at Hershey bars and gummy bears. But we still get our candy fixes in other ways. While Pepsi and Coca-Cola would like you to believe otherwise, soda pop has direct links to sherbets and sorbets. Cough drops are merely suckers with a hint of menthol or licorice added. And don't even get me started on the protein bars coated in chocolate or mints sold as breath fresheners. Many adults are candy eaters and simply don't have the courage to admit it. We can say we don't like the stuff, but all evidence points to us consuming all forms of candy, those made for both children *and* adults.

The thing is, we have always been this way. We have had a love affair with sweet foods since before the age of agriculture. Kenneth F. Kiple and Kriemhild Coneè Ornelas note, in the *Cambridge World History of Food*, that "wild cherries played a role in the human diet eons before the invention of agriculture and the beginning of recorded history. Our Neolithic ancestors extracted—and presumably fermented—cherry juice before it was discovered how to make wine from grapes." And roughly the same time that *Homo sapiens* began putting down roots and plowing the earth, some twelve thousand years ago, one of the first crops that we domesticated (after grains) was the cherry tree.

While our ancestors undoubtedly found benefit from fermenting cherry juice, there had to be a reason why they put the cherries into their mouths in the first place. The best answer is the simplest: because it tasted good. Yes, the cherries would have been tart. But there would have been an element of sweetness to them as well. In fact, Paleolithic humans would have been drawn to the sweet cherries over the tart ones. Why? Danielle Reed, a researcher who studies the biochemistry of taste at the Monell Chemical Senses Center in Philadelphia, explains:

> The ability to taste sweet really starts when a sugar or another kind of sweet molecule touches the sweet receptor on the taste receptor cell. And that sets off a chain reaction that's perceived by the brain as sweet. There's only one sweet receptor, but it's actually quite elaborate because it allows us to taste sweetness from molecules that have a whole different molecular structure—from just simple sugars to more unusual things like the high-intensity sweetener saccharine, or aspartame, and so forth. Being able to sense sugar is a very useful thing to do for animals that need carbohydrates for energy. Sugar is not only a good source of energy because it's very easy to absorb, and rapid, but it's also a very safe source of calories.

There it is in a nutshell, so to speak. While other tastes such as bitter or sour almost always come from a variety of sources, from a biological perspective, sweetness, for lack of a better term, has almost always come from a sugar, regardless of how it manifested itself. Sugar providing pre-agrarian humans with energy in the form of carbohydrates was either instinct or a winning evolutionary lottery ticket. Either way, once we were able to discern the good fruits from the poisonous, we found ways to domesticate the plants that held these fruits. From there, we were able to indulge our developing sweet tooth at our whim.

Unfortunately, my sweet tooth wasn't really calling out to me at the moment. That honor belonged to my general state of grogginess. This needed to be addressed before searching the streets of Palermo for candy. After finding the requisite amount of energy to adequately present myself to the world, I escaped the confines of my hotel and went out into a morning of Sicilian chaos.

When I think of Italy, I have to admit that Palermo does not leap to the forefront of my mind. Rome, yes. Tuscany, certainly. Heck, even Venice jumps out at me as an important city. But Sicily? Sicily was the place from which many of my neighbors back in Pittsburgh had emigrated. In the reptilian areas of my mind, this worked out to mean, logically, "If you found yourself in Palermo, you'd rather be somewhere else." Of course most of my neighbors had immigrated to the United States prior to World War II, so they likely had more pressing concerns than those of a twenty-first-century food writer.

That concern was getting in touch with that moment of joyous innocence that I had as a child. I had to get caffeinated and then find myself some genuine Sicilian confectionery. I wandered slowly down one of the major thoroughfares of the old town, Via Vittorio Emanuele.

Around me, in the noon sun, was a sort of choreographed chaos. The main road was claustrophobic in nature, with the various styles of buildings rising up four to six stories. The road was barely wide enough for two cars, and the sidewalks were a mere three feet across. The back alleys, clearly the result of a civic planning commission whose approach was based on the philosophy that it worked back in the eleventh century, seemed even more crowded, as if each building was caught in the others' gravitational pull. Through all this a multitude of scooters, low-end motor bikes, and cars no larger than a kitchen table ran with great purpose and noise, following traffic rules that were more hints and suggestions than laws.

It was like watching a hornet's nest writ large. Several times I had to walk out into traffic in order to walk around a car or scooter that had "parked." It was through this action that I came across my first Italian café.

Technically, it was more of a restaurant than a café, but the local clientele were nowhere to be seen, choosing instead to hover around the front coffee bars, quickly sipping their espressos and macchiatos before heading back into the chaos. I chose to sit and peruse the menu, skipping briefly over the coffee choices and instead trying to interpret the Italian options available under *gelati*.

It was on this menu list that I read of flavors both common and new. Chocolate was there, to be sure, as was pistachio. Also on this list were lemon, peach, and pineapple. A question occurred to me. Are fruits the first candy? Granted, the idea seems a bit naïve on the surface, but resolving this seemingly easy query opens up many other questions. For example, if we're going to ask whether something is candy, we should have a clear idea of what candy is.

I ordered a macchiato and asked myself this very question: what defines candy? This isn't as easily answered as we would like. I know, I know—starting a book with a definition of the book's primary subject is a hackneyed technique that we all outgrew back in the tenth grade. But with candy, the approach yields interesting and often contradictory results. People in different parts of the world think of candy in different ways. Even Merriam-Webster's definition that candy is "a confection made with sugar and often flavoring and filling" leaves out items such as cocoa-powdered almonds, sugar-free gums, and the infamous salted licorice found in the Netherlands. Are these candies? For many, the answer is yes; but if so, then Merriam-Webster's definition is, at the very least, incomplete.

Candy is one of those food items that fit into the category of "I know it when I see it, but I'll be damned if I can tell you what constitutes it." This lack of a concrete definition makes knowing what, exactly, is candy, a tad bit difficult. Even taking a good long look at the Snickers bar, one of the most popular pieces of candy in the United States today, offers little in the way of clues.

It's easy to see why the Snickers bar is tremendously popular. It's little more than a bar of egg whites mixed with sugar that is then topped with roasted peanuts, covered with roasted sugar (caramel), and enrobed in milk chocolate made from cocoa, cocoa butter, and sugar. But these are merely ingredients, none of which define candy outright.

Perhaps it's the sugar used to mesh these ingredients together? But this discounts candy made from honey or syrup, but includes pastries. Is candy "crystallized sugar formed by boiling down sugar syrup"? It can be, but the six-year-old in all of us knows of products that exceed this perspective. Is candy "a confection made with sugar and often flavoring and filling"? Well, yes, but so are turnovers, cupcakes, and macaroons. For every characteristic one can give to candy, an exception can be found.

Perhaps it is its portability? But then this would include products such as cookies and exclude classic candies such as Pixy Stix, which are nothing but sugar and a bit of citric acid combined together in a straw. Without that critical bit of packaging that is the straw, Pixy Stix would be nothing more than a simple baking ingredient that is difficult to transport.

From my perspective, candy is a product whose definition is dynamic. What constitutes candy differs from person to person, and from culture to culture. Baklava is considered "candy-like" in the Middle East. Confectionery in India includes an extensive use of milk and clarified butter.

The word "candy" does somewhat help clarify the definition, but only a little. According to the *Old English Dictionary*, the word goes back at least two thousand years, all the way to the Persian word *qand*, which was the word for the crystallized juice of the sugarcane. Using that definition, it's possible to trace back the word even further, to the Sanskrit *khanda*. That the word has changed very little over the past two millennia, and yet still connotes roughly the same meaning, is remarkable.

What this means is that the first candy was literally nothing

Kate's Candy Bag

PIXY STIX

The bane of parents everywhere in the United States, Pixy Stix are pure sugar mixed with a bit of citric acid and a touch of flavoring, packaged in drinking straws. As a child, I loved Pixy Stix, especially the jumbo size, sold in an eleven-inch plastic straw with enough sugar to kill a small hamster. Pixy Stix were the only candy that were strictly regulated in our household.

Candy Exchange Rate:
7 Pixy Stix straws = 1 York Peppermint Pattie

more than the crystallized grains of sugar. From that product, which is a mere by-product of the sugar cane, a multibillion-dollar industry was born. Judging from its etymology, the history of candy starts with the history of sugarcane.

This view is problematic, however, as it implies that indulging in one's sweet tooth didn't occur on a cultural level until granulated sugar made its way into various societies across the world. Yet time and time again we find that ancient cultures around the world found ways to bring sugary products into their diets on a regular basis, whether through the use of honey, fruits, syrups, or other crops that yielded a sweet product.

Acknowledging this dilemma, I have my own definition. It's incomplete, but it gives us a starting point. First, the product must be the result of a manufacturing process of some sort. The process may be as complex as a million-dollar assembly line in a factory in Hershey, Pennsylvania, or as rudimentary as someone drying fruit.

Second, the product must be enjoyed or consumed for reasons other than the primary reason for eating—overcoming hunger. This rule will thus cover foods that are eaten as treats as well as those consumables that were created under the auspices of medicine.

Third, the product should be easily portable and have an extended shelf life.

Fourth, a sweetener of some sort should be added as part of the process.

Fifth, and somewhat related to the fourth rule, it has to have more than one ingredient.

Finally, any culture may have one or two candies that do not meet one (and only one) of the above criteria. Let's call this the "salted-licorice rule."

So let's go back to fruit and apply these rules. Is a box of raisins, say, a candy? Drying fruit, although a process learned from nature, is now done on a mass scale via factory processes. It's a bit questionable as to whether raisins have ever been eaten for reasons other than to satisfy hunger, but let's give them the benefit of the doubt.

Raisins also have an extended shelf life and are easily transported, although they are more susceptible to mold and rot than most candies.

These dried grapes are also sweetened, albeit naturally. One could make the argument that, for rule four, the product should be unnaturally sweetened.

But there's only one ingredient; thus, raisins fail that requirement.

Finally, there's the salted-licorice rule. Do we, as a culture, allow for raisins to be seen as a candy? Only if you're an evil dentist

Kate's Candy Bag

SALTED LICORICE

Evil in confection form. There are some people who swear by the goodness that is salted licorice, but I am not one of them. The licorice is salted. It's salted with ammonium chloride instead of sodium chloride. Even the salt tastes weird. That it is popular in the Scandinavian countries, where culinary delights such as fermented herring still remain a viable option at the dinner table, should surprise no one.

Candy Exchange Rate:

10,000 salted licorice pieces = 1 York Peppermint Pattie

giving out treats on Halloween. So, for this reason, raisins (and dried fruit in general) do not meet the definition of candy.

But with these criteria in place, many foods do start to look like they would fit the definition.

Dried fruits have been around since the beginning of humanity. Flowers themselves have been known to be dried and eaten for pleasure, with varying degrees of success, and great pieces of candy can be made by doing nothing more than heating the sap of certain trees and allowing it to harden in the sun. In fact, if you're the type of person who wants to know the first of everything, the hardened sap makes an excellent candidate for the first "true" candy in the history of humanity.

But in today's world, flowers and tree sap are rarely used in food. The sweets we indulge in today, for the most part, primarily contain some combination of sugar, chocolate, nuts, herbs (for example, mint), and real or artificial fruit flavorings.

Let's talk about the sweetener that made its way into pantries and storehouses several millennia before cane sugar found its way into the Middle East, Europe, and Africa. Honey.

Yes, honey is actually a sugar. Honey gets its sweetness from the monosaccharaides fructose and glucose and has approximately the same relative sweetness as that of granulated sugar. It was gathered, according to some, as far back as the end of the Ice Age. In the Altamira caves in northern Spain, there is a Mesolithic rock painting showing two female honey hunters collecting honey and honeycomb from a wild bee's nest. Experts have stated that these drawings go back ten thousand to fifteen thousand years. As to how the honey was used, that information is lost to the ages.

When we discovered how to domesticate the honeybee our diet became far more intriguing. There is some question about when this domestication occurred. Some experts say that we had regular access to honey as far back as 5500 BC, while others say 2400 BC. Most agree that this occurred in ancient Egypt, so looking for evidence of candy in that culture seems logical.

Alas, while there is plenty of circumstantial evidence to suggest that honeyed treats were being made, it is not currently known whether the Egyptians combined nuts or seeds with honey, baked the mixture, and created the first granola bar. This might have happened. Certainly the ingredients and technology were there. But historians can't say with any definitive response that, yes, the Egyptians were granola-munchin' hippies.

Those of you quick of wit will note that I've subtly implied that granola is, as a point of fact, a candy. Readers who carbload on Nature Valley Sweet & Salty Nut granola bars may regard this as a bit of blasphemy. To you folk I say, look at the previous rules. Granola is portable, is sweetened with honey or sugar, is manufactured, and has more than two ingredients. The fact that the Quaker Oats Company feels compelled to coat its granola with chocolate doesn't help you argue your case that this is a health food.

Since there is no evidence to turn to from the Egyptians, where can we turn to demonstrate that people ate sweets long before Julius Caesar took one in the back? For this, we have to introduce one of the extended trading partners of the Egyptians—the Indo-Aryans.

Indo-Aryans existed roughly three thousand years ago in what is today the Afghanistan-Pakistan region. They later migrated into what is today northern India. According to ancient Sanskrit texts, the citizens of Arya would offer guests to their home a treat called *madhuparka,* a mixture of honey, curds, and clarified butter. The Sanskrit text detailing this activity is the first evidence of sweets being offered as a means of hospitality.

Honey mixed with curds is not something we would recognize today as a candy—in fact, it wouldn't pass our five-rule test, as it would have had a limited shelf life. But Sanskrit does contain something that is of massive interest to those of us with a sweet tooth: sugar and sugarcane are both mentioned several times.

But the Afghanistan-Pakistan-India region is not where sugar cane comes from. That honor likely belongs to what is present-day New Guinea. Botanists have placed the cane (known as *Saccharum officinarum* if you are keen on sounding learned) on that island roughly ten thousand years ago. From there it took two thousand years to make its way to the Philippines, through trade and other similar means; and then it took another millennium or so before it got to the west coast of India.

But sugar cane is no more sugar than an apple is apple juice. To get at the by-products of these crops, the agrarian technology must have reached a certain threshold. When that occurred for granulated sugar is difficult to say. What historians do know is that Dioscorides, a Greek physician who lived between 40 and 90 AD, wrote in his pharmacopeia of a "kind of concreted honey, called *saccharon,* found in reeds of India and Arab Felix, like in consistence to salt, brittle and to be broken between the teeth, as salt is. It is good for the belly and the stomach being dissolved in water and so drank, helping the pained bladder and the reins."

There's so much noteworthy information in that last paragraph that it's difficult to pick out where to start. First and foremost, given its comparison to salt, I think it's safe to say that by the first century AD, granulated sugar not only existed but was produced in enough quantities to send it along the various trade routes. The reference to "Arabia Felix," an idiom often used to describe the southern parts of the Arabian Peninsula, including modern Yemen, is interesting, as there is no evidence of sugarcane fields in that region at that time. But the area was a waypoint when it came to trade, not that a physician in Greece would have known this at that time. In all likelihood, any sugar that came from Arab Felix originated in India.

Another important point to consider is that it's not as if the process to create granulated sugar was discovered one day, and then three weeks later a Greek doctor found himself musing on its properties. The time it took to figure out how to extract the sugar crystals from the cane, then for those crystals to gain enough popularity in that region so that they were worth exporting, and then for that process to repeat itself from trading port to trading port was likely generations, if not centuries. So while Dioscorides may have had access to sugar in 70 AD, the innovation needed to create granulated sugar most certainly took place a few centuries beforehand.

Yet there's little historical evidence out there to account for this. As Sidney Mintz, in his book *Sweetness and Power,* notes, "It is not until about 500 AD that we get unmistakable written evidence of sugar making." And that evidence was found, of all places, in a Hindu religious document called the *Buddhagosa*.

This may be unmistakable evidence, but it's certainly not the first possible time period. Sadly, the lack of adequate archaeological evidence or ancient manuscripts detailing this burgeoning industry leaves us merely with speculation. The only evidence that I've been able to find surrounding the white table sugar we know and love today comes from a Sanskrit tablet circa 375 AD that mentions *sito sarkara churna*, or "powdered white sugar." Yet this is still long after Dioscorides looked at his saltlike substance and scratched his chin in contemplation.

What we do know about this era is that the Indian culture benefited greatly from sugar, and it became the linchpin from which all other sugar cultures developed. One of the generals of Alexander the Great reached India in 325 BC and wrote about "a reed in India that brings forth honey without the help of bees, from which an intoxicating drink is made though the plant bears no fruit." By 200 BC the sugar cane is well known in China, after having been brought there by traders. By 262 AD, after perfecting a necessary irrigation technique, the Sassanid king, Shapur I, paved the way to bring sugar into the Tigris-Euphrates river valley, where the Nestorian Christians later developed the means to standardize the process to create crystallized sugar.

It is not known who discovered the means to efficiently extract the sucrose crystals from the cane juice, but the inventors probably came from either Indonesia or India. Most likely it happened by accident, as evaporation of water from the juice would have left a more viscous liquid. The greater the evaporation, the more supersaturated the resulting product, until somebody somewhere ended up with a product that we would recognize today as blackstrap molasses. Further heating and evaporation would result in a treacly ball, a type of sugar that the Indians called *gur*. Letting these balls dry out would result in something resembling brown sugar.

Additional processes were created to remove the darker aspects of sugar, leaving chemically "purer" forms. Each process led to a new by-product, each one used to its benefit in whatever region it was discovered and implemented. The ultimate ideal of pure, white, granulated sugar is interesting but not reflective of what probably happened. Sugar was sugar, regardless of how white or dark or how liquid or solid.

But if sugar tasted so good, why is it rarely mentioned, if at all, by the Greeks and the Romans? As the statement by Dioscorides implies, they had access to it, although likely in limited quantities. But it's not like the Romans or the Greeks to dismiss an imported item simply because it's expensive. After all, many of the more interesting aspects of their histories have to do with their excesses, especially when it came to feasts and banquets.

There are two answers to this question. For one, they already had a sweetener. Honey was (and is) a perfectly acceptable means of sweetening foods, and it was already ensconced in each of their cultures. Granulated sugar, because of its high cost, never had a chance of overthrowing honey as the sweetener of choice, regardless of its grade or purity. As such, sugar was relegated to the sidelines where various men of intellect could study it and determine its value. And what was their conclusion?

Let's look back at the statement by Dioscorides: It is good for the belly and the stomach being dissolved in water and so drank, helping the pained bladder and the reins."*

In other words, it may have been too expensive to sit on the everyday dinner table, but it was perfect for medicine. And

---

* "Reins" is an archaic term for kidneys. In other words, Dioscorides thought that sugar water helped with kidney stones.

because it tasted so good and hit the sweet tooth just right, it would have been far more palatable to those looking for curatives.

The Greeks and Romans weren't alone in this outlook. As Tim Richardson notes, there was a second-century Indian medical book called *The Charaka Samhita* that called out a drug whose ingredients included "ginger, licorice, long pepper (more aromatic than black pepper), gum arabic, ghee, honey, and sugar." This concoction was to be served like a soup and would be seen as a preventive medicine rather than restorative. From my twenty-first-century perspective, it sounds like it would have made quite an interesting soda pop—minus the gum arabic, of course.

Sanskrit texts show that the authors believed that sugar had other medicinal qualities, improving everything from digestion to semen production. It is not only possible but likely that when sugar made its way around the trading circles, it was sold primarily, if not exclusively, as a medicine rather than a foodstuff. This would affect how we looked at sugar for the next eighteen hundred years. To find the historical path of candy, it's not enough to look at treats and pleasures found in the diets of our past. We have to look at the history of sugar first, and then at the history of medicine.

From my point of view, this is akin to going to the dentist before heading out trick or treating. From a historical perspective, this might be a logical step, but for me, in the search for whatever joy confectionery might bring, I would only go to a drugstore if I had to.

I finished up my macchiato. Energy and anticipation coursed through me as I paid for my caffeinated beverage of choice. I now had a plan. I knew what I was looking for, and where to look for it. "*Grazie,*" I said to the men behind the counter as I went out into the Palermo afternoon.

Chapter 3

Land of *Torrones*

●　●　●　●　●　●　●　●

$\mathcal{I}$ have to admit to becoming fairly introspective when I come across a city that is older than one thousand years. Not that one thousand years is a magical line, one where anything newer than a millennium is passé, while anything older is mystical. It's just that it's around one thousand years that my perception of time starts to warp into a deeper abstraction. One hundred years? That's more than a lifetime. Five hundred? Heck it's been that long since Columbus's voyage. One thousand years? Yeah, it's at this point that I'm losing a strong definition of how long a millennium actually is.

And when I think about Palermo? My head begins to spin.

Of course, much of this head spinning could be attributed to sitting in the back of a taxicab on my way to various areas of the city, wondering why the drivers of this old city approach their traffic laws the same way Americans approach nutritional labels—the information is important, but only for other people, not for me. To avoid thinking about any impending death, I thought about why I was in this ancient urban area. Hopefully this would give me enough of a distraction to avoid wondering why I was being tossed around in the backseat with the same fervor as a popcorn kernel on a hot plate.

I found myself in this great Sicilian city, picking up the trail of candy left by the Moors, who invaded and conquered this strategic port in 831 AD (after several attempts over the previous two centuries). By that time, this area of the world had already seen fifteen hundred years of history. It was here that the Moors conquered the Byzantines, who had conquered the Ostrogoths, who had conquered the Vandals, who had picked up the pieces left by the Romans, who had defeated the Carthaginians, who had settled there with the Greeks, who had bested the Phoenicians, who are reputed to have been the first to settle the region way back around 700 BC. Over the course of those fifteen hundred years, both Palermo and Sicily were under constant threat of invasion, and rare was the time when it could be said that its citizens had lived in peace.

Looking at a map, it becomes clear why this was the case. Sicily sits smack dab in the middle of the trade-heavy Mediterranean Sea, making it of vital strategic importance to anyone looking to export and import goods throughout the area. It is also a stepping-stone of sorts for anyone who wishes to invade Europe from Africa.

Palermo and Sicily have been so important from a strategic point of view, that they seem to have always been in somebody's crosshairs. This importance of its location brought with it near constant risk of invasion, making it difficult to administer from a government perspective. In other words, its value as a target paradoxically made it less valuable for any ruling government to invest in the area over the long term.

Paradox—that's the word that describes Palermo to the letter. It's a city that screams order in chaos, poverty in wealth, rubble among construction. It's a city where traffic laws are more akin to suggestions than rules. It's a city where buildings bombed during World War II sit one street away from the renovated commercial district. It's a city that retains as much from previous cultures as it can while still looking to establish itself in our modern era.

The old town of Palermo showcases this paradox in its most concentrated dosage. For it is in this area that one can still see remnants of past cultures, from the Bourbons to the Normans to the Moors.

When the Moors enter the Mediterranean, history gets really interesting for candy fans. Europe's culinary landscape changed rather dramatically when they brought sugarcane with them.

How did the Moors end up the bearers of the sweet cane? That takes a bit of explaining. Until the Moorish expansionism of the seventh and eight century it's unlikely that sugar making was done much farther west in Asia than Persia. When Byzantine forces attacked Khosrau II in 628 and looted the Persian king's palace, they documented that they found pepper, silk, ginger, and sugar, which they described as an "Indian luxury." Had they been more familiar with sugar, or even sugar making, the sweet powder would never have been given the "Indian" designation.

The new Moorish empire, taking advantage of the Persians and Byzantines beating each other over the head, used this opportunity to expand, defeating the aforementioned empires left and right, heading west all the while, until they found themselves on Europe's doorstep, making inroads into the Iberian Peninsula in 711 and, after a few false starts, Sicily in 831.

At the time of the Moorish conquest, the majority of Sicilians were happy to see them. Having been under the rule of the disinterested and arrogant administrators of the Byzantine Empire, and before that, the Vandals and the Goths, the locals must have seen their new rulers as a welcome change because the Moors started developing the island's infrastructure and actually investing in local lands.

And develop the lands they did. For the Moors, having kicked around the deserts of North Africa, the arable lands of Sicily must have seemed like finding gold. With their extensive knowledge of irrigation (necessitated by their quest for food in desert regions), Sicily's lands soon blossomed. Crops that required excessive work elsewhere in the Moorish Empire seemed to require little effort on this island, and the new overlords took full advantage of this. After ensuring that durum wheat (whence pasta was developed) could feed enough of their citizens, they introduced several new crops, including melons, eggplant, saffron, almonds, pistachios—and sugarcane.

I gave myself a quick and easily obtainable goal. I would see if I could find some sugar in the form of a confection that I could tie to the pre-Islamic era in Sicily.

Cars and scooters flashed by me to my right as I walked up the street. As I could read only very few words of Italian, I let the products in the window tell me of the various wares that the local businesses were selling. I passed places that were selling soccer jerseys, gift shops selling postcards and cheap sweatshirts, and restaurants that would not open until the early evening. There was one place whose name intrigued me, a location called Carne Equina, which, if my Latin was up to snuff, was a place that sold horse meat.

Around a corner, there was a place that had some delicate-looking sweets in their window. But the store looked to me more like a jewelry store than a candy one.

I opened the door, ringing the bell that was connected to the top of the door frame, alerting the older woman dressed in designer clothing behind the counter. As I was about to speak, the scent of potpourri wafted through the air, waking me up to the fact that the only Italian I knew was "Io non capisco l'italiano. Parlate inglese?" which loosely translates to "I am too lazy to learn any of your native language in great depth, so I'm hoping that you know enough English that we can communicate."

The woman behind the counter started off the conversation instead. "Benvenuta!" she said.

"Uh. Hello," I said. "Parlez-vous anglais?" My inner self face-palmed as rudimentary French stumbled out of my mouth before I could stop it.

The woman, with her impeccably styled slivery black hair, looked at me with amusement. "Could . . . I help . . . you?" she asked.

"Yes," I said, relieved that there were benefits to the general ignorance of foreign languages by most Americans. "Do you sell . . ." I racked my brain for the correct word. "Confezioni?"

She looked at me, a tad confused. "Sì."

"In the window. I saw some beautiful candy. Could I . . . buy some?"

We were pressing upon the boundary of our crosscultural communication capability. The woman was straining to find the right word. "Are . . . you . . . planning . . . wedding?"

A wedding? What? Wait. No, no, no. This wasn't my version of *Eat Pray Love*. I just wanted to try some candy.

"No. Ha. No. I'm writing a book. About candy." There was no way she understood what I was trying to say.

"We . . . make . . . weddings," she said.

It seemed I had stumbled into the storefront of a wedding consultant. My first attempt at acquiring candy in a foreign land, and here I was, inadvertently attempting to plan my own nuptials.

"No. No. Por favore. Scuse. No wedding. No wedding." I bowed to her for reasons known only to my subconscious. "Grazie. Grazie," I said as I backed out of her store, onto the three-foot-wide sidewalk with the chaos of the street immediately behind it.

Holy hell. This was not the way I wanted to start my search. I looked at the storefront in order to see where I had gone wrong. The only word I could make out was *confettificio,* which roughly translates into "confetti." I had clearly entered the wrong establishment. Rather than risk further miscommunication, I decided to explore the rest of the city. Finding candy should not be this trying.

Walking through Palermo, hell, most any large city in Italy, it's not difficult to find a confection that has a tie to the deep past. One needs to look no further than the *torrone.* I knew little of Italian candies, but thanks to my deep love of nougat, I was already somewhat familiar with the joys of this treat.

The legend is that torrone was invented for a medieval wedding in the Italian city of Cremona. The candy dates from 1441, the wedding of Francesco Sforza and Bianca Maria Visconti, members of two powerful fifteenth-century families. So powerful, in fact, that the dowry was the city of Cremona itself. The wedding feast served thousands of people, the elite of the region's elite. The master chef, finding himself with an excess of egg whites after preparing thousands of pastries, is said to have created the dessert out of necessity, in order to not let these egg whites go to waste. He made a wedding cake in the shape of the bell tower of the Duomo of Cremona, which was called the Torrione. This translates into English as, roughly, "the big freakin' tower."

As with most legends in food, it is charming and a little bit romantic, and it gives the city of Cremona, a small town in northern Italy, something to be proud of.

The problem is that it is, at the least, a tad misleading, and at worst an out and out fabrication. The basic concept of a torrone is dead simple. Egg whites, whipped into a froth, are mixed with nuts and then sugar or honey for sweetness and bulk. That's pretty much it. Circumstantial evidence indicates that the processes and ingredients to make this recipe would have existed thousands of years before the wedding.

As I stopped in café after café and then, finally, confectionery after confectionery, one thing became immediately clear: torrone no longer (if ever) has to be strictly made with egg whites. Certainly the classic version of torrone, with its soft, marshmallowy look and its deep woody aroma of pistachios or walnuts, was available nearly everywhere I stopped. For a lover of nougat, the amount of these treats available to the general public is almost— *almost*—obscene. The area of my brain that houses my id made itself known immediately upon seeing these candies out on the shelves. "Oh. My. God," I heard myself say out loud to no one in particular, but my comment raised the eye of one disinterested woman behind the counter of a gift shop that I had wandered into. To make up for this small distraction, I put a few bars of different flavors of these torrone into my basket. I sized up my haul. I had found a bar of pistachios, one of almonds, another with sesame seeds, and still another that was of the traditional nougat-looking style, dotted with what looked like pieces of citron.

I explored the collection of candies that this gift shop had available. Next to the more well-known candies such as Mars bars and Kinder eggs were items that looked like versions of brittle, albeit made with seeds or nuts. There was the *torrone di semi di sesamo*, a torrone that looked remarkably like those small sesame seed candies made by Joyva that one tends to find from time to time in health food stores or Jewish delis. There was the *torrone ai pistucchio*, a bar of pistachios that had been set in a deep, rich molasses. Here was a collection of torrones that looked nothing like nougat, adding a small amount of credence to the idea that these candies were less the result of an emergency cake made from the mind of a sophisticated fifteenth-century chef and more the name of a simple confection. These were no longer the towering cakes of legend, but simple bars of candy. Whether or not they contained egg whites was secondary to their definition.

These varied types of torrones opened up an entirely new path for discussion—brittle candies, which likely have an even older history than nougat. Mixing nuts, beans, or seeds into honey and then baking would have been the simplest of processes, and in fact we see types of brittle throughout the world.

If we are to believe that torrones include brittles, then we have to acknowledge the variations of the sweetened seed "bars" that were reported to have been known of in China around 500 BC. A more solid bit of history states that around 116 BC, Marcus Terentius Varro mentioned the delicacy "cupped," a

 ### Kate's Candy Bag

PLANTERS PEANUT CANDY BARS

The most popular torrone bar sold in the United States is not even recognized as such. But if we're going to look at the example that I found in Palermo, the Planters Peanut Bar would be known as a torrone ai arachide, *essentially a peanut torrone. They never had much value to us kids in the neighborhood, because they were missing a crucial ingredient—chocolate. As an adult, I can't get over how much this candy bar looks like a granola bar minus the oats.*

Candy Exchange Rate:
2 Planters Peanut Bars = 1 York Peppermint Pattie

sweet made with honey, flour, cooked wine, and sesame. The names *cupeta* and *copeta* are still used in the regions of Campania and Calabria, respectively, to identify torrone.

There is stronger evidence that suggests that the treat has its roots in either Arab or Persian culture. Between 1100 and 1150, the Italian Gherardo Cremonese published *De medicinis et cibis semplicibus,* a translation of a work by the Arab physician Abdul Mutarrif of the Iberian Peninsula. There he extolled the virtues of honey and a sweetened medicine called *turun,* used to treat sore throats, coughs, and indigestion. Some believe that *torrone* is a variation of the Arab *cubbaita,* made with honey and toasted sesame seeds. The toasting component, in any case, is seen as the basis of the Latin etymology of the word: to toast in Latin is *torrere,* in Spanish *turrar,* and thus *turrón.* The Arabs, in fact, introduced this way of making the sweet to the Mediterranean countries where they had political or economic influence: the south of France and all of Spain, as well as Sicily, likely within a mile or so from where I purchased modern-day versions of these treats. If my goal was to follow the history of candy in order to find some sense of innocence, I was on the right trail.

I paid for my several candy bars, left the gift shop, and tried to find an area in Palermo where I could enjoy them with a modicum of peace. The hectic pace of the city made this task difficult, but I was able to find a place with some semblance of order at the Villa Bonanno, a park near the Porto Nuova at the far end of old town. What with the plethora of palm trees and park benches, it was a small but effective tract of land on which to escape the chaos of the city.

I opened the bag of confection and went not for the classic torrone but instead with the *torrone ai pistacchio,* as it seemed a more apt choice, considering the Sicilian predilection for the nut. I unwrapped its ribbon and cellophane and inhaled the deep, woody aroma of the pistachio, mixed with a rich, dark sweetness. The cloying aroma of molasses hung in the air like excess perfume on a humid summer day.

For a second, I felt as if I should commemorate this moment, as this would be the first "foreign" candy that I was going to consume on this trip. But my indulgence got the better of me, and before I could formulate an appropriate bit of prose in my head, I bit into the torrone.

It was a delight. It tasted new to my palate, yet familiar. Yes, it had all the aspects of a basic brittle. It was a deep, rich sugar, baked to a point where it could crunch enough to make my dentist shiver. The taste of lightly salted pistachios mixed with the sugar just enough to give a slight tug of war between these two tastes.

It was over just as quickly as it started. Soon, the typical dilemma of the sweet tooth kicked in. I wanted more. Not just more *torrone ai pistacchio* but more sugar. I looked into the bag and saw several other options that were immediately available to me.

"No," I thought. "This can be saved for later."

Sometimes immediate gratification is our worst enemy. I was not going to succumb to it so easily, at least not so early on this trip.

But I did have a question. Why did the Moors find sugar so important that the sugarcane fields had to be close by? Surely confections weren't that important, especially with honey so readily available. And trade relations with other states and kingdoms were weak connections at best, so importing it was financially risky. If sweeteners were such a priority for them, they surely could find some in the plethora of honey from local domesticated beehives.

The Moors grew crops wherever they could because, while their domain was huge—extending at one point from the Iberian Peninsula of southwestern Europe all the way to what today is known as Pakistan—the amount of arable land was limited. Maintaining the infrastructure to keep this empire fed and supplied was an enormous undertaking. Any land that demonstrated it could grow crops well after the implementation of any new Moorish advances in agriculture was fully taken advantage of.

But that still doesn't answer the question, "Why sugar?" The answer lies in two arenas, one culinary and one medicinal.

For a relatively young empire, energized by a relatively young religion, the Moors made and maintained advances in science and technology that put them in the same league as many of the historical dynasties we Westerners take for granted. Between the eighth century to the twelfth, they influenced the introduction of everything from crop rotation to free markets to scalpels, forceps, and sutures. The Islamic Golden Age left impressions on our Western history that are still being felt today. But to understand why they were making improvements in these areas, it's important to know where they were coming from, from a scientific belief perspective.

From our currently enlightened position of knowing a bit about nutrition, and even more about human physiology, it's easy for us to look at our past and assume that since our ancestors did not know these things, they didn't equate food with health. Ironically, this would be an unenlightened position in and of itself. Most foodstuffs were considered when it came to health, and few, if any, foods were seen to have no effect upon it. To understand this, we need to look at the underlying philosophy of medicine from that time. And that means talking about the humors.

It is said that it was the ancient Greek physician Hippoclater, and later Claudius Galenus (also referred to as Galen), who helped develop the humorist approach to medicine. This approach was in use in both the Western and Arab worlds all the way into the nineteenth century. So it's an idea that has been around for quite some time, through the Roman ages, past the Dark Ages, up to the Renaissance, and easily into the industrial age. It's an idea that had legs, and it wasn't truly discredited until the development of microscopes, which helped us see what was truly going on under our skin.

The core ideal of humorism that was expanded upon by Galen was this: the human body is balanced by four humors, fluids that in health were naturally equal in proportion. They were blood, yellow bile, black bile, and phlegm. Too much of one fluid would mean that a person would take on characteristics related to said fluid. Disease would be the result of an excess of one of the fluids or a deficiency in another. Doctors (and barbers) would treat a person based on the characteristics they displayed. For example, if a person was easily angered or bad-tempered, he was thought to be choleric and suffer from an excess of yellow bile.

Diets and medicines would be recommended that would help alleviate these unwanted characteristics and illnesses related to the humors. As being phlegmatic was thought to be a result of being too moist and cold, foods that were considered dry and warm would often be prescribed. Dry, warm foods included pork, apricots, truffles, pumpkins, and ale. If you were phlegmatic, pumpkin pie and ale were supposed to do wonders.

Most every type of food and spice had a humor associated with it, and many recipes from those periods ended up being a balanced equation created to fit not only the people eating the dish but the time of day it was eaten, and the time of year. For example, if the recipe was a roast chicken with lemon and garlic, chicken would be for those who were sanguine (too much blood), while garlic helped suppress the choleric (yellow bile), and lemon balanced out those with too much black bile. What would be the perfect time of year to serve such a dish? As chicken was the primary ingredient, the meal should be consumed during the time of year which was considered most sanguine, which would be the spring. A good cook would have to know all of these little nuances and take them into account when creating a meal.

The Arabs had bought fully into this philosophy, and it shaped their approach to developing various cures and remedies for an entire bevy of ailments. They also had learned from previous scholars the benefit of the use of sugar in the creation of various medicines. It was this approach that helped lay the foundation for the field of pharmacology.

One of the more famous of these early pharmacologists was a man who lived in the ninth century. Al-Kindī introduced Hindu numerals to the Islamic and Christian world, translated Greek texts into Arabic, and dabbled in the relatively new school of pharmacology. He was the gentleman who developed a scale that apothecaries could use to quantify the strength of a drug.

As I pointed out in Chapter 2, using sugar in medicines was nothing new. The writings of Buddha indicate that he believed that it was no sin for the ill to request it. Several classical Greek and Roman writings also extol the virtue of sugar for medicine. As the product became more widely available, the natural progression was to put it into more and more medicinal products. Most physicians recommended bitter herbs and spices as remedies. Adding sugar to them made these unpleasant products more palatable. And what were the mediums in which these medicines were offered? Powders, pills, and syrups. Each of these approaches would eventually evolve into sugary treats of its own.

Tim Richardson notes in his book *Sweets: A History of Candy* that one thirteenth-century powdered medicinal formula described by al-Samarqandī is to be mixed with the following formula:

It is mixed with a ratl of sugar, two dirhams of pulverized Indian aloeswood. It is placed over a fire. To it are added saffron, clove, cardomon, and so on, one after another. The sum total

depends on the need. It may be mixed with lemon rob in quantity to make it pleasant. Lemon juice may be used instead. It is
yellow and pretty. (p. 163)

As Richardson explains, not only does it sound like a medicine,
it "also sounds like something you could bag up and sell as a
sweet."

But the Arabs didn't offer just powders and pills as medicine.
They offered syrups as well. Sometimes this was done under the
guise of medicine; other times the line between "medicine" and
"delicious treat that might have a bit of a socially unacceptable
fermented kick to it from sitting out an extra day or two" was
often cloudy.

It was also the Arabs who figured out a beneficial purpose for
high-boiling cane sugar to a point where it turned brown. Rolled
into little balls of sugar, these were used as a hair removal product, that, it is supposed, a woman would spread or roll along the
area that needed . . . ah . . . pruning. Called *kurat al milh*, this
product is often considered the first recorded instance of caramel.

Alas, the use of sugar in Moorish Sicily is merely supposition,
based on circumstantial evidence. We know that the Moors
planted sugarcane on the island, we know that pharmacology
was taking off in the Moorish world. We also know that the
Moors had a rather short residency as rulers of the Sicilian island.
While they first started their invasion in 827, they weren't able to
kick out the Byzantines fully until 902. The Normans looked toward the island in earnest in 1061. That means that there were
only 160 years of Arab rule, quite a short era for an island that has
a history going back almost three millennia.

And what culinary records remain from the century and a
half they ruled this land? None, according to John Dickie, writer
of *Delizia! The Epic History of the Italians and Their Food*. There
are no medical texts, there are no cookbooks, there is nothing

we can point to that gives us any evidence of their use of sugar. All we have are pharmacologies from other parts of the Islamic empire and archaeological evidence of sugarcane fields in Sicily. What was there that tied the sugar fields to Sicily? Why did they need to have sugar so close at hand?

One of the few other areas of Palermo that had some semblance of order isn't found in the city, but in the port, which can be seen from the park that is located just through the Porto Felice and across the Via Cala. From this location one can see the organization involved in loading and unloading cargo ships, unloading fish from trawlers, and travelers from the ferries that to Sardinia and Corsica. As I watched the choreographed ballet of ships and boats entering and exiting the harbor, the ancient value of this area became clear. I imagined the multitude of galleys that had made their way here and left filled with whatever bounty could be collected. Sugar was here—it's never really left. I looked about the panorama to see whether I could pick out where the cane fields would have been.

Nope. Not here. Whatever crop lands that may have been here have long been swallowed up by civic expansion.

I looked out at a cargo ship and a thought came to mind. What would have happened if someone got ill on an extended trip? Surely there would have been some form of medicine on board.

There it was. Trade! This must be how confections made the jump from Moorish Sicily to the warehouses of Venice. Say you ran a galley that made runs from Palermo to various ports of call throughout the Tyrrhenian and Adriatic seas. Oarsmen for your ship may be easy to find on land, but when you're in the middle of the sea, sick crew members mean a drop in speed. What was the solution to this problem? Keep them from getting too ill, if possible, by feeding them medicines, various lozenges, troches, and syrups that you were able to keep on board.

When you arrive at your final port of call, when you're trying to get as much profit as you can, you see whether there are any buyers for whatever medicines are left over. Suddenly, Venice, Genoa, and Cagliari all have new products to sell to their customers and you've created a new need for sugar. Not only that, but these new ideas of "pharmacology" are suddenly taking root in countries where regular stops have been made.

The evidence is circumstantial, but it is there. A fair amount of trade is known to have occurred in Palermo. And the Venetians, expanding their reach throughout the Mediterranean, would have most certainly visited here at some point, as well as the many other areas in this great sea region that had access to the cane. Whatever limited amounts of sugar that were available, the young trading empire would have immediately seen the economic benefit of such a commodity. It is no coincidence that a sugar warehouse was established in the city of Venice roughly around 966.

If I was going to follow the history of candy, I needed to follow the trade routes. And if I needed to do that, I needed to get to what was once the largest merchant city of the Mediterranean.

Chapter 4

The Spice Trade

• • • • • • •

I arrived in Venice with all the fanfare of a large wet sponge. The rain had been falling for about two days before I arrived and showed no sign of letting up. Looking around on the *vaporetti,* the ubiquitous Venetian water buses, I saw that I was the only one without rain boots. Misery seemed always present. This was a far cry from the balmy weather of the Mediterranean that I had just experienced in Palermo. This weather was more akin to what I could find in my hometown of Seattle. Cold rain is never pleasant, regardless of how romantic the city may be.

Most people come to Venice because it is the city of romance. I had come to Venice because when one talks about trade in the early Middle Ages of Europe, the City of Canals is *the* place to go. Of course I realize that those of you who share my perspective are likely to be as big a nerd as I am. Sure, sure. When *normal* people think of Venice during the modern era, they have visions of a romantic getaway, or perhaps a playground of the wealthy. But Venice had to have gotten its wealth from somewhere, and long before there were operas, casinos, and Bellinis, there was trade.

Starting out as a small, salt-producing region of 117 islands that banded together to defend themselves against the Lombards and the Huns, the Venetians developed their (for all intents and purposes) independence when the Byzantine Empire either left or was forced out of northern Italy (depending upon who you believe).

Located on the east coast of Italy, in the upper northwest of the Adriatic Sea, Venice had several things going for it. First, the city is situated in a region that gives it ready access to and from the northern regions of Europe. If the Germanic regions wanted cotton, black pepper, or, later, sugar, they headed to Venice, as long as they had silver or other valuable products to trade.

Second, Venice, although not containing more than 100,000 people at its height, had resources available to it that allowed it to not only defend its lands but threaten and cajole other regions into giving the Venetians theirs. At first the threat was backed up by being the westernmost outpost of the Byzantine Empire. Later, after they turned on their masters, the Venetians could simply pay for large navies and armies to get their point across.

This leads me to the third advantage they had—money. They had lots of it. Through a series of events, the Venetians were unlike other regions in the area, as they were influenced only a little by the church and even less so by royalty. The ruler of their city was the doge, a term that is related to the English word "duke." But to the Venetians, it was as far from royalty as our term CEO is from "politician" in our world today.

Doges were elected (albeit for life), which meant that the title was not inherited. What influenced the voters was how much money a potential doge could bring into the city.

For example, in 932 when the Venetian leaders determined that the far more successful salt producers in Comacchio were affecting the sales of Venetian salt, they decided that the best course of action was to invade Comacchio, burn down its church, and massacre its citizens. Anyone who survived was taken back to Venice, where their options were either to swear fealty to the doge or lose their heads. This is a corporate takeover at its most literal.

Using these sophisticated techniques and advantages, the Venetians became successful traders in the Mediterranean and Venice evolved into one of the wealthiest cities of Europe.

With their Byzantine connections and vast merchant fleets, the Venetians had their fingers in many pies. From seafood, to salt and black pepper, even to positions within the church, everything that could be bought or sold was. This would include such things as medicine, fruits, and the one ingredient that tied these both together: sugar. And where sugar had a hold, medicines containing the ingredient were close by.

I was feeling the need for medicines myself, as the rain continually plopped on me and the city. I was getting antsy. I was hoping to find a way to avoid the unpleasantness that weather such as this can bring to one's state of mind. Recognizing that nothing gets accomplished when no action is taken, I decided to take control of the day. I gathered my jacket and waterproofed myself as best as I could. I would go out into the rain, come hell or high water. I was going to find me a candy shop.

Although I didn't have to worry about hell, high water was most certainly a concern, as many streets and alleys were flooded to some extent or another. Either I had to walk on the elevated catwalks that the city saw fit to put up in order to have pedestrians avoid the ever-growing puddles, or I had to find detours to the several streets that had been closed outright. The careful planning that I had done for this impromptu journey had been ruined by the rain. When I left the confines of my hotel room, I had a fairly good idea where I was going thanks to a map that the concierge had provided. A mere thirty minutes later, and an innumerable amount of unplanned right turns, and I had no idea where I was. Compounding the problem was that the day was quickly dwindling into early evening, and the close confines of the walkways made Venice appear quite dark. At first I would look at each business I passed, trying to find that one place that might sell confections. But as the day turned to evening, I became more intent on trying to figure out just where in the hell I was.

When I located a business with bright displays in its front window, even though others around them had closed for the day, the shop appeared as if it was an oasis. It was only when I looked at the display case and saw torrone after torrone that I realized I had accidentally come upon exactly what I was looking for. As I peered deep within the shop, my realization was confirmed. I had found the first true candy shop on my trip.

The shelves were stocked full of torrones of different sizes and ingredients. The walls carried chocolates from Lindt and Caffarel. There were baskets full of tiny pieces of chocolate-covered hazelnuts called *nocciolotto,* and *caramelle,* which I easily recognized as traditional caramels. Each piece was individually wrapped; 300 grams' worth could be had for only three euros. On the top shelf of each display were several different types of a dense cake known as *panforte,* an Italian version of our traditional Christmas fruitcake.

I shook myself like a retriever that had just stepped out of a swimming pool and looked for a basket to begin my shopping. It was then that the older gentleman came out from the back, said something to me in Italian, and made a gesture that seemed to indicate I was to go back out into the rain.

"You're closed?" I asked.

I had no idea if he understood me or not, but he nodded and walked out from behind the counter, indicating to me that it would be best if I was on the other side of the door.

I stole a glance at a clock on the back wall. It was the top of the hour. I had indeed entered the establishment exactly at closing time. I nodded in agreement, bowed for reasons that I have yet to understand, and left into the darkness of Venice. The candy looked precious, even more so now that I knew that I could not have any. My mind flashed back to when my parents would deny my requests for chocolate bars, and I became flooded with an eerie sense of déjà vu.

As I walked through the city in search of anything that seemed familiar (so that I could make it back to the hotel), I understood that sometimes merchants didn't wish to sell their wares. Sometimes the promise of a good meal at home or an inviting drink at the local tavern could be more important than trying to sell another ten euros of product.

Sugar was never the primary focus of the Venetian merchants. That honor goes to black pepper. But from the point at which they established the first sugar warehouse in 966 to 1204, when they took over Crete and introduced the sugarcane in order to fulfill demand, many of the Venetian merchants realized that Europeans' love affair with the new sweetener meant that not only was it here to stay but it would likely outsell honey at some point.

What was it exactly that made sugar a better sweetener than honey? There are several reasons. For one, it was moderately easy to produce from sugarcane, as long as people were willing to put in long hours in front of a large, boiling cauldron.

Number two, sugar in its crystalline form is far more portable than honey and quite a bit lighter. Therefore it's easier to transport and, thus, to trade.

Finally, there's its chemical makeup. Refined sugar consists of sucrose, a disaccharide that is composed of two mono-saccharides—glucose and fructose—linked via a chemical bond. The result of this setup is that it reacts differently when put into different environments.

Let's take water. Add sugar to water and it breaks down, or, more specifically, a small proportion of the sucrose hydrolyses, a process better known as hydrolysis, a chemical reaction during which molecules of water (H_2O) are split into hydrogen cations (H^+) (conventionally referred to as protons) and hydroxide an-ions. The result is that the sucrose yields a solution of fructose and glucose. To put it into terms that we nonscientists know, it becomes a simple syrup, and a very versatile one at that.

Heating this syrup shows exactly how sugar trumps other sweeteners. The process, known as sugar boiling, is a method of progressively concentrating the syrup. It's a process anyone can see in the kitchen. All you need is a pot or pan that distrib-utes heat equally and a syrup in the ratio of roughly two parts sugar to one part water (too much water and the refined sugar will not dissolve until the syrup has been heated).

The more sugar within the syrup, the higher the temperature at which it boils. This is when the magic happens. Most of the stages are defined by the physical properties of the boiling sugar syrup when a bit of it is poured into cold water (see sidebar).

You will notice that I called out very specific temperatures. This is all well and good for us living in our modern age, but for cooks around the turn of the first millennium this was a bit prob-lematic as access to thermometers would not be available until the sixteenth century. Working with sugar in the several stages listed would have been considered an alchemic skill, a talent that would have put such knowledge into high demand. Thus, a fair bit of the history of candy involves the story of the discovery and improvement of talents and technologies surrounding sugar boiling.

STAGES OF SUGAR BOILING

1. Thread: 215°F–235°F; 108°C–118°C. At this stage, the sugar is less a solid and more a viscous syrup, often providing the base for icings, jellies, and, well, syrups. Few, if any, candies are available in this state, as it's more liquid than solid. Between 230°F and 235°F the boiling sugar creates small bubbles, which indicate a little more "stickiness." The syrup will spin a two-inch thread when dropped from a spoon, a trick pastry chefs everywhere take advantage of.

2. Soft Ball: 235°F–240°F; 118°C–120°C. A small amount of syrup dropped into cooled water forms a soft, malleable ball that is easily shaped by hand or equipment, or even by looking at it crossly, so much so that gravity will flatten the ball for you. It is at this stage that candies and sweets such as fudges, fondants, and pralines are made.

3. Firm Ball: 245°F–250°F; 123°C–125°C. Drop a bit of sugar cooked to this temperature into cold water and it will form a firm ball, one that won't flatten when you take it out of the water. Instead, it will retain some level of malleability and will flatten when squeezed. It has a bit more structure to its form than sugar cooked to the soft-ball stage. Many caramel candies use sugar cooked to this stage. But don't confuse the caramel candy with the boil stage mentioned below. The two are different beasts.

4. Hard Ball: 250°F–265°F; 125°C–133°C. It is at this stage that the sugar will form thick threads as it drips from the spoon. The sugar concentration is rather high now, which means there's less water in the syrup. A little of this syrup dropped into cold water will form a hard ball, one recognizable to most of us as a hard candy. If you take the ball out of the water, it won't flatten, instead retaining its shape. However, it can be molded to a specific shape. This makes molded candies an option, as we can see in many of the confections made with sugar at this stage, including nougats, marshmallows, gummies, divinity, and rock candies.

5. Soft Crack: 270°F–290°F; 135°C–145°C. The cooked sugar becomes less "smooshy" and more "stretchy" at this stage. Depending upon the temperature, the sugar can be worked, but it stretches and requires some effort to do so. At this point one can make taffy and pulled sugar candies such as candy canes.

6. Hard Crack: 300°F–310°F; 150°C–155°C. There is almost no water left in the sugar at this point, and it becomes quite difficult to work with. Often candies cooked to this stage are left to harden, and that's all the work that's done to them. Or a bit of acid can be added to the concoction (citric or tartaric, thank you very much) to create even more types of candies such as acid drops. At this level you have your brittles and toffee.

7. Caramel: 320°F–335°F; 160°C–168°C. Caramel is defined here not as a type of candy, but rather as the change that occurs when the Maillard reaction takes place. Think the crispy bit of browned sugar on top of flans and you'll have a basic idea of what caramel sugar actually is. Getting to this stage is almost akin to stepping right up to the cliff's edge; one more step would be catastrophic. I say "almost" because, let's face it, sugar boiling isn't an extreme sport.

The liquid, viscous nature of the sugar syrup would have been a familiar vehicle for cooks and alchemists alike. Additionally, the physical similarities between sugar and salt would also have been noted, and in fact, there are records of sugar being referred to in various Roman texts as "Indian salt." Because of these similarities, it's not a stretch to conclude that cooks would experiment with sugar in the same way they used salt *and* honey.

What their experimentation would have uncovered was that granulated sugar works quite nicely as a preservative, which was particularly helpful when dealing with fruit. Sure, one could have salted or smoked the fruit in order to preserve it. But drying it out was still the preferred way of extending the shelf life of whatever fruit was available. Because, let's face it, who wants a salted kumquat?

Imagine the delight of cooks when sugar came onto the scene and they discovered how it affected preserving fruit. What happens when granulated sugar is spooned onto a slice of fruit? The water within the fruit dissolves the sugar via hydrolysis. Then it binds up the water molecules, drawing them out of the fruit's living cells. With limited or no water remaining in the fruit, bacteria have no place to live, no place to thrive. The bacteria's food supply literally dries up, which either cripples or outright starves the remaining bacteria within. Voila! Preserved fruit.

Kate's Candy Bag

FRUIT ROLL-UPS

Fruit roll-ups came on the scene in the mid-1970s, and everyone who didn't wish to contribute to the obesity rate, or the cavity counts of children, felt obliged to hand these out at Halloween. For my siblings and me, we felt that these candies were nothing more than trade bait, the "player to be named later" when it came to our candy swaps.

I can remember how several parents in our neighborhood lauded the technology necessary to create such a confection, not realizing that the means to produce fruit leather has been around since the time of the Egyptians.

Candy Exchange Rate:
3 fruit roll-ups = 1 York Peppermint Pattie

The folks who discovered this method of preserving fruit found that the sugar complemented the taste of the fruit. The texture of the fruit turns chewy, almost gummy. The flavors within grow more concentrated. The added sugar mitigates any tartness that may be within. The fruit almost ceases to be fruit; certainly, it becomes different in taste and texture than dried fruit. It becomes almost candylike.

Store these fruits in an abundance of granulated sugar, and the sugar then takes on some of the characteristics of whatever is being held within. Place an orange peel or six in your jar of sugar at home, and in a few weeks, your sugar will contain a faint yet distinctive taste of orange. Try dried plums or rose or violet petals, and the sugar will impart a plum, rose, or violet taste.

It was through this process that violet and rose sugar came into being. Plop a bouquet of flowers into the sugar, and the sugar will take on the characteristics of the flowers both in smell and taste. The popularity of rose and violet sugar was such that often households that could afford these treats would keep more flowered sugar on hand than white sugar.

Confectioners at the turn of the first millennium would likely have stored fruit in sugar syrup, similar to the way that honey was used. In doing so, these folks were laying the groundwork for candies that were developed three to five centuries later.

There was one more, less acknowledged benefit of cane sugar over honey. For many of the domesticated honeycombs, smoke was used, often to excess, in order to tame the bees when the honeycombs were gathered. As a result many honeys contained not only the taste of sweet but also the taste of smoke. Sugar, refined from a less flavor-intrusive process, was pure sweet—no smoke added.

These were the benefits of sugar. It was more adaptable, it had a more "pure" sweet taste than many honeys, yet it still provided the preserving benefits. The immediate benefits of fruit preservation are obvious: a family can store a preserved fruit far longer than one that hasn't been preserved. To merchants, the preserved fruit held value for a longer period of time than fresh produce, so much so that they could export these fruits to other cities and countries.

This wasn't a new idea. Merchants had been doing this for ages with honeyed fruit. But place a piece of fruit preserved by sugar next to one preserved by honey, and the simple benefits become clear: less mess; less space taken up on ships and caravans. Place it next to sugar itself, and suddenly even the simplest of merchants could see the benefits.

The Arab merchants used this tactic quite well throughout the Mediterranean. They exported whatever meager amounts of sugar they could afford to, and they also traded any confection that could last the long travel time on the Silk Road or on merchant crafts on rough, open seas.

And if, say, a merchant saw enough value in sugar to create a sugar warehouse, then he would see the value of the medicines the Arab traders stowed on board to keep their galley slaves alive and marginally healthy.

By 1150, business for the Venetian apothecaries, or *spezialis* (from *spezie*, for "spice") was so brisk that they could afford to outsource their pill and syrup making to third parties. As a result Venice's first confectioners took root in the city. Later, when people realized that they could skip the middle man, they would go directly to the confectioners for these medicines. This led to disputes among the guilds and merchants—but I'm getting a bit ahead of myself.

As more and more people became exposed to sugar and the confections that were made from the commodity, the demand for the product grew. Many historians point to the First Crusade as sugar's turning point, believing the crusaders' exposure to cheap sugar, and the many products made from it, while stuck in Jerusalem made them crave the sweets once they returned home.

The reality is likely more nuanced. Sugar had reached southern Europe by the ninth century. Sugared sweets and medicines, although quite expensive and limited in availability, would have made it to various trading points throughout Europe at least one hundred years or so before the First Crusade.

Using Venice as one of the staging areas for the Crusades would have been just as influential as exposure to sugar in Jerusalem. For it was in Venice that the average crusader would have seen sugar, fruits preserved with sugar, and medicines made from sugar, and these products would have been affordable.

From the point of view of the confectioner and candy historian, Venice's role in the Crusades was critical to the expansion of the demand for both sugar and the ideas and products surrounding it.

By 1100 AD candied fruits were popular, although they were just as likely to be made with honey as with sugar at that time. By 1150 AD, Venetian traders were introducing comfits—tiny sweets made from single seeds, nuts, or pieces of fruit covered in layers of panned sugar—to merchants throughout the continent. By 1319 AD, Venetian traders were selling fifty tons of sugar per year to England, at a value in today's money of more than $20 million. During these two hundred years, sugar took off in ways that would change the culture of many a European country.

By this time the Italians started taking the lead in pharmacology and its associated skills. By the twelfth century, Arab pharmacology began to diminish in quality, both in the East and in the West, with only a few exceptions. One region of importance during this decline in efficacy and influence was Egypt, where men such as Kuhin al-Attar and Ahmed al-Antaki documented their approach to medicines and the confections that they made.

What made this region so important? The Mamluks, a lower caste of slave soldiers who successfully controlled the trade routes through the Red Sea. The Mamluks were a major trading partner of the Venetians.

The Mamluks acquired so much power that they eventually became a powerful military caste in many Muslim societies. They ruled in various capacities in the Levant, Iraq, and India, where they acquired and then held their political and military power. Most notably, the Mamluk factions seized the sultanate in Egypt and Syria; the Mamluk sultanate thrived between 1250 and 1517.

It is from al-Attar and al-Antaki via the trading routes of the Mamluks that pastilles were introduced into Europe. Of course, they weren't called pastilles, a name that is as French as it looks. They called them troches and, later, lozenges. These were small

Kate's Candy Bag

ALTOIDS

Altoids are one of the few candies that I developed an affection for as an adult. It is also the best possible example of the modern-day troche this side of the Necco Wafer. I was never a fan of peppermint as a kid (unless it had a chocolate coating). But as I grew older, something clicked which made me seek out more and more peppermints. When I found one that advertised itself as "curiously strong," I had to try.

The phrase "curiously strong" has always struck me as an odd one. I could never imagine the Nestlé company advertising their candy as "strangely chocolate."

Candy Exchange Rate:
1 tin of Altoids = 1 York Peppermint Pattie

oval, round tablets, roughly the size of a quarter. They contained seeds, herbs, or other medicinal agents incorporated in a flavored, sweetened mixture or fruit base. Pastilles are meant to dissolve in the mouth, which, in theory, helps to slowly release the "drug."

However, whenever I've had pastilles, my impatience overrides any recommended consumption instructions, and invariably the candy will be chewed almost immediately after being put into my mouth. My logical side says that I don't have time to wait seven minutes for a candy to melt. In truth, my id loves it when I crunch things.

Looking through a variety of Islamic formularies from the twelfth and thirteen centuries, we find a litany of different recipes for pastilles available. There's *qurs al-banafsaj,* a pastille made of violets, yellow myrobalan, turpeth, licorice, anise, gum traga-canth, scammony, and sugar; it was used as a laxative. Then there's *qurs tabashir kafuri,* a concoction that includes rose petals, licorice juice, mucilage from flaxseed, and sugar (supposedly good for coughs and chronic fevers).

Confections and pills were also a large part of the Islamic pharmacist's repertoire, with the typical recipe for a "pill" similar to this for a cough: gum arabic, licorice, broad beans, chickpeas, flour, starch, almonds, myrrh, gourd and watermelon seeds, and aniseed, all crushed and then boiled together with sugar.

The pharmacists of this age also worked directly with traders of spice. The raw ingredients that they used or sold reached Egypt via the Red Sea trading route, and the quality of their products was only as good as the quality of spices that they could acquire from Yemen and India. This trade was of the utmost importance to the Mamluks and was a major source of revenue for Egypt during this period. Of course, according to the more fundamental Catholics in the Vatican, these were heathen traders. When Saladin was able to conquer a great part of Jerusalem in 1291, the pope retaliated in the only way he could: he prohibited trade between Catholic Europe and Muslim Egypt.

Venice was displeased and advocated a return to the trade routes. This was permitted in 1345, and by 1395 the volume of spices reaching Venice via the major Mediterranean ports of Alexandria and Beirut dwarfed that coming via the Black Sea port of Tana that they had acquired from the Byzantines.

The Egyptians who benefited most from this were the Karimi merchants, a group of wholesale merchants who special-ized in spices. They were the great international merchants of their day, and they found themselves profiting from their role as middle men in the trading between Egypt, India, and several Italian city-states (primarily Venice). They were most prominent during the fourteenth century, until the sultans realized how much money (and thus, power) there was in the spice trade, and gradually began usurping control from these merchants in the private sector. Eventually the sultans began to monopolize more and more of the spice trade, not only out of greed and a thirst for power but also because of a long-term decline in the population of the sultanate caused by the Black Death and subsequent outbreaks of the plague. This decline in population meant a decline in income from revenue-producing land allocations, which caused the Mamluk leadership to come up with other streams of money. They turned to higher taxes, then later confiscation of high revenue–producing trade routes and sugar plantations, and finally, exclusive government monopolies of the spice trade and sugar industry in order to keep themselves in power.

The spice trade, however, was a transitory trade, and Egypt's control of it was dependent upon its control of the Red Sea route to the east. Egypt could only preserve its own geopolitical importance by ensuring exclusive access to this trading route. When the Portuguese reached India by going around Africa in the early fifteenth century, the Egyptian fortunes ran out. Venice ended its partnership with Egypt, and the Venetians' role as primary supplier of drugs and spices to Europe, which had been the raison d'être of the city-state, ended as well.

The mark made by the Arabs on the sugar and confection history was an impressive one. For six hundred years, Arab medicine influenced the West, either through innovation, education, or economic trading prowess. How strong was the influence of Islamic medicine upon the Western world at the start of the Middle Ages? A great many of the Latin pharmacological works were dependent on translations from the Arabic texts. The most

famous center of learned medicine in Europe before the arrival
of the Arab medical tradition was in Salerno, in southern Italy.
Already by the tenth century Salerno had the reputation for excelling in practical medicine, and during the eleventh century,
Salerno physicians started producing new medical texts.

It was here, in the monastery of Monte Cassino, that the first
wave of translations from Arabic into Latin took place through
the efforts of Constantine the African. By 1065, he began to translate the medical works of Greek and Arab authors into Latin.
Some of the massive amount of work he accomplished included
formularies and pharmacopoeias. These pharmacopoeias ended
up in the hands of the apothecaries throughout the peninsula.

These trends in Salernian medicine spread to the whole of
Europe by the thirteenth century, and further translations occurred, as well as growth in the number of physicians and pharmacists. The material chosen to be translated was determined
by its supposed usefulness. The changes these translations added
to the European world of medicine were seen as a leap in the
pharmacological discipline. But it likely had less to do with
the efficacy of these new confectionary cures and more with
the "exoticness" of the ingredients used. That it also helped
fuel the spice trade was just an added benefit.

It was after the Italians started translating these texts that the
second major variable in sugar's popularity came into play. At
some point during the latter part of this era, the perception of
sugar underwent a transformation. The evidence of this comes
from a medium that was rare in thirteenth-century Italy—the
cookbook.

The distribution of recipes via the written word has been
around since the time of the Babylonians, who put the recipe for
beer in a poem on a clay tablet. But for the most part, conveying
the ingredients of a dish was primarily an act that fell into the oral

tradition. Writing down recipes required three things that your average everyday cook was unlikely to have: literacy, wealth, and time.

Because of this, finding historical documentation surrounding food is rare, and when it is found, it often exclusively describes the eating habits of the wealthy. But since we've already determined that sugar was primarily a commodity for the wealthy, looking for Italian cookbooks is a logical path.

The one book that stands out is a Venetian manuscript written in the mid-1300s. Known in today's Italian as *Libro per Cuoco* ("Book for Cook"), we can see where and how sugar was used in the kitchens of the Venetian elite. What's interesting about this book is that, for the most part, honey is still the primary sweetener in the kitchen. When sugar is used, it is as a means of mitigating the saltiness of cured meat products.

However, in the late thirteenth century, in a Neapolitan work, *Liber de Coquina* ("Book of Cooking"), honey is used primarily as an addition to sauces. Sugar takes on a larger, more direct role in cooking, one that we're still using today. Somewhere between the late 1200s and the late 1300s, sugar became more important in Italian kitchens.

This transformation of sugar usage is key to the development of candy because, although apothecaries still used the powder in their medicines, sugar also became a tool in the cook's repertoire. Soon the two seemingly disparate trades would cross paths, when people would try to replicate in their own homes the medications that they purchased from the apothecaries.

I finally made it back to my temporary residence, but as the hotel had no dinner service, I was forced to go out into the rain once again if I was going to have anything to eat that day. I wrapped myself up in my jacket, placed a cap on my head, and headed back out into the storm.

Rather than risk the touristy restaurants around Piazza San

Marco, I stuck to the back alleys and minor thoroughfares until I found a place that seemed to be completely devoid of tourists. I was in a miserable mood, and did not want to be bothered by those afflicted by wanderlust. I wanted alcohol, I wanted silence, and most of all, I wanted to be warm and dry. I entered the first place that seemed like it would sell me food and leave me alone.

The restaurant was empty, save for the lone hostess behind a counter and presumably a cook in the back.

"Scusi. Capite l'inglese?"

She paused for a moment. "Yes," she said.

"What would I eat here if I were a Venetian?"

She smiled, pulled out a menu, and pointed at one dish in particular. I took the menu to the table and considered the use of sugar in Venetian cooking.

Still damp, I ordered a glass of red wine and a plate of what she recommended—*sarde in saor,* fried sardines that had been marinated in vinegar and sugar. Whether truly Venetian or not, this local delicacy screamed to me "Made for long sea voyages." Was sugar a traditional ingredient in this dish? I did not know. But I hoped that the rain was temporary and that tomorrow would bring sunshine. And I would wake up early enough to find that candy store.

Chapter 5

The Merchant City

● ● ● ● ● ● ● ●

*W*hen I woke up, it was readily apparent that the day was to be a better one than the previous because the sun was permeating the darkness of my hotel room. A quick look outside confirmed my joy—blue skies. I dressed quickly and left the confines of my dry, warm room for the bright day ahead. My goal? Return to the candy store that I had found the day before.

There was one problem. I didn't know where the store was located. I did not let this dissuade me from my purpose. I was sure that I could stumble upon its location again. Venice is little more than a collection of islands. How difficult could it be to find one store?

More difficult than one might expect. There's little rhyme or reason for the paths throughout the city, and as horses—and then cars—have never been a permanent part of the Venetian landscape, there has been little need to rezone the city for it to make any ordered sense. As it has worked for over a thousand years, there is little need to change now.

I tried retracing my steps, but the overcast skies of the day before had hidden the smaller, more important landmarks that I could have used to navigate the pathways. I looked for the cat-walks, but they had been removed now that the flooding was receding with the tide. When I believed I had found a place that looked familiar, it turned out to be a similar, yet altogether different location from where I wanted to be. A street that I was sure had a church ended up having a tobacconist. A place I was sure was the candy store turned out to be a high-end shoe shop. Either the candy shop existed in a Venetian version of Brigadoon, or I had no idea how to navigate the back streets of Venice. My money was on the latter.

As I walked around Venice, it became apparent that it was designed (or redesigned, as we shall see) to allow tourists to imprint their own version of the city. Want to view the religious history of the island state? There are churches everywhere. Care to explore art from different periods? There are museums that cover everything from the Renaissance to modern art. Want to live the life of the nouveaux riches? Venice has high-end shopping and dining that appeals to the powerful and the easily awed.

What you won't see in Venice is any obvious evidence of its mercantile roots. Not unless you're looking for it, that is.

My search for the candy store had taken me to the Mercato di Rialto, the open-air market found just off the Grand Canal in the center of the city. One of the great markets of Europe, possibly of the world, it compares easily with the Borough Market of London or Pike Place Market in Seattle. Except that here, the fish is taken right off of the boat and placed in the market stalls. It is here that the tourists take pictures and the locals get their fresh fruits and vegetables.

Ah, tourists. Being one myself, it's difficult to be too critical of them. If you don't mind large crowds while you are investigating a foreign city, then you probably have no beef with their presence. If you love the thrill of traveling but despise excessive crowds, then you probably avoid activities that would increase your odds of being labeled one yourself. If you have the urge to purchase garish T-shirts, cheap shot glasses, poorly photographed postcards, and other similar bric-a-brac, then not only are you a tourist, you would likely have no problem having that moniker flashing over your head and a siren alerting others to your traveling habits. It is these Tourists with a capital *T* who are the traveler's equivalent of the fans who wear face paint and blow vuvuzelas incessantly at sporting events. These are the people who have that ever-impressive ability to be both harmless and annoying at the same exact moment.

The Rialto in Venice is full of such people. There were Americans taking pictures of themselves or their loved ones on the bridge. There were Canadians laden down with all manner of overpriced knickknacks. There was a British couple trying to haggle down the price of pasta that they would take back to England.

I looked upon this crowd the way that an Olympic skier surveys a downhill run. If I cut around that couple, made a quick right by the shop, jumped over the spilled gelato on the pavement, worked my way past the crying child, and then sprinted behind the people in front of the stand selling cheap *limoncello,* I might be able to make it across the Rialto Bridge and into the Mercato di Rialto with limited difficulty. I took a deep breath and dove into the throng.

The Rialto is the heart and soul of Venice. It's the one area of the city where residents and tourists are forced to comingle. It is the financial and commercial center of Venice and has been so for centuries. Yes, there are stores for the tourists here, and there are several shops selling loads of overpriced Venetian trinkets, but this is the primary place where fresh fish and produce is sold to the local populace. As space in Venice is at a premium, there's simply no other place to put the market, which has been here in some fashion or another since 1097.

Having done my fair share of market shopping in Europe, I'm used to visiting shops and even some businesses that are older than the United States. But as I walked around the periphery of the market, I realized that it is rare for me to be in places of business that have been around longer than Great Britain has been a country.

Right off the market, slightly to the southeast, is a smallish street called Ruga degli Speziali, which roughly translates into "street of the apothecaries," or "street of the spicers." This location is as close as Venice gets to taking notice of its roots. Looking around, at the boats loading and unloading directly onto the Mercato a mere fifty yards or so from where I was standing, I could easily see how this area would have thrived.

There's a store here called the Antica Drogheria Mascari, a relative newcomer to Venice, having only opened in 1948. It wasn't the candy store from the evening before, but I was drawn to it all the same. Some of this was due to its location and the wanderlust it instilled. Some of it had to do with the acknowledgement, real or accidental, of the store's ties to the apothecary shops of ages past. Mostly the appeal of the shop was due to the several variations of torrone that had been put on display in the window, each variant representing a different region of Italy. There was *torrone con nocciole e miele* from the Piedmont, *fondant con frutta candita* from Florence, *torrone con pistacchi, mandorle, e miele* from Sicily, and *torrone con mandorle e miele* from right here in Venice. Displaying these in the window was like a beacon to me, and I felt the desire to explore their store.

Upon entering, one could easily be forgiven for thinking that this store had been around for centuries, what with the spices on the back wall, and the nuts, dried fruits, liquors, and jams shelved throughout. From my own perspective, the owners of this store had created a modern-day version of the apothecary, and my mind easily filled in the picture of patrons of years past entering this location for their pastilles and pennets. I had to remind myself that this shop had only been open for some sixty years.

Ah yes, the *pennet,* one of the first modern medicinal candies of which we have direct evidence outside Italy, in part due to Venice's reach of trade.

By 1319, we have the first recorded major importation of sugar into England when ten thousand pounds of sugar and one thousand pounds of sugar candy were brought into Southampton from Venice. But there are records of sugar and sugar candy in England for many years prior to this. King Henry II had sugar budgeted into his kitchen costs in the mid-1100s, and by 1288, the royal family was going through sugar and sweets to the tune of six thousand pounds in one year. From these records, we can guess (and really, owing to limited records, guessing is the best we can do) that sugar in some form was introduced into northern Europe and England at the end of the 1000s or start of the 1100s, and that the residents were interested enough in the product to keep looking for it when the traders visited.

Rare or not, it seems as if those who could afford sweets and sugar were still using it primarily as a medicine. When Edward I's son John took ill, he was prescribed, to no avail, licorice, rock candy, and the pennet. It's hypothetically possible that his doctors also prescribed manus Christi, a medicinal hard candy made from sugar, flowers, and rose water, sometimes with gold leaf or pearls added for reasons difficult to fathom in today's age.

Let's focus on pennet, or pennid, for a moment, because it's one of the first candies of which we have clear evidence. The word itself is derived from the Arabic *al-fanid,* a term dating back to the thirteenth-century, Moorish-occupied Iberian peninsula. Roughly translated, the word means "pulled sugar, shaped into discs."

We can deduce that by this time confectioners and medicine makers were boiling sugar to at least the soft-crack stage. Someone, somewhere (probably in Persia) had discovered that sugar at this stage remained flexible yet cool enough to handle. This allowed the sugar to be manipulated, stretched out, and then folded in on itself repeatedly. While we know that this process incorporates air into the sugar, giving it its sheen, back then, they must have initially thought it akin to magic. When they found that the sugar could then be sculpted by hand into various shapes, or that oils or flavorings could be added, well, they must have thought it borderline miraculous.

That pennets were prescribed to the sick child of Edward I is understandable. To those of us who suck on a cough drop or even a piece of Werther's Original, the basic theory is the same. The sugar, brought to body temperature, melts and, while it won't cure the problem, it does provide temporary relief to aggravated areas of the throat.

From a merchant's point of view, this meant that pennets held some measure of value, one of which they would surely have taken advantage of. Pennets (which traveled very well) and all of their variants would have accompanied sugar and preserved fruits to all the major trading posts of Europe in the medieval era.

It's this chase for medicine in medieval Europe to which candy and other sweets owe their debt of gratitude. Once the idea of Arab pharmacology took hold in the minds of the elite of Europe, the demand for their medicine took off.

For example, in 1390 there are records of the Earl of Derby paying "two shillings for two pounds of penydes." There's also an early Arab medicine called a *diapenidion,* made from ground penids, pine nuts, almonds, cinnamon, cloves, ginger, licorice, and starch, which was still being prescribed in the 1600s in England for flu, pneumonia, and tuberculosis-type illnesses.

Exotic sugars flavored with violets and roses imported from

Kate's Candy Bag

PEPPERMINT DISCS

On the end opposite the Altoids continuum is, quite possibly, the dullest candy on the planet—the peppermint disc. Often given to children by adults who have the best interest of the child in mind, under the misapprehension that "It's candy! Who wouldn't like candy?" peppermint discs are the first candy that teach children the idea of patience. For while we would have preferred Pop Rocks or a 3 Musketeers bar, we recognized the thought behind the gifts. This is also the candy most often handed out at restaurants.

In fact, I'm willing to bet that the majority of peppermint disc sales are to people looking to pawn off these candies on someone else. This is hardly a selling point.

Candy Exchange Rate:

18 peppermint discs = 1 York Peppermint Pattie

the Middle East were also popular as cures. A look at the books of the English royal household in 1287 indicates that rose sugar was far more popular a product than regular, granulated sugar—to a tune of 1,900 pounds versus a measly 677 pounds.

Was this store I had wandered into a tie to the Venice–England trade connection? Only in the loosest sense of history, but I jumped on that tie like a kitten jumps on the light of a laser pointer.

I looked around the store, my eyes brightened by the new and the exotic, overwhelmed by the options available to me. The child within me wanted to buy everything that I could, but the adult in the back of my mind kept having thoughts such as "luggage weight," "health concerns," and "insulin levels." The adult in my brain was being a killjoy.

That is, until I saw the marzipan.

While not unheard of in the United States, marzipan is certainly a lesser known product and does not carry the popularity of, say, a chocolate bar.

This is what we candy aficionados call "a shame" for it is from marzipan that one can mine enough sweetness for the child, yet enough history for adults that both end up satisfied with the treat.

Marzipan is another confection that is older than sugar's popularity. Recipes for it have been found in the *Kitab al-Ṭabikh*, a tenth-century Arabic cookbook, which not only shows it has been around for a while, it also ties the sweet to the history of lozenges. A section about making *lawzinaq* (literally, "almond confection") describes making two different types: *yabis* (dry) and *mugharraq* (drenched). A translation of the dry method, where skinned almonds are ground to a fine paste, and then sugar, water, and rose water are added, can be found in Rodinson and Arberry's book *Medieval Arab Cookery*, and comes preciously close to sounding like an early recipe for marzipan. While the end result is more akin to an almond brittle, it would not have taken much effort to play around with the water-almond-sugar ratio until something resembling the marzipan we know and love today was discovered.

The earliest evidence we have of the word "marzipan" being applied to this sweetmeat is in the 1300s, in the documents of Pegolotti, a Florentine merchant and writer. The word also meant a small box in which valuable trinkets and foods were carried. It derives from the Persian and Armenian word *marzuban*, which not only meant "governor of a region," but may also have referred to a unit of capacity that the size of the box specified, as directed by said governor. Such etymology, as suggested by

Maxime Rodinson in his essay "Venice and the Spice Trade," would indicate that the confection was a frequent gift put into a box by leaders and rulers; eventually the treat itself took the name of its container.

However, as with most of the confections prior to the Renaissance, much of this is pure conjecture. If you're not content with this path to marzipan, there are literally dozens of other theories. As there is little to no evidence that points to the exact moment when marzipan was created, the best most food historians can do is speculate based on limited existing evidence and word etymologies, an imprecise science at best.

When it comes to marzipan, the only thing food historians can agree upon is that no one can be absolutely right.

What we can be sure of is that marzipan took off in popularity in Europe, with several regions of the continent (incorrectly) assuming the mantle of marzipan discoverer, the most egregious example of which comes from the German town of Lübeck. The legend is that that a local baker invented this sweet treat during a great famine in 1407. As he had only four ingredients left in his pantry—sugar, almonds, eggs, and rose water—he made the only thing he could. He worked the ingredients together to make a paste that he fashioned into shapes to cheer up the town's hollow-eyed children. Considering three of those four ingredients originated in the Middle East, it either makes the legend quaint, or out and out ridiculous. I leave that to you, the reader, to decide.

The Spaniards have a better right to lay claim to marzipan's creation: the *mozarabes*—Christians living under Moorish rule— wrote in the eleventh century of getting together with fellow Catholics to celebrate the Mass of Christ and eating marzipan.

My guess, based on other circumstantial evidence, is that the Arabs invented marzipan, dropped it off at various ports of call within the Mediterranean, and the treat took off from there.

And one of those ports of call would have been Venice; specifically, no more than sixty feet from where I was currently standing.

That the Italians tend to shape marzipan into fruit shapes and colors, albeit bite-sized, made the treat seem that much more appealing to me than purchasing, say, a loaf of marzipan. Seeing the almond paste in the form of bananas, strawberries, and pineapples, I realized that this was what I was looking for. I went to the counter, shared an awkward round of "I don't speak Italian," "Non parlo inglese" with the kindly woman behind the counter, and yet still managed to purchase a small package of marzipan, a few peppermint pastilles, and a handful of espresso suckets, my nod to the pennets of years past.

I walked a bit more around Venice, trying to get a feel for the place and tie it to candy's past. In doing so, I could not but help feel elated. I was in the most European of European cities, on a bright, sunny day, and I carried a bag full of confections. I was thrilled. No, I hadn't found the store I was looking for, but I had come across a place that I could connect to Venice's merchant history of centuries ago.

I examined my joy as I walked around the throngs of tourists. Sure, I was one of them, but yet, not. I wasn't here to see the churches or the piazzas or to ride the gondolas. I was here to tie myself to the history of Venice and to sample it in a very literal sense.

This is what the best of food does. It ties us to our past, and for a far too brief moment, we are no better or worse than a merchant of Venice who wishes to soften a cough with a bit of mint and sugar. For all our technological breakthroughs in the past seven hundred years, there are moments when we can experience nearly the exact same things that an average citizen in the fourteenth century did. That I was walking on man-made islands that have been around for just as long, with buildings nearly as old, made me feel as if I was part of the past.

This was a far different feeling than I anticipated when I set off on this journey. Initially, I had expected to connect to that moment in my youth when I had no concerns beyond whether I should have a Hershey's bar with almonds or one without. Instead, I found myself thinking back much further in time. I was thinking as an adult who was slightly knowledgeable about history, but somewhere within me was a similar sense of awe and joy from my childhood.

One of the joys of Venice is the fact that it is an island, and that allows a certain sense of containment, one where people can get lost in the twists and turns of the streets and alleys and still be assured that they have a good idea of where they are. Many of the guidebooks I had read to prepare for my visit had suggested that not only should travelers resign themselves to the fact that they will get lost, but that the true Venice experience wouldn't occur until they found themselves in an area with no idea how they got there.

As I had been lost in thought, I realized that once again, I was having that requisite Venetian experience. I smiled, grabbed my bag of candy, and soldiered forward through the darkened passageways and over the sun-drenched bridges, looking for any pattern of streets that might look familiar.

But I did this only halfheartedly. Soon I found myself atop the Ponte dell'Accademia, a large footbridge that covers the Grand Canal before it opens up onto the bay outside of the Piazza San Marco. I opened my bag with the intent of sampling one of each of the candies. I placed myself at the center of the bridge and looked out at the gateway to the Adriatic Sea. Multitudes of passersby walked behind me, some intent on being elsewhere, others fully indulging in the joys of being a tourist, and still others with no clue as to where they were.

The packaging of the marzipan required that I put down my bag of candy and rip open the cellophane surrounding the brightly colored fruit facsimiles. A subtle hint of almond permeated the air around me. I picked up a piece that had been shaped and colored to look like a strawberry and tucked in.

Sweetness leapt across my palate along with a heavy dose of almond. The texture was near that of cookie dough, but far more fine. I closed my eyes to reflect upon the moment.

While marzipan is available throughout Europe, and many places designate themselves experts in the field, my heart will always belong to the Italian variant. Perhaps it is the faux artistry needed to have the marzipan resemble a banana, perhaps it is the fact that other European versions seem too clinical, too . . . manufactured (a silly idea at best, as the treats that I was currently enjoying were as manufactured as any found in Germany or Spain). Then there are the variants that are covered in chocolate, an idea that sounds wonderful in theory but in practice requires both marzipan and chocolate to be pitch perfect. No, sometimes it is better to be simpler rather than more complex.

In contrast, Italian marzipan seemed simpler, more vibrant, more . . . fun. Isn't that the essence of candy?

My activities garnered the attention of both birds and children in my vicinity, some of whom circled me under the belief that they might benefit from my largess. As I had vowed to bring these candies back to the States so that my friends and family could indulge in the treats I had found, I packed up my wares and this time intentionally lost myself in trying to find my way back to the hotel. I never found the candy store from the day before, but I found something else—a moment when I was no longer middle-aged. For an instant, I felt as if I belonged to the Venetian past.

There's a reason why Venice tries to hide its past—it was a

nasty business being the predominant power in the Mediterranean, a business that runs counter to the ideal of romance and art that the city sells today.

Having contacts with the spice routes and being the dominant power of the Mediterranean for nearly five hundred years meant that Venice was in a constant fight with those trying to take its power away. Wars with other city-states were a way of life, and rivals from Florence, Pisa, and Genoa were always looking for ways to usurp whatever they could from the Venetians. The idea was simple. Control the spices, and the world was yours.

Venice toyed with the idea of diversification. They looked to create crops of pepper, ginger, and sugar closer to home but only succeeded in introducing sugar close by, in Crete to be more precise.

In the end, it wasn't any one Italian city-state that took down Venice. Rather, it was the Portuguese, when they improved upon shipping technologies with the caravel, a small, highly maneuverable sailing ship developed in the fifteenth century. With the improvements to speed and capacity made possible by its triangular sails, these ships could and did circumvent the spice routes that crossed Asia. The Portuguese soon found themselves at the doorsteps of India, and they could deal with the source of the spices without having to pay all of the intermediaries that Venice had to satisfy. Venice's days as the trading capital of Europe were numbered.

At the same time, the Portuguese had difficulty in manning their increasingly large navies while colonizing various ports of call. Soon they found themselves having to make up their crews from other regions of Europe. One of the people who found himself hanging out in Lisbon was one Christopher Columbus, who had more indirect influence on the candy industry than one might imagine.

Chapter 6

The Age of Exploration

● ● ● ● ● ● ● ● ● ● ●

*T*here is a difficulty in talking about the history of candy, especially when one is trying to recapture moments of one's youth. Sugar, the primary ingredient in the majority of sweets, comes with historical baggage that cannot be ignored. The demand for the sweetened substance led to abuses of liberty and freedom of individuals that we are still paying for today. For a book that's supposed to talk about a topic as light as candy, it has to be acknowledged that the demand for sugar to make confections, medicines, and later rum resulted in an increase in slavery.

Slavery had been around for thousands of years prior to this time. By the time of the Crusades, when sugar took its place on the world stage, it was common practice for Muslims to be enslaved by Christians and vice versa. This later evolved to a point at which the religious distinctions used in the slave trade became blurred. The practice became so commonplace that Christian and Muslim merchants and consumers alike would buy slaves of any religion. For reasons too complex to address in this book, it became the belief among both the European Christian community and the Muslims of North Africa that the citizens of inner Africa had a higher value on the slave market. Soon they were considered status symbols and were prized as domestic servants in the very early stages of the Atlantic slave trade. Black slaves living in a white society stood out, and this made it hard for them to run away, which was a definite advantage from the owner's point of view. Furthermore, it was a popular assumption that black Africans were better workers. By the 1300s, slavery was widely practiced throughout the Mediterranean world and became an industry unto itself. This prompted the merchants of Europe to enter the Atlantic seeking new sources of slaves in sub-Saharan Africa and the Canary Islands, the way they might explore a new land looking for pepper or gold.

All of this was occurring as demand for sugar was rising, and governments were looking for ways to profit from this demand. As the Portuguese, with their new caravels that allowed them to travel farther and faster, moved into the Atlantic and followed the coastline south, they took the sugarcane with them and introduced the crop wherever they could. Sugar production was introduced on the islands of Madeira in 1452 by the Portuguese, with canes brought from Sicily and capital provided by Genoese financiers. It quickly proved a success and encouraged the Portuguese to explore farther south along the coast of West Africa. Soon, sugar cultivation could be found on the Azores, Cape Verde, and ultimately Brazil. With the intensive labor required for sugar production, slavery followed close behind.

It's not as if Portugal just up and decided to go exploring one day. Instead, what we have here is a marriage of convenience of sorts between Portugal, which had the technology, and Genoa, which had the finances to support exploration, as well as a deep-rooted desire to stick it to the Venetians, who had been kicking their asses in the spice market for centuries. While it is likely that the primary motivation for the explorers of the age was to find a new route to India in order to gain control over the pepper, ginger, and sugar trade, there would have been enough motivation to find areas closer to home where such crops could be grown.

So the explorers often had a secondary task of establishing plantations where one could grow high-return crops that would thrive in whatever local environment they encountered. The labor initially was provided by indigenous people taken into slavery. When aboriginal slave labor was soon found to be more difficult to enforce than the Europeans had thought, African slaves were brought in to fill the labor void. This is where the slave era begins in the Western Hemisphere.

What does all this have to do with confectionery? Demand, pure and simple. There were other sugar products that helped propagate the slave practice, chief among them rum. But the products of the apothecary, and later the many home remedies that were made to try to re-create the medicines, were all part of the initial demand that was the reason that the Venetians, the Genoese, and later the Flemish and British invested heavily in the trade.

I closed the books I had brought on the train from Venice to Genoa that explained all this history in great detail, and a deep sigh escaped from my lips. I opened a bag of mint pastilles that I had purchased on Spice Alley in Venice and contemplated their role in the escalation of the slave trade.

It wasn't mint that caused this escalation, that much was sure. Mint is one of the oldest flavors on record, starting out its culinary history as an herb, rather than the oil that is so prevalent today. Use of the herb had been recorded in ancient Egypt,

Greece, and Rome. It took few resources to grow, and evidence of its presence can be found in history from the Levant to England and everywhere between. If there was a high demand for mint, in all its varieties, it would have been easily met.

No, the cause was the sweetener itself. And the demand for it was coming from confectionery, not rum. For one thing, the timing is wrong: rum, from molasses, didn't become popular until the 1600s and 1700s. But here we were in the mid- to late 1400s, with historians telling us that people were making money from the sugar trade, and they were doing so at the cost of other people's freedom. The demand for sugar had to be coming from somewhere, and with rum yet to hit its popularity, that leaves us with confectionery.

I rolled the pastille through my fingers as the clickety-clack of the train wheels rolled beneath me. Here I was on a train to Genoa, nearly a third of the way through my journey to reconnect with my innocence, and the history of candy was letting me know that nothing about its role with sugar was very pure. I frowned at this realization.

Perhaps I was being unfair. While the basic recipes for candy may not have changed all that much in the past six hundred years, perceptions have. Should the candy of today or, more specifically, the candy of my youth, be looked at with suspicion and disdain based on events that occurred long ago? Various cultures have come and gone since the era of slavery. Behaviors surrounding how one interacts with commodities such as confectionery would have evolved as well. One needs to look no further than the original language surrounding these treats, much of which has disappeared from everyday use. Terms that were around for centuries suddenly went missing in a generation or two. Such is the fate of the term "comfit," a word that is likely only known to candy producers today.

Comfits were a food of the wealthy, a side dish used to provide a bit of Galenic balance to the meal. As mentioned earlier, these would have been the warm and dry aspects so valued by those who ate foods that were considered cold and moist.

These comfits were little more than a bit of spice or nut coated repeatedly in panned sugar, giving the central compo nent of the confection dozens if not hundreds of layers of sugar coating.

Le Ménagier de Paris, a medieval manuscript dated to circa 1393, mentions candied spices throughout the book, although they translate into "chamber spices." Included in these candies are ingredients such as candied orange peel, candied citron, red anise, rose sugar, and white-sugared and red-sugared almonds.

There are plenty of modern confections that can trace their roots directly to these chamber spices. If you've ever gazed longingly at a gobstopper, tasted a Jordan almond or a Good & Plenty, or admired the green shell of an M&M, then you know what they are. Even the term "sugarplum" relates to this type of candy. From a linguistic point of view, the disappearance of not just these terms but any term to adequately describe a piece of candy that is recognizable on sight speaks much to the state of candy in the corporate era.

The odd thing is that these sorts of candies were likely around before the sugarcane era in Europe. Before they were known as comfits, they were known as "dragées." Before that, they were known as something else. John Ayto, in his book *The Diner's Dictionary: Food and Drink from A to Z*, explains:

The word [dragée] appears to come ultimately from the Greek *tragemata*, "sweets," plural of *tragema*, which was derived from the verb *trogein*, "gnaw." These Greek sweets consisted typically of aromatic seeds, such as aniseed or fennel, coated in honey, and this was the association the word *tragemata* carried with it into Latin, and thence into Old French as

Kate's Candy Bag

M&M'S

M&M's, both the plain and peanut variety, were a type of candy that rated highly among my peers, but never seemed to be anyone's ultimate choice when it came to picking a favorite brand. The candy-coated chocolate was invented for the troops of World War II in order to provide them with a chocolate that could not melt. Even knowing this was not enough to convince us that it was our patriotic duty to make M&M's our top choice.

No, M&M's didn't become our top choice until my friends and I were in our early teens, when rumors emerged that the green M&M's were an aphrodisiac. Of course, with the hormones rampaging through our bodies, it was likely nothing more than a case of post hoc, ergo propter hoc. When I was thirteen, they may as well have said that Dr Pepper would make you horny. It was just as likely to be true.

Candy Exchange Rate:
1 small bag of M&M's = 2 Peppermint Patties

dragie. This was borrowed into English in the fourteenth century as *drege,* by which time sugar had replaced honey as the outer coating. *Comfit* soon replaced *drege* as the English term for sweets, but in the nineteenth century English reborrowed the French word, which by then had become *dragée.*

In the twenty-first century, the word "dragée" is still around, but it is used exclusively as a term for those silvery candy beads used for decorating cakes. Instead of being an all-encompassing term for sweets, the word has been relegated to a single confection known mostly to cake decorators.

So why have these terms diminished in importance? Laura Mason, in her book *Sugar-Plums and Sherbet,* suggests that the words "lost meanings as indicators of status and sophistication" as they, and the techniques required to make them, became popular. In other words, they became too commonplace.

Which is a bit of a shame, really, given their importance in the history of candy. For if any candy represents the turning point from pharmacology to sugared treat, the comfit we know and love is a great place to start. It is with the comfit that the idea of "candy for the sake of candy" begins to take hold in Western culture.

This turning point can largely be traced back to the magical properties contained in granulated sugar. As cooking techniques for sugar evolved and became more sophisticated, what could be accomplished by a skilled confectioner would have appeared as close to magic as one can get in the kitchen. A simple seed or nut, placed in heated syrup, coated, then removed and dried, would have been a commendable discovery. Taking that sugar-coated seed or nut and repeating the coating and drying technique dozens if not hundreds of times, per nut, would have been seen as exquisite. Variations of the sugar-to-water ratio within the syrup would result in different finishes. This would include anything from a dull, matted look, to a pearl-like shiny appearance, from rough in texture to smooth as glass. Add to all of this the use of food dyes, and suddenly the world opens up to the confectioner. A talented maker of sweets could make candies with different fillings and present them in a variety of colors.

Evidence of this knowledge dates back as early as 1475 and

was likely known for several generations before that. According to Mason, by this time, comfits would have been readily known as "a spice or a nut, covered in a layer of sugar." The most popular would have been a candy we still recognize today—the Jordan almond.

In their most classic form, Jordan almonds are exactly the candies mentioned in *Le Ménagier de Paris* as sugared almonds. But in Italy, they are referred to under the generic name *confetti*, along with other panned pieces of comfits made with cinnamon bark, anise seeds, pine nuts, and citron peel. *Confetti* have nothing to do with the English word "confetti," which we take to mean bits of colored paper tossed into the air by someone who has no responsibility to clean it up.

Confetti can be traced back to the Romans, who apparently had a predilection for offering, and then throwing, seeds and nuts at festive events, including weddings and birth announcements. It was *confetti* that was on display in the window of the wedding consultant in Palermo.

This was a tradition that made it all the way to the Renaissance, but by that time the recipe for comfits could be found in multiple Italian cookbooks, and the *confetti* were not just for ceremonial use; they were offered as a component of feasts.

In 1487, more than 260 pounds of *confetti* were consumed at the wedding banquet held for Lucrezia Borgia and Alfonso d'Este, the son of Ercole I d'Este, Duke of Ferrara. If true, this story illustrates that *confetti,* and the sugar used as its primary ingredient, were still popular among the wealthy and ruling classes.

In the middle of all of this exaltation of treats among royalty and the wealthy is one Cristoforo Columbo, better known to us Americans as Christopher Columbus.

This is why I found myself on a train to Genoa, the presumed hometown of the legendary explorer.

Columbus has a surprising connection to both chocolate and sugar, one that makes him the ideal representative of this era of exploration and exploitation.

By the late 1400s, Columbus found himself hanging out in the court of King João II of Portugal. He had reason to feel good about himself. He was an up-and-coming navigator, he had married into a Portuguese family, and, according to legend, he had his own ideas about reaching the spice regions of India.

Contrary to what you may have been taught in school, educated people of the Renaissance did not believe the world was flat—that the earth was round had been determined by the ancient Greeks. The question of the day was how *big* it was. According to one eminent Florentine geographer of the time, the earth was a mere ten thousand miles across at the equator. Using this number, Columbus made the calculation that you could get to India much faster by sailing west than by going south and east.

There is some indication that King João II didn't cotton much to the Italian adventurer, but what eventually damned his proposal in Portuguese eyes was the preposterousness of the numbers. The frequent trips down the coast of Africa had given the Portuguese navigators a pretty good sense of how big the earth was from pole to pole. If Columbus's numbers were to be believed, the earth would have the improbable shape of a football. All the same, as Columbus's father-in-law was the respected Bartolomeu Perestrello, the Portuguese explorer who had claimed Porto Santo Island for Portugal, the king let a commission decide whether Columbus's idea was worth his time. The commission gave it the thumbs-down.

It's probable that the Portuguese navigators already knew what lay beyond the western horizon, and it wasn't India. There is some evidence of this in the form of two Portuguese maps that show Brazil as early as the 1430s. But let's set those aside for the moment as anomalies. Consider the idea that Portuguese sailors spent the years between colonizing the Azores in 1431 and Vasco da Gama's first journey to India in 1497 exploring the Atlantic. Giving the current and winds, it's almost impossible that they didn't at least have sight of South America. When the Vatican helped shape the 1494 Treaty of Tordesillas, which divided up the New World between Portugal and Spain, there was considerable push from King Joao to have the dividing line moved west in order to have the eastern part of South America in Portugal's domain. This placed Brazil in the Portuguese sphere six years before Brazil was officially "discovered." But Joao did not have the resources to explore both the New World and a trade route to India simultaneously.

So instead, Columbus went next door to Castile, where he talked the king and queen into backing his plan. But his trips to the New World were an unlikely event, made doubly so by the reticence with which Ferdinand and Isabella approached exploration. They had never been fully interested in the Atlantic, as there were still regions and cities to conquer on the Iberian Peninsula. But once the cape route to India had been shown to be feasible, and a weakness in the Venetian trade monopoly had been exposed, the Spanish monarchs must have felt a certain urgency to act so that they wouldn't lose out. When Columbus showed up, they likely needed to be convinced not of the profitability of owning a trade route, but rather whether Columbus was the right man for the job.

That's the story most of us are familiar with, along with Columbus's exploration, fall, and then atonement. But Columbus likely had a secondary agenda; or at the very least he was aware of a way to make his journey pay for itself. For explanation, we need to revisit his knowledge of his father-in-law's past.

Let's consider Bartolomeu Perestrello, who had helped settle Madeira as well as Porto Santo. It was at Porto Santo that Senor

Perestrello became the first *capitão donatário* by regal donation in November 1445. He oversaw the planting of the sugarcane and sugar plantations surrounding it, and would have had a hand (either directly, or as an advisor) in the establishment of similar plantations on other islands in the area. Columbus, who had cut his navigational teeth in these islands, would have been intimately aware of the family's history and its path to royalty.

Fast-forward fifteen or twenty years. While Columbus was keen on finding a shorter trade route to find black pepper as his inroad into nobility, he was just as keen on finding lands that would allow for optimal growing of sugarcane. We see evidence of this on his second voyage across the Atlantic, when he introduced sugar to the New World by taking some sugarcane cuttings to the Caribbean colony of Santo Domingo (now Haiti) for trial plantings. The crop briefly flourished in the sunshine, fertile soil, high humidity, and subsequent heavy rainfall. The reason for its eventual failure was not due to the quality of the land but to the poor oversight offered by Columbus. It did not take long for his ventures into the world of sugar plantations to fall behind those elsewhere in the region, and soon the land went fallow.

This is the first way that Columbus influenced the confection industry—by finding and propagating sugarcane. While his successes in this endeavor were limited, he serves as an admirable personification of the mind-set of the era.

The second way he influenced the industry was really more of a lost opportunity. It's ironic that for someone who was looking for a means to become a successful explorer and bring riches to his patron, Columbus had outright ignored one of the most important commodities of our modern era. Columbus was likely the first European to come across chocolate.

After his arrest during his third voyage, Columbus was exonerated and looked to get back to his explorations. Admitting that he had not discovered a distant part of the Far East, this time his goal was to find a strait through the New World and find passage to India and the other spice islands.

Columbus set sail on his fourth journey on May 9, 1502, with four caravels and 150 men. His fleet traveled to Hispaniola (where he was denied permission to port his ships by Spanish colonists), weathered a hurricane, and explored the waters around Jamaica. He eventually went to the west, where he sighted land on the modern-day island of Guanaja, some thirty miles north of the Honduran mainland. What happened next is to be found in the account penned in Jamaica in 1503 by Columbus's second son, Ferdinand.

On August 15, 1502, the admiral had sent a reconnaissance party ashore on the island, where there appeared a dugout canoe, said by Ferdinand to have been as long as a galley. Amidship it had a shelter fashioned of palm leaves, "not unlike those of Venetian gondolas," under which were placed the children, the women, and the cargo. Admiral Columbus immediately ordered its capture and met with no resistance.

Later historians have speculated that the vessel he had captured was probably a Mayan trading canoe, most likely belonging to the Chontal-Maya–speaking Putún. Its cargo included clothing, weapons, and bells cast of copper. Ferdinand stated in his journal:

> For their provisions they had such roots and grains as are eaten in Hispaniola [these would have been maize and manioc], and a sort of wine made out of maize which resembled English beer; and many of those almonds which in New Spain [Mexico] are used for money. They seemed to hold these almonds at a great price; for when they were brought on board ship together with their goods, I observed that when any of these almonds fell, they all stooped to pick it up, as if an eye had fallen. (Coe, *The True History of Chocolate*, p. 104)

What's interesting is that the Spaniards had no way of knowing that these "almonds" were used to manufacture the New World's most royal of beverages (nor could they have known cacao's use as money, that bit being a likely embellishment from later translations). What made the event notable to Columbus, father and son alike, was the value the Mayans had placed on these beans.

In what must have been one of the world's greatest missed opportunities, Columbus didn't follow up on this encounter, let alone taste the chocolate. He let the canoe go and headed toward Panama.

This was what I was about to find in Genoa, during my candy trip. As my train pulled into the station, a brief thought filtered into my head. Legends never live up to their reality. Columbus was likely a status-seeking explorer who had no qualms about exploiting and conquering in the name of God and the highest bidder for his services. And we have exalted him into American sainthood.

I wondered if I had made a similar error in trying to understand the topic of candy. Is the legend of our nostalgia far more palatable than its reality?

Chapter 7

The City That Columbus
Left Behind

• • • • •

I had arrived in Genoa a bit weary from the week on the road. I was still unsure as to why I was there. I had come to the city to, I don't know, pay homage to Christopher Columbus? That seemed both gratuitous and unwarranted. I suppose I came to see the result of Columbus's influence, if any, upon his hometown's confection scene. But I had no explicit plan to follow. My approach was nothing more than to play tourist, look for signs of Christopher Columbus, and then indulge in some confections. Veni, vidi, candy.

Part of my reluctance to commit to anything explicit in regard to Columbus is due to my own baggage surrounding him. Sure, when I was a youth, we celebrated his "discovery" of America every year in October. The education I received dutifully reported aspects of his initial voyage with the *Niña*, the

Pinta, and the *Santa María,* and how he demonstrated that the world was round and not flat. To my eight-year-old self, Columbus seemed heroic, the grandfather of America's pioneer spirit.

The image of him changed drastically over the course of a generation, as legend gave way to historical fact. First off, there was a general belief in 1492 that the world was round, so he was hardly the first to discover that tidbit of information, which anyone with a passing interest in astronomy could have figured out. Second, he never set foot in what was to become the United States. Third, many other cultures, including the Portuguese, whose favor he curried, likely arrived in the Western Hemisphere before he did, not to mention the millions of aboriginal peoples who had been there for thousands of years. Finally, Columbus was very much a man of his era, which is to say he treated various non-Christians as commodities—slaves, really. These he used to help pay off his debt to the Spanish.

Add to all of this the fact that many of the leaders of Europe who had had audiences with him to hear his proposal for a shortcut into India thought he was a bit of a jackass. These perspectives have left me with the impression of Columbus as a social-climbing opportunist who was a bit of a bastard.

Of course, bringing these facts up to the Genoese would be akin to going to the Alamo and proclaiming to the local populace that Jim Bowie was the reason the fort had been lost. I promised to keep my opinions to myself. Instead, I would visit Genoa and see what would happen.

We pulled into the Genova Piazza Principe railway station and I gathered my luggage, walked across the street, and checked into the hotel that sat directly behind the Cristoforo Columbo monument at the Piazza Acquaverde. Apparently finding Columbus's legacy would not be difficult at all.

What I truly wanted to find at that moment was a cup of

coffee. The travel had me awake early, and opportunities to have a macchiato were missed thanks to my rush. I dropped off my luggage and set out for some much-needed caffeine.

One of the great things about Italy is that finding good coffee is nearly as easy as finding breathable air. The Italians don't mess around with the stuff. They don't weigh it down with twelve ounces of milk or cover it with blended ice topped with a heaping amount of caramel and whipped cream. They give you a shot or two of espresso. If you wish to temper the beverage, they will add a bit of milk or cream to the cup, but even with that, I'd be surprised if the drink ends up being anything larger than six ounces.

They also don't like to hang out in coffee shops for any great length of time; this is contrary to how we folk in Seattle get our coffee shop action on. They stand at the extended bar, order their drink, consume it in a minute or two, and then get out. Bing, bang, boom.

A lot of this has to do with the seating charge that these places are obligated to enforce. If you take a seat at one of these places, another euro or two per person will be added to the final bill, essentially adding a 100 percent markup to the drink simply because you wanted to take your time.

I wanted to take my time, and I had no issue with the added charge, for there is another aspect of the Italian coffee shop that I had come to appreciate over the past few weeks: this was where one could find candy for sale.

I'm not talking about your low-end, mass-marketed, Mars bar/Ferrero Rocher chocolates either (although some of the cafés do sell these items). I'm talking about everything from torrone to locally made chocolate to sugar-coated flowers.

As I walked in, everyone at the coffee bar turned to see who had entered. I gave them a brief yet awkward hand wave, con-

vinced that if I pretended that I knew them they would not pose
a threat. Seeing that I was someone they did not know, they all
turned back to their espressos and breves while I walked to the
candy counter.

Before me stood a display that would rival any average candy
store in the United States. In the front counter sat several pastries and chocolates. Behind the counter were dozens of glass
jars filled with mints, pastilles, and *marrons glacés*, sugared chest-
nuts. Oh, the selection of candies that were readily available!

Looking at this array, I hit upon a realization: most people
know that Italians do not carry a whole lot of guilt surrounding
their food, regardless of how good or bad it may be for one's
health. Candy and confections are an extension of that worldview.

They even have a hierarchy of outlets that carry confections.
This hierarchy can be listed as follows:

1. **Tobacconists:** Generally speaking, the tobacconists are
   where you go to find your mass-produced candy. They
   are light on chocolates, heavy on mints and digestives,
   especially the anise-flavored ones.
2. **Grocery stores:** Not in the markets, but in the chain
   grocery stores you can find more mass-produced candies, with a bit more emphasis on the major world players
   in candy (your Mars and your Haribos can be found
   here). Honestly, in the two grocery stores I visited, the
   candy sections seemed like afterthoughts. This makes
   sense, considering the next option.
3. **Cafés:** Many of the cafés I walked by in Palermo, Venice,
   and now Genoa had confections in their windows,
   looking to draw people in. The majority of these were
   pastries, but many places offered simple sugar confections
   that they either made on site or, more likely, outsourced

to a local producer of some sort. The point is, there was candy in these locations. And because they had to compete with the aesthetics of the pastries, many of them were gorgeous—big, fluffy meringues, huge loaves of colorful torrone, and many other types of near-artisanal confections can be found here. My experience tells me that if coffee is an everyday ritual in Italy, then their primary means of interacting with sugar confections is at these cafés.

4. **Confectioners:** These are the high-end shops, where confections are purchased for special occasions. Getting married? You can buy *confetti* from these locations. Attending a dinner party? Here you can pick up sugared fruits dusted with candied flowers, all wrapped beautifully by a salesperson on site. These shops render the confections found at cafés merely pedestrian. There are likely no American counterparts to these types of shops, at least not anymore (although I've seen other similar shops elsewhere in Europe).

Honestly? There are few American counterparts for the cafés either. Sure, we have coffee shops, but we treat coffee shops here (at least the non-Starbucks varieties) more like pubs for caffeine fanatics than we do as a brief respite from the day. Part of this is cultural, of course, because of the aforementioned seating charge. It doesn't take more than a fifteen-minute visit to an Italian café to understand that most people prefer to stand at the bar, have their coffee and pastry, and get out in five minutes, saving their euros for other items.

We also rarely sell candies at our coffee shops, choosing instead to focus on pastries of some sort. And if candies are sold, they are smaller, prepackaged candies. I cannot recall ever seeing a huge glass jar of sweets that needed to be pulled off a shelf full of other candies while ordering my Americano in my home-town of Seattle.

This is the confection environment in which the Italians find themselves. It's easy for them to dismiss mass-marketed candies because they are seen more as lower-end impulse buys than arbiters of the confection quality that we kinda-sorta have here in the States. When the marketplace regularly offers a higher-quality alternative to the mass-produced candies, at only a nominal expense, the Italians seemingly have no problem in choosing the higher-quality item.

When I, as an American, wander into this environment, it's like . . . well, it's like being a kid in a candy store. If a forty-something woman eats candy in Italy, it's simply another day at the coffee shop. If it's eaten in the States, either it has to be a higher-end confection, or it has to be explained away with an embar-rassed "I have a sweet tooth" explanation. Although adults account for 63 percent of candy consumption in the United States, we are loathe to admit it. Furthermore, the advertising of candy to adults is exponentially smaller than the marketing to children. Marketers will tell us that, by the time we hit adulthood, our brand loyalty is nearly set. They will tell you that they would only be throwing away good money by trying a high-profile campaign to get thirty-somethings to switch from Nestlé Crunch to Hershey Krackel. But these messages are coming from the same industry that tries to sell me on the idea that Atkins bars are not confection-ery, but instead are a viable means of nutrition; I find their premise difficult to swallow, not to mention those Atkins bars.

I reminded myself that the Italians have had one thousand years of confection in their backyard and have had far more time to deal with whatever impact it has had on their cultures. Meanwhile, back in the States, we still have to deal with chocolate-covered fondant being called "energy bars." These are two very dissimilar environments.

Kate's Candy Bag

MERINGUE

The recipe for meringue is dead simple. Fold whipped egg whites into boiled sugar, shape, and then set in the oven until dry. There is no flour, little mess, and the meringue can be good for a couple of weeks unless hit with moisture. In Italy, meringue can be found in many, many confection shops.

When I was a child, meringues were things my Italian neighbors handed out for treats, either at Christmas or Easter. Depending upon the skill of the cook, they were either dipped in chocolate or filled with crushed nuts of one form or another. We took them when offered, only to be polite. After eating some, we invariably asked for more.

Candy Exchange Rate:
3 meringues = 1 York Peppermint Pattie

I purchased a small bag of chocolates and a similarly small bag of meringues, went to the counter, downed a quick espresso, and went back to my hotel room to rest for the next day.

Genoa was an easy city for me to like. There's a certain feel that cities next to major ports have, one that nonport cities miss entirely. Part of it has to do with the sheer diversity that enters and exits the city every day through the ports. It matters not if that diversity is in the shape of people or products from distant lands. There seems to be this feeling of "Let's just get things done, and let others get their things done as well," that is prevalent in many of these cities. Seattle has this feel to it, as do San Francisco, Boston, New York, and, seemingly, Genoa.

Yes, there were major tourist areas, specifically in the old town and the newly gentrified docks that border it. But beyond this area of the city were the docks to the Mediterranean and areas that reminded me that there were hundreds of thousands of people in the region who likely thought of me in the same way I thought of the folks who flocked to Pike Place Market or the Space Needle: "Thanks for coming, please spend your money, and please stay the hell out of my way." I was a tourist, and there was little evidence that could convince me otherwise.

I still had the goal of seeing where Christopher Columbus grew up, so I perused the Internet and picked up directions to his house. I reflected upon this for a moment.

One of the great things about Genoa is how walkable it is, as long as you're not averse to climbing a hill or two. With Columbus's home being a mere two miles from my hotel, I used the opportunity to walk to the old town, then through the Piazza de Ferrari, and down Via Dante to the "casa di Cristoforo Columbo."

It was a beautiful day for the walk, with a crisp chill in the air but a bright blue morning sky above me. It took me no time at all to make the distance, and I soon found myself outside a skinny, three-story house that looked over five hundred years old. I paid my six euro to enter the house and began to look for any hint of the influences on Signore Columbo's life.

What I found instead was two interesting pieces of information. The first came from a sign, a cement plaque, really, set above the small, centuries-old house.

It read:

Nulla Domus Titulo
Degnior Paternis In Aedibus
Christophorus Columbus
Pueritiam Primamque Juventam Transegit

Translated, it means roughly "No house is more worthy of consideration than this in which Christopher Columbus spent within the walls of his father, the first youth."

It's a rather touching sentiment. Too bad a photograph found within this small building shows this exact plaque at several other locations in Genoa over the past 120 years.

Add to this that whatever building that may have belonged to the Columbus clan was likely destroyed in 1684 when the French invaded. At best, the location of the Columbus house was nearby, maybe even spot on, but the house was most certainly a re-creation.

I contemplated this for a moment and came to a conclusion. I was okay with this. When it comes to Columbus, the legend has always overshadowed reality. Genoa wasn't selling tourists the reality. They were selling the legend. The house was a perfect representation of such. It had been re-created to fit the time and to supply both the United States and Genoa with a hero. The legend of Columbus reflects our ideals, and the reality reflects ourselves. That the Genoans wish to make a buck or two off that—well, what was more American than that?

Besides, from my perspective, he still had a strong influence on candy's history.

I mulled over this idea as I walked back through the old town of Genoa. The old town is a series of city back streets that have been around since time immemorial. These are the paths that were created when the town was first founded, around which

homes, merchants, and, soon afterward, churches had been built
and grew into the city of Genoa. It's an area of the city that had
fallen into a bit of disrepair until a recent infusion of cash, which
was invested to help clean up the area, with the hopes that tourists
would come and bring along with them a return on the investment. As I studied the groups of people who were wandering the
streets, it appeared as if this is exactly what had happened.

The end result of this update to the old town of Genoa is that
this area of the city comes across as a cleaner, less wet version of
the back streets of Venice. Businesses and markets are everywhere and, as the streets are narrow, it allows only for foot traffic in many of the areas. Like Venice, its size is quite manageable
for someone on foot, but unlike the city of canals, getting lost is
never an issue. While the old town can still have a claustrophobic feel to it, what with the dark, Gothic, five-story buildings
crowded next to one another, it is quite pedestrian-friendly. The
area comprises an incredible amount of tiny streets and alleys
called *caruggi*. Walking through this area, it just feels as if these
were buildings and streets that had been around for centuries,
albeit adapted and updated for the modern era.

All the while, I thought of what I was trying to accomplish
here. I wanted to go to Genoa, Italy, and see how this city represents Columbus, and if I could gain any insight on this man
from the Genoan perspective. The hunger in my belly let me
answer with a "You did fine. Could we move on to a higher
priority?"

That priority was looking for a specific high-end confectioner found in the deep recesses of old town. Its name? Pietro
Romanengo fu Stefano.

The confectionery is not on one of the several major thoroughfares of the city, but after a few wrong turns and a few moments of backtracking, I soon found myself pressing my nose
up against the window and looking at the store's wares.

This was a candy store that seemed made for royalty. The display was placed upon a fabric of deep violet, and several of the wares in the shop had been placed on it with the delicacy usually employed by a museum curator. The window was festooned with bright, colorful, and clearly handmade confections and everything from marrons glacés to candied flowers was on display.

I went into the store and started looking at all the products on the shelves and displayed in the counters. These weren't candies made for children. These were confections that were meant to celebrate, to share, and to impress. These candies (if I dare call them such) were meant to instill a sense of sophistication.

Think about that for a moment. We live in a world of M&M's and Haribo gummy bears. There is nothing sophisticated about these products, unless you count their marketing processes. I hesitate to bring the element of "class" into the discussion, but the confections in this Genoan store communicated a nuanced aesthetic that Hershey and, heck, even Godiva could only dream about. The closest experience I'd had prior to this one was in a chocolate shop in Brussels, yet even that is akin to saying that one has experienced Manhattan because one has visited Hoboken.

I spoke very little Italian, and the woman behind the counter spoke no English, yet I was still able to get the purchases I wanted, each selection wrapped in a royal blue paper and bound delicately with string, just enough to provide a handle of sorts. The process of buying confection here was less a transaction and more of a ritual—one that I, a clumsy American, was loathe to disrupt.

I purchased several items from the woman, including a box of candied apricots and figs and a small assortment of *pâtés de fruits*, which struck me as a high-end version of Chuckles. I also purchased some candied violets and rose petals, and even a small bag of Genoese dragées, which held a selection of sugar-coated almonds, pine nuts, pistachios, citron peels, and bits of cinnamon stick. But there is one item that I purchased that I believe best represents this shop.

On display was a confection known as *lacrime d'amore,* which translates to "tears of love." These little treats are no more than the size of a large caper or peppercorn and are as delicate as tissue paper when put into the mouth. Press down too hard on their outer shell, or bite them, and they instantly disintegrate, leaving behind a smallish amount of liqueur. Each color has a distinct flavor, from pink representing rose water to white for anise to a pastel yellow indicating lemon. Unlike most confections, which have bolder, stronger tastes, what makes these candies unique is both their delicateness and their subtlety.

Even under the briefest consideration, it is clear that these candies were not made for children. The nuances would simply be lost upon them. No, these candies are for those who have a more delicate palate. I later passed these candies around to friends and family back in Seattle, without comment, along with other, more traditional Italian confections. These were talked about more than any other—they are *that* intriguing. From my perspective, one that includes trying to write a book on candy, these were a revelation: I felt that no candy better demonstrated the dissonance between what candies were and how we perceive them today.

Pietro Romanengo fu Stefano was founded in Genoa in the second half of the eighteenth century by Antonio Maria Romanengo, not surprisingly as a drugstore. The company was so well regarded that it often provided the royal families of Europe with their sweets for both private and official functions. Giuseppe Verdi was a tremendous fan of their work and marvelled over Romanengo's candied fruit in several of his letters (which are preserved at La Scala opera house in Milan).

I had come upon one of the more distinguished candy shops in all of Europe. I indulged in as much as I could, again with my inner adult letting me be aware of everything from calorie intake to the money I had budgeted for this trip. Here I was in one of the better candy—no, confection—shops that I had ever been in, and my inner child was still struggling to be heard over the litany of responsibilities that I, as an adult, felt had to be addressed.

The entire trip in Italy had been this way to some extent. While my inner child had made brief appearances throughout this journey, more often than not I held myself to the very adult responsibilities that come with traveling. There were moments of brief awe surrounded by multitudes of budgets, schedules, e-mails, and writing obligations.

I noted this observation in my notebook back at the hotel room and hoped that on the next stop of my journey, the United Kingdom, I would be better able to connect to my inner child.

Chapter 8

From Portugal to Great Britain

• • • • • • • • • • • •

I looked at the clock, where it sat on the end table, silently mocking me with its display: 4:30 AM.

Damn.

I closed my eyes to see whether I could squeeze out a few more minutes of sleep, but it was not to be. Those of you who travel a fair bit, and even you insomniacs out there, will recognize this as the "Ah shit, my body is rebelling against my brain" moment.

I had arrived in the United Kingdom with a specific goal in mind: to find a candy shop. Not just any candy shop, mind you, but one that matched the image of candy shops that I had created in my youth and had refined over the course of my life. This ideal had been battered during these many years, mostly by reality, but somewhere in the back of my mind was a candy business that would awe children into silence and make adults giggle in anticipation of the treasures to be had within.

In this fantasy candy shop, there are shelves upon shelves of candies of all sorts. Because of the amount of candy being sold, the business is rather large, but not overly so. There are candies from around the world, and rare sweets can be found right next to the more popular varieties. The counters are staffed by matronly middle-aged women wearing overly starched aprons and providing each customer with perfect suggestions. The candy sold is both familiar and rare. Names such as "fizz bombs," "bonbons," and "twirly bangs" ring out as necessary, pleasing everyone within the shop.

I initially blamed Gene Wilder for this fantasy, which has been in my head for over a generation. His performance as the title character in the movie *Willy Wonka & the Chocolate Factory* showed a world where candy ruled supreme. The lessons of moderation that the movie tried to convey were lost on me. Only rivers of chocolate, Everlasting Gobstoppers, and Three-Course Dinner Chewing Gum stuck with me. What other types of candy and confection were to be had in Wonka's factory?

Soon after viewing the movie, I found out that Mr. Wilder was not the true instigator of these fantasies. That title actually belonged to one Roald Dahl, and his book *Charlie and the Chocolate Factory*.

First, Mr. Dahl had a gift for naming candies. Nut Crunch Surprises, the aforementioned Everlasting Gobstopper, and the Fudgemallow Delight (which contained Charlie's golden ticket). He made up names of candy that I wanted to try.

Second, his story was quintessentially British. This I was to learn a long time after reading it, when I finally understood what "quintessentially British" could mean. At least with regard to candy—or as the Brits call it, "sweets."

This is why I found myself in a hotel room in Edinburgh, at four thirty in the morning, contemplating how I could find the candy shop of my dreams.

Yes, Edinburgh. Edinburgh, Scotland.

I realize that, to the uninitiated, the idea that Scotland has a distinct candy tradition sounds as plausible as Kansas having a robust seafood trade. After all, Great Britain's climate couldn't produce a viable sugarcane crop given its distinct lack of tropical rain forests.

But for a period of nearly three centuries, people in the British Isles consumed sugar as nearly no others in the history of this planet. Sugar helped define the line between rich and poor, provided an economic foundation for the British during their years of colonization, and created wealth for the merchant classes.

Among the roll call of the new wealthy was one Henry Tate, who started life as a grocer and migrated into sugar refining, making enough money to become one of the more powerful men in England during the nineteenth century. You may better know him as the man for whom the Tate Gallery and the Tate Modern museum were named after he donated his collection of contemporary paintings to the government in 1889.

The end result of this fascination with sugar is a litany of candies and sweets that are unique to this nation. Some of them would be recognizable to Americans under the category of "Grandma candy."

When I was younger, I believed that there were two standards for candy. First and foremost, there was candy that we kids enjoyed: Snickers, Reese's Peanut Butter Cups, and other similar brands that we purchased with our meager allowances and hoped beyond hope to receive on various Halloween solicitations.

The second standard applied to any candy that our grandmothers offered us. These candies were ones that were never instantly recognizable, and we looked at them with skepticism. It was common for us to be reminded by the adults in the room that what we had in our hands was candy, and that we liked candy, and why were we looking at it in such a strange manner?

One of my grandmothers had a predilection for purchasing hard candies from other countries, candies that had words from faraway lands plastered on them. Often these candies were made with honey, licorice, or some bizarre amalgam of the two. Once I put them into my mouth, I quickly determined that the candy was meant to be sucked on, like a Life Saver.

My other grandmother made her own candy, proudly boasting that it was "hard-tack candy," which made it seem, somehow, less appealing.

 ### *Kate's Candy Bag*

BUTTERSCOTCH DISCS

Butterscotch discs are the ultimate in Grandma candies. A child doesn't go looking for these sweets, but instead is given them with a nod and a wink, letting the kid know that they're about to be let in on a sweet secret.

The child, wishing instead for Bubble Yum or a Twix bar, accepts the candy begrudgingly. After unwrapping the cellophane and popping the treat into his mouth, he realizes exactly what secret he's been let in on: grandparents can have a sweet tooth equal to those of their grandchildren . . . and they're willing to share.

Candy Exchange Rate:
15 butterscotch discs = 1 York Peppermint Pattie

And missing from all of the Grandma candy was any mention of the words "chocolate," "nougat," "fizzy," "sour," or any other candy word that would cause children to burst into a fit of delight and make parents reconsider allowing their kids to even look at sugar again, let alone consume it.

But we ate the Grandma candy anyway, for two reasons:

1. We never, ever wanted to disappoint Grandma. Because in the battles of kids versus parents, a grandmother was often a worthwhile ally.
2. When you're a kid, eating candy—any candy—is better than not eating candy at all.

What I was about to discover was that much of the candy that I called Grandma candy has its roots in Great Britain.

The question is, how did this island nation in the North Atlantic become the center of the confectionery universe? After all, by the time Columbus left his mortal coil, it was Portugal and Spain, not England, that were making the big bucks in the sugar business. England had yet to garner its own direct connection to a sugar supply.

The Portuguese were rolling in the stuff, and much of the wealth created by the Iberian nation came from sugar. And the royalty of Portugal made sure that the rest of Europe knew it.

In 1565, twenty-year-old Alexander Farnese, son of the governor of the Netherlands, married Princess Maria of Portugal at the Palace of Brussels. This was clearly a marriage of political opportunism. The Spaniards, who were the ruling class in the Netherlands, were forging a strong tie with the exceedingly wealthy Portuguese. Alexander, with his ties to Spain, could help the Portuguese diplomatically. Marriages of political convenience were the common practice of this time.

What makes this marriage unique was the celebration.

Like many of the royal marriages of the time, it was celebrated in grand fashion. The difference? The Portuguese had
made much money in the sugar trade, and the banquet tables
demonstrated this. Alexander's mother, the regent of the Netherlands, Margaret of Parma, walked around the tables full of
crystallized fruit from areas near (Spain, Portugal, Genoa, and
Naples) and far (Africa, the West Indies). These candies were displayed in dishes, jars, plates, and cups, with matching knives and
napkins. The evening was lit by candelabras and chandeliers. All
of these were for show, all were made of sugar, and, ultimately,
all were meant to be tasted.

This scene, as majestic as it was, wasn't even the centerpiece of
the evening. That honor was for the display in the next room,
where several tables were set up with scenes of Princess Maria's
voyage to Brussels, complete with modeled city gates, shipwrecks,
carriage processions, and palaces. The detail was so intricate that
one could see tiny modeled kittens and parakeets in some of the
windows. All of this was also made with sugar.

As I said, the Portuguese were making a killing in the sugar
business. I mean this both figuratively and, because of the slave
trade, literally.

The display of such massive amounts of sugar, estimated at
roughly six thousand pounds, may seem gratuitous to us today,
but by the time of this marriage, such displays of sugar (and by
association, power) were commonplace with the elites. Sugar
sculptures were invented roughly around the late fifteenth century, once the material became available in excessive quantity.
Such displays, ironically called "subtleties" even though they
were anything but, were seen in the courts in Italy, Portugal,
Spain, and later Hungary, France, and England. One such feast
was held for Philip II where, along with lightning, thunder-
bolts, and a hail of comfits, three tables descended from the ceil-
ing, each with displays of a multitude of sweetened preserves.

One table contained a rock made from candy sugar, with five trees, also made of sugar, carrying blooms of sugared fruit.

This was conspicuous consumption on full display. And although many food historians try to paint sugar's growth during this era as a response to the gaining popularity of new imports such as coffee, tea, and even chocolate, the fact remains that sugar already had demonstrated its usefulness outside of these mediums. Sugar, in all of its personas, was popular long before tea's introduction in the seventeenth century. In the sixteenth century sugar found its tipping point. Supply was such that it was no longer restricted to either medications or minute consumption for pleasure. It was a full-on colonial commodity, one that the Western European states both desired and demanded.

Such displays weren't restricted to the Portuguese wealthy. The British had their own sugar subtleties. The physicians of the era proclaimed that sugar's humoral qualities were unequivocal—it was perfectly balanced, dry, warm, and, once consumed, it went throughout the body. Its delight was such that "if sack and sugar be a fault," wrote Shakespeare, "God help the wicked."

Once the countries of the Iberian Peninsula began to cultivate sugar in the Canaries and Antilles in the mid-1400s, the quantity of available sugar in Britain surged. Shipped in cones weighing up to thirty pounds, it had to be broken into chunks with nippers and ground in a mortar before it could be used. It cost about a shilling per pound, or a laborer's daily wage—special enough to make an ideal present. But as merchant wealth grew, the taste for sugar inexorably trickled down to the gentry and yeoman farmers and consumption expanded: the pound of sugar that lasted a whole year for an entire household in the early 1400s would hardly have been enough for one person in the 1500s.

Sugar's cachet came from its taste, its conspicuous expense, and its lusty reputation. And it had one more crucial characteristic: like honey, it acted as a preservative. As pungent spices began to lose their allure and the Tudor palate woke up to the soft taste of butter, the tingle of citrus, and a more pronounced use of nutmeg, the final course at medieval feasts evolved into a final sweet course called, confusingly, the banquet. This banquet, which we think of today as a form of royal feast, back then was a selection of confectionery and candies—a hallmark at the feasts of the well-to-do.

Bristol was the port of entry from the Canary Islands during Henry VIII's reign. By the sixteenth century, Antwerp became a major refining center, importing crude sugar from Lisbon, and sugar into England became easier to obtain. After Antwerp was captured by the Duke of Alva in 1567, the refining switched to Amsterdam, and sugar became even more available.

The price of sugar in England during this era reflects this growing availability. From 1259 to 1470, the average retail price was about 17 pence per pound. Around 1480 the price dropped to 8 pence; in 1490 it went down to 6 pence; in 1500 to 4 pence; and in 1510 to around 3 pence. One can see in cookbooks of the period the increasing use of sugar, especially for subtleties and confections.

What are subtleties? Go into the bakery section of any major grocery store in the United States, and you'll invariably be drawn to the cakes of many shapes and sizes. But it's not the cakes themselves that are of interest. It's the cake decorations. Little sugar sculptures, sometimes in the shape of a flower, other times, letters and numbers used ostensibly to spell out "Happy 5th Birthday," "Congratulations," or even "Merry Christmas." They are all sugar, or more specifically sugar paste, and they play a distinct role in candy's tradition. One of the earliest recipes containing sugar paste comes from the documents of Alexis of Piedmont in 1562, who was both English and, not surprisingly, an apothecary.

By this time in history, sugar usage by apothecaries was fully established. The benefits were twofold. The medieval pharmacists had found that sugar paste was a near perfect medium to deliver measured quantities of drugs and tonics. Consumers of the drugs found that the sugar soothed the throat and made their breath less rank. By the Renaissance, fashion for sweets would rise and fall, but the apothecaries' need for sugar would remain constant.

Sugar paste had the benefit of being less labor-intensive than typical boiled or pulled sugars. All that was required was sugar ground down to a near powder and a bit of gum arabic or gum tragacanth. Once combined, the resulting paste could be molded or sculpted like clay and had a nearly indefinite shelf life.

Alexis's recipe went something like this: steep some gum tragacanth in rose water; mix in a mortar with a small amount of lemon juice, egg whites, and sugar; and knead like dough. The result? Sugar paste that could be rolled out into a "plate of sugre, whereof man may make all manner of fruites, and other fyne things with theyr forme, as platters, dishes, glasses, cuppes and such like thinges, wherewith you may furnishe at table."

Think about this for a moment. Here we have an apothecary making edible "platters" and "cuppes" made from the still rather expensive commodity of sugar. This would be akin to us today eating dinner off paper plates made of twenty-dollar bills and then throwing them into a fireplace for disposal. Nothing sends the message that someone is very wealthy indeed than eating meals from expensive and disposable tableware.

These types of tableware could be ornately decorated with flowers and family crests made with additional sugar paste. The sugar could be made aromatic with flower petals and herbs. Dyes could allow for specific aesthetics, everything from delft ceramic ware to marble.

Pasting skills became rather refined over the course of the years, to the point where people were adding cinnamon to the recipe and then shaping and coloring the paste to resemble a cinnamon stick. It didn't take long before sugar paste flowers, castles, and even fish, were being made, displayed, and sometimes eaten.

I say sometimes because there was a fine line between edible sugar paste and inedible gum paste. Gum paste was far more malleable than sugar paste and had a greater range of uses. Confectioners who were more keen to have their work appreciated for their looks left sugar paste behind and began using gum paste, causing much confusion on just what was allowed to be eaten at the dinner table.

Much like the earlier subtleties, these sculptures, regardless of whether they were made from sugar paste or gum paste, were made to get people talking. To make a feast or banquet memorable, one needed to make an impression, and nothing did that faster than saying something with style. Telling an honored guest that he and his accomplishments were memorable was one thing; communicating the guest's feats and accomplishments so all other guests could read and point to them throughout the evening was something else entirely.

Someone, early on in the sugar paste fad, had the bright idea of mixing established confectionery techniques with that of sugar paste. Sheets of paste were pressed into two halves of molds, filled with comfits, and stuck together to provide surprises for diners.

Beyond medication and gratuitous displays of wealth, what was sugar used for? One theory is that of conserving of fruit and jam making. While preserving fruit with sugar was not new (mixtures with honey were common long before sugar arrived on the scene), the methods involving sugar were. It spread from royal courts to the kitchens of more modest social groups such as shopkeepers, artisans, and even peasants. Later, the making of these preserves could provide supplemental incomes for those in the merchant classes, especially if they had ready access to gardens and orchards. The recipe for preserves was so accessible that women found to be in need (whether widowed or abandoned) could sell preserves to provide a small income. Jam making took on a feminine aura, similar to that of lace making.

What is notable about the above is that it demonstrates, over a course of a few generations, the migration of sugar from the royal class to the bourgeoisie to the distinctly lower class. This shift in sugar consumption between social classes plays a key role in the history of candy as it shapes how we look at candy today. There are people today who will gladly consume a seven-dollar piece of salted caramel, yet ignore the one-dollar Snickers bar. This attitude starts here, during this transition.

It is likely that convents—which were multiplying in number in Catholic Portugal and Spain while being threatened or outright closed in Protestant England and Holland—were partly responsible for introducing sugar to the lower classes. These convents, lavishly provisioned by the churches and royal houses, found themselves entertaining their benefactors with trays of sweets in order to maintain good standing. They would, in turn, use that same sugar to make confections that ended up in the pantries of the less well off. Under the idea of symbolic and spiritual valorization, the nuns would distribute fruits, flowers, and jellies fit for a king to the underclass. The idea that was being communicated was that the underclass had just as much right to the pleasures of God as kings did.

But it was more than preserves that were becoming more popular. As more and more sugar was imported into Lisbon from Portugal's colonies, more and more confection and pastry shops opened. By 1552, there were close to thirty *tiendas de confeiteiro* (confectionery shops) and ten *tiendas de pastéis* (pastry shops) in Lisbon.

Over the course of the next generations, the trade of confectionery, influenced by the Italians and then fed by the sugar supplies of the Portuguese, blossomed across Europe. Cities soon began extolling and promoting candy "made" within their confines. Candies such as the *calisson d'Aix*, a candy made of a thin paste of melon confit and almonds ground together and topped with icing; *cotignac*, a small cube of quince paste from Orléans; and preserved mirabelle plums from Metz were all developed and popularized in this time and are still around today.

With confectionery taking off, the general public soon developed its own discerning palate. One myth has it that when Marguerite of Burgundy married King Louis X and became queen, she had her personal confectioner make some mints. The result was substandard, and the queen ordered the confectioner to distribute the poorly made candies to the common folk of the northern French town of Cambrai, under the pretense of including the lower class in the marriage celebration. When the candy was discovered to be of poor quality, the legend goes, they threw the candy right back at the ones offering the sweet treats. Effigies of the poor confectioner started showing up at various festivals soon after, and assorted candies were tossed at his representations. These candies were later known as *bêtises de Cambrai*, or "idiocies of Cambrai." While this story is likely untrue (the era of Queen Marguerite was in the early 1300s, long before sugar was plentiful enough to just give away), the story itself is indicative that candies were being developed to the point where quality could be discerned and a value given to the candy based on said quality.

The Britons were not immune to this new indulgence. Henry VIII also loved his sugar. His cooks furnished the royal table and receptions with all sorts of confections, including spices coated with sugar, marmalades, marzipan, sugar plates, and subtleties shaped in the form of soldiers, saints (including a St. George on horseback), and St. Paul's Cathedral. Under Elizabeth I and James I, the sugar banquet evolved into a standard element in court entertainment.

This heavy reliance upon the Portuguese and Flemish sugar put the British in an unenviable position, one where the demand for sugar was at the whim of the suppliers. The government of England soon decided that it needed to get into the sugar business for itself.

After the British defeated the Spanish Armada, they indulged in sugar in all of its forms. Confectioners took on the role of artists as much as producers of treats. Subtleties became de rigueur in the English court, and Henry VIII loved these so much that he entrusted the sugar creations to only one person. Elizabeth I had such a sweet tooth that by the time she was sixty-five years old, Paul Hentzner, visiting her Greenwich court from Germany, wrote:

> Next came the Queen, in the sixty-fifth year of her age, as we are told, very majestic. Her face oblong, fair but wrinkled, her eyes small, yet black and pleasant, her nose a little hooked, her lips narrow and her teeth black (a defect the English seem subject to, from their too great use of sugar). (Mintz, *Sweetness and Power*, p. 134)

With the royal court and the upper class of Britain clearly enamored with sugar, the foundation for their fascination with sugar candy had been set. Queen Elizabeth's sweet tooth was the reason that I found myself exploring the tradition of sweets in Great Britain. I was in Edinburgh in a quest for the most rudimentary of all British sweets—Edinburgh Rock.

When ten o'clock rolled around, I headed out to see what Edinburgh had to offer. Three stops were on my itinerary, and my hopes were that each would bring forth some different treats.

Edinburgh is defined, at least from a tourist's point of view, by the Royal Mile, a medieval street that runs between two important landmarks in the history of Scotland. At the top of Castle

Rock sits Edinburgh Castle, the old home to Scottish royalty. A mile down the road are the ruins of Holyrood Abbey, an abandoned Augustinian abbey on the grounds of the Palace of Holyroodhouse. In between these two landmarks, Edinburgh rose from a small village to the center of the Scottish nation.

Now, several centuries later, the Royal Mile is lined with restaurants of varying qualities, souvenir stands selling cheap trinkets, and, every now and then, a church, a house, or a mews that reminds the tourist just how old the city is.

In the shadow of Edinburgh Castle, just north of Princes Park, is a small, nearly camouflaged store, up the stairs from the street. Its name is I Love Candy. With a sobriquet like that, I had to visit.

The store was defined by its size, or rather, its lack of it. It had one aisle, with room for only one person to walk. The white walls reflected multicolored streamers tied to deflating balloons, bags of sugar candies in the shape of various foods, and pieces of boiled sweets. On the floor were a multitude of buckets, each filled with a dizzying array of sweets, from marshmallows to lollipops, from Kendal Mint Cakes to Orange Fizzes, the whole store containing a dizzying array of sugar confections that I had never heard of before. The kicker? Chocolate was nearly impossible to find. The candy found in this store would be relegated to the back bench in the United States, owing to our preference for all things cocoa.

I had several items on my list of things to purchase. Number one was Edinburgh Rock. Ah, Edinburgh Rock. This was the reason why I chose Scotland as my point of entry into Great Britain. Here in the Scottish capital, one could find sweets unavailable anywhere else on the island. The Scots had their own candy tradition, one that held up quite nicely against that of England. But the one that had caught my attention back in my office in Seattle was little ol' Edinburgh Rock.

To understand what Edinburgh Rock is, one first should understand what "rock" is. Rock is a type of hard stick-shaped boiled sugar confectionery most usually flavored with peppermint or spearmint. It is commonly sold at seaside resorts throughout the British Isles. Think candy cane without the hook, and you're getting close. It is a stick candy with a sheen and usually a name of a city or person literally embedded within. The most famous rock sold today can be found in souvenir stands in the seaside town of Blackpool on the western coast of England.

The story behind Edinburgh Rock is that it was first made in the nineteenth century by a man named Alexander Ferguson. He learned the confectionery trade in Glasgow and then moved to Edinburgh to set up his own business. It is said that Ferguson discovered Edinburgh Rock by accident. One day he came across a tray of sweets that had lain forgotten for months. He tried a piece of the softened results, found it to be delicious, and so Edinburgh Rock was born.

Much like many such stories about amazing discoveries in candy, it's more urban legend than fact. Candy tends to lend itself to "amazing discoveries" or finds itself named specifically after events that couldn't have possibly happened. In fact, since the 1500s, confectioners had known that letting pulled sugar sit for months would result in the product softening.

What makes Edinburgh Rock unique and the perfect representation of candy is the fact that it uses tartaric acid, also known as cream of tartar. Way back then, centuries before the legend of Edinburgh Rock was born, confectioners knew that sugar by itself had physical limitations. After boiling sugar to the point where you can make pulled sugar, also known as rock, its chemistry will result in its reverting to its crystalline state. Candy in this state will become brittle and fall apart, becoming more akin to its natural, granular state of sugar. This process is called "graining," and it's typically seen as an undesired aspect in candy making.

There is a way to prevent graining: add acid. This process of adding acid of some sort, called "greasing," took off in Britain during the rise of the British Empire. But its roots are across the English Channel, in France. J. Gilliers, in the book *Le Canname-liste Français*, published in 1751, wrote:

> Once your sugar has reached the *casse* [crack stage] add the amount of color you think appropriate along with four or five drops of lemon juice, according to the amount of sugar, to prevent it from graining.

Gilliers called this recipe *graisier,* from which "greasing" evolved. By the time that Alex Ferguson was slinging candy, adding tartaric acid was already a well-known aspect of candy making. The method of letting his creation sit for a few extra months was also well known, as back in the day when these treats were medicines, demand for the product would have been based on the wellness of the individual, rather than the impulse of delight. What Alex Ferguson had come across wasn't a new innovation, but an old one—one that might have lost favor with the confectioners as more immediate demand was coming from the marketplace.

One thing that is true is that Edinburgh Rock is one weird confection. It looks like a child's writing implement, sort of a cross between a crayon and a piece of chalk. Depending on its quality, it could have a texture near to that of taffy or be more like chalk. If you get the taffylike consistency, the candy is a treat.

The candy can also be made with any flavor available to the confectioner, from mint or cinnamon to rhubarb or even Irn-Bru, a local soft drink known for its somewhat citrusy flavor, being cut with quinine, and its bright fluorescent orange colorings that are illegal in several other countries. I picked up a basket and selected a package of Edinburgh Rock.

I looked at the wall covered with small plastic barrels, each containing treats I hadn't heard of before. Soon into my basket went Aniseed Balls, Frying Pans, Bullseyes, Kola Kubes, Berwick Cockles, Fairy Satins, and Soor Plooms. Here in front of me, in all their glory, were candies that the typical American had never heard of. For a moment, I felt like I had discovered a lost treasure. I smiled at my harvest. This was what I had come to Edinburgh for.

These items also trace their history back to the addition of acid to the sugar, and the results of this would change the way that the consumer would look at sugary confections. For one thing, the grain would go away, making the heated blob pliable, and thus easy to manipulate into shapes and molds.

Second, the resulting candy would appear nearly see-through, giving it a gemlike appearance.

Finally, the acid would give a very distinct taste to the resulting candy, quite different from the pennet candies that had been flavored with herbs and oils. These new candies would taste almost fruitlike.

Physically what was happening was that the acid was preventing the sugar from recrystallizing. It would solidify, sure. But it would not crystallize. This was a handy thing to have happen.

Now consider the following: here we have, at some time in the Middle Ages, a confection that was not only tasty, but visually stunning. No other product in Europe at the time had a look as opulent as these fruit drops (as they were later called). Sure, subtleties and marzipan required a fine touch, and both had a manufactured aesthetic about them that was borderline artistic. But translucent confections were different. Seeing a product in an apothecary shop that had the look of a precious gem would have been as close to seeing a real piece of jewelry as some people would ever get. Demand, based on the exotic nature of these treats, would have grown.

What makes the candy in Britain so brilliant, even today, is its simplicity. Most are no more than boiled sugar with a bit of flavoring and coloring added. The Soor Plooms could be mistaken for green apple balls, what with their DayGlo green color and their bright, acidic flavor. When I pop a Soor Ploom into my mouth, my faith that mankind can create delight in the smallest of packages is confirmed. The Scots were doing sour candies centuries before we Americans caught on.

Additionally, the name itself brings forth a smile. Soor Ploom! Clearly a derivation of "sour plum." The legend goes that these treats were named to commemorate an incident at Galashields, a burgh on the Gala Water River in the Scottish Borders. In 1377, while eating unripe plums, which abounded in the district, a band of English invaders were surprised and routed by the local Scotsmen.

As with the story behind Edinburgh Rock, the truth is likely much more mundane. The word "plum" is the key here, as it used to be a synonym for sweet. Hence, a sugarplum (as in "visions of sugarplums danced in their heads") is a sugared candy, and a sourplum is a candy that is, well, sour. But whenever they have to choose between promoting the legend or promoting the truth, candy makers far prefer the legend.

The dictionary defines a sugarplum as a small round or oval piece of sugary candy. English being the flexible language it is, the name could have come from the resemblance to a small plum. Or it could have come from actual plums preserved in sugar, a relatively new idea in sixteenth-century England. Prior to this time, sugar was so expensive that it was used very sparingly, much as we would use an exotic spice today. In the 1540s, however, sugar started being refined in London, and this lowered the price considerably—although only well-off families were able to use it lavishly. Preserving with sugar allowed the sweet fruits of summer to be enjoyed all year round, especially during the holiday season.

But the prices weren't lowered that much. And most common folk would not have been able to afford to use sugar in such copious amounts. Preserving fruits, including plums, with sugar would have been strictly a task for the upper class, or, more likely, their servants.

So instead, they turned to a confection maker, asking, "Could you make us a reasonable facsimile of a true sour plum?" (I'm paraphrasing here). And someone (likely an apothecary) somewhere (likely here in Scotland) figured out how.

I took my candy haul back to the hotel room and considered my next step. Part of me wanted to open up all the bags onto a bed and roll around in the candy, much like Uncle Scrooge did with his gobs of money. But I quickly dismissed that as unsanitary and, quite frankly, a little creepy.

I compromised. I did pour out the bags of candy onto the bed. From there, I assigned a value to each piece, which would later determine just when said candy would be eaten as I drove down to Pontefract.

And no matter how many times I calculated and portioned the candy, the aniseed balls, with their black licorice flavor, always ended up on my personal "candies that are most likely to get spat out" list.

Chapter 9

Of Cookbooks and
Housewives

● ● ● ● ● ●

*I*n 1440, the German Johannes Gutenberg invented movable type by developing foundry-cast metal characters and a wooden printing press. In 1455, he followed up with this invention by printing his first book, a Latin Bible. Twenty years after that, the Englishman William Caxton produced the first book printed in England, the *Recuyell of the Histories of Troy*. From there, the English book publishing industry took off.

This was the start of the newly developing genre of books that we know today as cookbooks. With the development of movable type, suddenly information became somewhat economical to pass on to others via the printed word. I say "somewhat," because although these books were often affordable to the middle- and upper-middle class, the lower class did not have the financial resources to take advantage of this new technology. Then there's the question of literacy, something that wasn't really a priority for the government of the time.

Of course, back then, cookbooks didn't look like the bound hardback with glossy illustrations we see today; instead, they were rather rudimentary by today's standards, sometimes nothing more than several sheets of paper sewn together. But what they accomplished was nothing more than revolutionary, introducing both new and traditional recipes to the English "huswife."

I realize that the idea of "huswife" is so common to us now that trying to explain the concept can come across as a bit, well, patronizing. But what we know of as a housewife today is a little different from how they were defined in the sixteenth century. The idea of "managing" a household wasn't unknown, but it took on a different look in different types of homes. In the palaces and houses of the medieval aristocrats, men made up the bulk of the housekeeping staff, with women only taking on the roles of nursemaids and laundresses. In the lower class there were different roles for the different genders, but the act of actually managing the household was likely a shared responsibility between the patriarch and the matriarch.

The concept of a housewife only took form with the landed gentry. In these households, the matriarch of the house directed the housekeepers and oversaw the management of the home. Activities would have included making sure the household was fed, the house was clean, and the family was healthy.

It was this last activity that is of importance here. As Gilly Lehmann wrote in her book *The British Housewife: Cookery Books, Cooking, and Society in Eighteenth-Century Britain:* "[The] Mistress and upper servants shared in the preparation of remedies, and of the confectionery that went with remedies."

So, during the sixteenth century, confectionery in aristocratic households was made, in part, to demonstrate their wealth. Among the gentry, confectionery started with a more pragmatic purpose, one that had been around since the beginning of granulated sugar—making the medicine go down.

The newly developed publishing industry gave these new housewives access to recipes both local and from the Continent.

Ladies of the middle and upper classes transformed the produce of their kitchen gardens and fertile orchards into preserves, candies, and "banqueting stuffe," assisted by the swathe of confectionery books that showed them how. The first of these was a translated book from Italy that arrived on the scene in 1559, the first year Elizabeth I came to the throne. Bartolomeo de Sacchi di Piadena (otherwise known as Platina) published *De Honesta Voluptate* in Venice. This was translated into German, Italian, and French and frequently republished throughout Europe. About 250 of Platina's recipes were borrowed from a manuscript written by Martino of Como, who lived between 1450 and 1475. Martino's recipes were reprinted in *Epulario* ("Of Feasting") two hundred years after their origin.

Soon strictly "English" books began to appear, promising to unlock the secrets of sugarwork and confectionery. Interest in the slim, pocketable guides was so intense that they were best-sellers—practical guides in a world where even the rich hoarded high-class preserves against crop failure and hunger. But the books did more than that. They sold a lifestyle, an ideal of what it meant to be the "lady of the house." In this way, they were no different than the books sold today by Martha Stewart or Rachael Ray.

This would include people like Sir Hugh Platt, one of the true nerds of the British Renaissance era. Oh sure, he presented himself as a gentleman of the highest order. But when one writes books that devise ways to make coal fires less smoky and publishes essays on ways to keep walnuts moist for a long time, that person is, almost by definition, a nerd.

Sir Hugh Platt wrote perhaps the most charming and well-written sweets recipe book of all, dedicated to the ladies of leisure who were his target readership. The art of preserving and candying fruit had by this time become a ladylike diversion as well as a professional business; because of the high price of imported sugar, sweets were still an expensive luxury enjoyed only by a few. Among Sir Hugh's recipes is a way of candying rose petals on the bush by pouring syrup over them and letting them dry in the sun. His dedicatory poem is a useful inventory of sweets in favor in the sixteenth and early seventeenth century, including *sucket* (candied lemon and orange peel) and *marchepanes*, a type of hard marzipan modeled into diverse shapes for the table, and not always edible when ingredients were added to keep the shape longer than a year or so.

The recipes for confection captivated the upper middle class and aristocracy of the nation. This, in turn, raised the demand for sugar. These books helped release candy from the apothecaries and the upper class and made it accessible to a much wider audience. Genoese pastes, lemon marmalades, candied fruits, and many more soon began appearing on tables throughout Britain.

For anyone who has spent time trying to make candy, the first thing one learns is that the process can be time consuming. For confectioners in the Tudor era, it was doubly so. If money allowed, some homes soon found themselves with rooms dedicated solely to the purpose of making confection. Oftentimes these rooms would be next to the ingredients, namely those found in the kitchen gardens or orchards. Into this room they would take the sugar, often a less refined variety as there were only two sugar refineries in England during the mid-1500s. There the ladies of the house would clean and refine the sugar themselves, often via the traditional methods that had been around for over a millennium by this point—with either egg whites, if one could afford it, or cow's blood if budgets were a concern.*

Once the sugar was refined to a point where the women were satisfied, what would they make? Often they would look to re-create the recipes found in these cookbooks, which themselves were re-creations of what was purported to be found on the tables of royalty. This meant marchepan, comfits, and even smaller-scale subtleties (thanks to the availability of gum tragacanth).

They would also follow the fashion of the era by preserving fruits as either jellies and jams or candied fruit. Although today it may be logical to believe that the popularity of preserving fruit would have followed the popularity of fruit itself, in fact the reverse was true. Prior to the fashion of fruit preserving and candying, fresh fruit was looked upon with great suspicion by the medical establishment. The speed with which fruit rotted once picked made many uncomfortable in consuming the sweet produce. If the fruit did not have a long shelf life, then there was little practical need for it—even less if the rotted fruit had a history of making one ill.

Sugar changed all that. Within a generation or two, the art of preserving and candying brought forth a greater demand for fruits of all sorts on the British Isles. With sugar giving fruit a longer shelf life, suddenly fruits once thought of as risky were now desired. Peaches and apricots, a rarity in England, made their way into the marketplace, as did melons, figs, and even pineapples. It didn't hurt that the sweetness that the sugar pro-

---

* The albumin in the egg white and the plasma of the cow's blood can be used to pull the various impurities out of the sugar. Stirring albumin into a combination of heated water, sugar, and limewater causes the albumin to coagulate. As it solidifies, it collects most of the impurities together in a sort of a scummy film, making it easy to remove them from the liquid sugar.

Kate's Candy Bag

DRIED, SUGARED PINEAPPLE

Dried, sugared fruit is often left to trail mixes and granola bars today, which is a shame really. It's a long fall from the banqueting tables of Europe to the backpacks of health-food junkies trying to assuage the demands of their sweet tooth. Whenever my mother got into one of her "we need to eat healthy" kicks, dried pineapple found its way into the Bermuda triangle of our pantry. There, it would be lost behind the jars of sauerkraut and cans of beets that I always thought we stored in case we needed food for the coming apocalypse.

The pineapple remained unbothered for years, until the pantry needed to be cleaned, and one of us found the sweet, seemingly unchanged from the day it had made it into our household food supply. It mattered not. We threw it out anyway.

Candy Exchange Rate:
78 ounces of sugared pineapple = 1 York Peppermint Pattie

vided helped maintain, and in some cases, even improve the fruits' taste.

Vegetables and flowers also found their way to the confection rooms for the exact same reasons. It was common to see candied carrots or candied orange blossoms. If it could be grown in a garden, someone in England during this period likely sugared it at some point. Whether they discovered these processes on their own or the idea came from Italy or the Middle East, the fact remains that the convenience and adaptability of sugar had reached its tipping point.

Confectionery was one of the results of this tipping point. People discovered that these remedies tasted great on their own, regardless of whether they were ill. The addition of the new course at the dinner table, called the "banquet," showcased the confectionery skill of the mistress of the house, as well as the wealth of the master. A typical banquet could have everything from preserves of fruit, to marzipan; from molded sugar in the shape of snails and birds to the grand subtleties of royal tables.

During the Tudor era, throughout the Stuart reign, and into the English Civil War, the pantry of the bourgeoisie changed to include sugar. It was no longer a luxury; it was a necessity for the pantry. This demand would end up changing the way England did business in the era of colonization. The history of candy was right behind, following in the wake of England's insatiable need to indulge in its sweet tooth.

Chapter 10

Land of Black Licorice

● ● ● ● ● ● ● ● ● ●

T am not a fan of black licorice. I never have been. I have lived with this fact for quite some time. For a while, you could even say that I was at peace with this knowledge. But unlike any other candy out there, black licorice comes with extra baggage—namely, the fans of black licorice.

American fans of black licorice always feel the need to let those of us who don't like it know how wonderful their candy is, implying that those of us who fail to kneel at the altar of these candies are little more than unsophisticated heathens.

One night at a dinner, I asked Kelly—a friend of mine and purported fan of black licorice—a simple question: "Can't I be allowed to not like a piece of candy?"

"Of course, but only after you've had a licorice that was made properly. It's possible that you haven't had the right type," she responded. In the back of my mind, I wondered if fans of

Kate's Candy Bag

CANDY CORN

A waxy fondant shaped like corn kernels, candy corn was created in the late 1800s as a means to disappoint future generations of children as they went door to door trick or treating.

It's quite possible that candy corn was better when people used marshmallow as a binding agent along with the sugar and corn syrup. But during my lifetime, whatever the major companies have been using, it makes these Halloween sweets taste like little more than candle wax with autumn colors added.

Candy Exchange Rate:
1,476 pieces of candy corn = 1 York Peppermint Pattie

candy corn were out there chastising others for eating the wrong "type" of candy corn.

"So, what is the correct type?"

"Well, nothing American that I can think of," she said. "There are some good Dutch versions out there. There are some Swedish varieties I like as well. England has Pontefract cakes, of course."

She rattled off the name of a few brands, but I mindlessly nodded at her observations. While on the outside, it looked as if I was participating in polite conversation, internally I was wondering if her response was an elaborate hoax. Who on earth would have sampled that much black licorice, outside those who had done so on a dare?

Perhaps I was doing it wrong. If there were so many varieties, either we have collectively decided as a global society to
keep trying to make black licorice until we get it right, or there
are some versions that really are better than others.

This is why, weeks after this conversation with Kelly, I was
heading to Pontefract, Britain's home to all things licorice. It is
one of the few regions in the world that I can blame for the banc
of the candy world—black licorice. The next morning, having
settled on a selection of candies to eat for the day, I picked up a
rental car and drove through the northeast region of England. I
traveled into Yorkshire and, finally, into the small town of Pontefract. This city is the home of black licorice and the home of
one of the more infamous English apothecaries, the gentleman
whom I blame for all of this nonsense.

Throughout this book, I've talked about apothecaries and
their role in medicine and candy, but it's worth delving into
their past a bit more in order to get a feel for where they sit
in the class hierarchy. After all, they were not doctors, nor were
they entirely profit-driven. Apothecaries fell somewhere in between. They were tradesmen who worked at creating products
to make their community better—but often at a price.

The word "apothecary" itself is derived from *apotheca*, meaning a place in a community where wine, spices, and herbs were
stored. Sometime during the thirteenth century it came into
use in England to describe a person who was in charge of keeping these commodities.

The apothecaries of London were initially members of another English trade association, the Grocers' Company, which,
in turn, can be traced back to the Guild of Pepperers, an association formed in London in 1180 to help mitigate prices of spice in
England. Once again, we see strong evidence of the pharmacy
in the spice trade.

The Guild of Pepperers eventually split into two factions.

One was made up of the wholesale merchants who dealt with product *en gros* (which is where the word "grocer" comes from). In 1428, this faction was incorporated into the Worshipful Company of Grocers. The other faction, dealing with trade in spices or with pharmaceuticals, became independent of the grocers and led to the emergence of apothecaries. These members were the ones who had stored and sold spices, confectionery, perfumes, herbs, and drugs and were the ones who took the responsibility to make these products and dispense them to the public.

Before the Reformation, Arabian pharmacology, via the Latin translations that took place in the eleventh century, was the primary school of thought when it came to the making of medicines and the dispensation of "medical" confections. But with the discovery of printing, and the ready access of information through the medium of books, came the study of Greek classics, including Hippocrates and Averroes. Treatments with medicine shifted from preventive care and into the realm of "to be used only when sick." The services of the apothecary became less in demand.

But there's a bit of a chicken-and-egg question here because the position of the pharmacist in England was a relatively high one. Medicines created by the apothecary still held value. It's quite possible that the shift in medicine from preventive to restorative had as much to do with the economics of spices as it did with the sudden accessibility of information via the book. After all, medicine is cheaper if one only has to take it when one is ill.

By the sixteenth century, the separation of pharmacology from medical practice was complete, and the status of the apothecary had risen throughout Europe to some measure or another, but specifically in England. William Boleyn, supposedly a relative of Queen Anne, was a prominent apothecary. In order to add credibility to his job, he wrote down the following rules for the practice of pharmacy:

The apothecary must first serve God; foresee the end, be cleanly, and pity the poor. His place of dwelling and shop must be cleanly, to please the senses withal. His garden must be at hand with plenty of herbs, seeds, and roots. He must read Dioscorides. He must have his mortars, stills, pots, filters, glasses, boxes, clean and sweet. He must have two places in his shop, one most clean for physic and the base place for chirurgic stuff. He is neither to decrease nor diminish the physician's prescription. He is neither to buy nor sell rotten drugs. He must be able to open well a vein, for to help pleurisy. He is to meddle only in his own vocation, and to remember that his office is only to be the physician's cook. (Quoted in Lawall, "Pharmaceutical Ethics")

These rules still have value in the modern-day pharmacy, but it's the last one that I'm interested in. Squabbles between physicians and pharmacists exist to this day, but back in the 1500s, the divide helped set the course for both modern medicine and candy shops. Many apothecaries believed they were the only ones who had insight into the physical well-being of man, and that physicians were nothing more than quacks. Others took the opposite view, believing that it was the apothecary who served the physician. It's telling that Boleyn believes that an apothecary was no more than the "physician's cook."

That divide between physicians and apothecaries, and the way that each European government dealt with those disputes, helped set the course of confectionery in Europe.

The English apothecaries, with their specialist pharmacy skills, petitioned for several years to secede from the Grocers' Company and were eventually granted such license. By 1617, the Worshipful Society of Apothecaries of London was incorporated by royal charter.

We can guess the likely reasons for their need to separate

from the grocers and to have their guild given an air of authority. The condition of the drug trade in the rest of Europe can be sussed out by reading testimony of the druggists of Nuremburg, in 1581, to the city council, who were responding to explicit charges made by the physicians of the area. Many complaints about the business of the pharmacy trade made by the apothecaries paint a distinct picture, quite interesting to anyone looking for the evolution of candy:

> May it please the Honorable Council to lend ear to our complaints, and in conformity therewith to see fit, in such a manner, to protect our interests, that henceforth we shall not be unduly oppressed by the physicians, and that each of us shall be enabled to enjoy the just results of his labors. The following, honorable sires, forms the substance of our complaint:
>
> 1. The sale of all confections, formerly dispensed by us, has now fallen into the hands of the sugar dealer.
>
> 2. Counter sales are now made by all the large spice and cheap corner grocery shops, thus robbing the druggist of a source of profit that he is justly entitled to.
>
> 3. The sale of sundries, such as sealing wax, fumigating pastiles, paper ink and pens, is now taking place in common huckster shops.
>
> 4. The sugar dealers are not only selling confections, but also all kinds of fruit juices, electuaries of quinces, and all such preserves that do not deteriorate in the course of a year.
>
> 5. All distilled waters, oils, and the like, which were formerly kept by druggists only, are now indiscriminately sold by any

ignoramus who imagines himself qualified to engage in this traffic.

6. Unguenta and Emplastra, which certainly belong to the exclusive field of pharmacy, are now dispensed by barbers and ignorant physicians, who are neither justified by precedent nor by qualification to handle these things.

7. Now, many expensive medicamenta are, every year, carried over and deteriorate, because the doctors do not prescribe them, and they prove a total loss to the druggist. Of such medicines we will but enumerate the fruit juices, the purging elixir of roses, etc. (Quoted in Peters, *Pictorial History of Ancient Pharmacy*)

You know things are bad for a group when they feel that they have to call their competitors "ignoramus."

The Nuremberg complaint made against the spicers and sugar bakers indicates that grocers and druggists were becoming separate, distinct occupations, and that pharmacists were assuming more the position of professionals and less that of tradesmen. The *spizieri* and *confectionarii* of the thirteenth century had become merged in the fourteenth but were now beginning a final separation into grocers, spicers, sugar bakers, and apothecaries.

King James I justified his decision in the House of Commons in 1624: "I myself did devise that corporation and do allow it. The grocers, who complain of it, are but merchants; the mystery of these apothecaries were belonging to apothecaries, wherein the grocers are unskilful; and therefore I think it is fitting they should be a corporation of themselves." In other words, the grocers weren't smart enough to make drugs and therefore shouldn't be selling them.

This is all well and good, I can hear you thinking. But what has this got to do with candy? Consider this: as a prominent apothecary wrote in the sixteenth century, "Ryff [family physician] said: 'Honey and sugar are the druggist's chief stock in trade. He uses it for his confects, electuaries, preserves, syrups, julips and other precious mixtures.'" Sugar, moreover, was one of the main sources of income for the sixteenth-century druggist.

The Pharmacopoeia of the London Colleges first claimed sugar for medicinal uses, which must have played an important part, judging by the well-known proverb that a person standing in need of some essential possession that he lacks is "like an apothecary without sugar."

In 1704, the society won a key legal suit (known as the Rose Case) against the Royal College of Physicians in the House of Lords, which ruled that apothecaries could both prescribe and dispense medicines. This meant that they could do so without direct oversight from physicians. In essence, they were allowed to create and innovate new medicines. And they did. Many of these ended up being new confections and candies that are still found today in both Britain and its colonies, including such items as barley sugar, rock, and mint cakes.

Contrast this with France. In the dispute between apothecaries and physicians, the physicians won. Enraged at advice being given by apothecaries, the physicians determined to starve them out, and by prescribing only simple remedies from herbalists they subdued the rebel apothecaries, obliging them to take the following oath:

> I swear and promise before God, the Author and Creator of all things, One in Spirit and divided in Three Persons, eternally blessed, that I will observe strictly the following articles:
> First: I promise to live and die in the Christian Faith.
> Second: To love and honor my parents to the utmost; also,

to honor, respect and render service, not only to the medical
doctors who have imparted to me the precepts of pharmacy,
but also to my teachers and masters from whom I have learned
my trade.

Third: Not to slander any of my ancient teachers or masters, whoever they may be; also, to do all I can for the honor,
glory and majesty of physic.

Fourth: Never to teach to ungrateful persons or fools the
secrets and mysteries of the trade; never to do anything rash-
ly without the advice of a physician, or from the sole desire of
gain; never to give any medicine or purge to invalids afflicted
with acute disease without first consulting one of the faculty.

Fifth: Never to examine women privately, unless by great
necessity, or to apply them some necessary remedy; never to
divulge the secrets confided to me.

Sixth: Never to administer poisons, nor recommend their
administration even to our greatest enemies, nor to give
drinks to produce abortion, without the advice of a physician,
also to execute accurately their prescriptions, without adding
or diminishing anything contained in them, that they may in
every respect be prepared *secundem artem*.

Seventh: Never to use any succedaneum or substitute
without the advice of others wiser than myself; to disown
and shun as a pestilence the scandalous and pernicious prac-
tices of quacks, empirics and alchymists, which exist to the
great shame of the magistrates who tolerate them.

Lastly: To give aid and assistance indiscriminately to all
who employ me, and to keep no stale or bad drug in my shop.
May God continue to bless me so long as I continue to obey
these things. (Quoted in Peters, p. 39)

Here, the apothecaries had committed to follow physicians' instructions or risk, at best, ostracism, and, at worst, being labeled a

blasphemer. In sixteenth-century France, any innovations in the apothecaries' job were dictated by physicians.

If one were to review the various pharmacopeia published between 1600 and 1850, one would find various recipes and concoctions in which sugar played a vital role. These recipes include everything from syrups to lozenges.

Consider this recipe for lohoch commune, a sugary paste found in an Edinburgh dispensary around the time of the American Revolution:

LOHOCH COMMUNE

Take of Fresh-drawn oil of almonds,
Syrup of marshmallows, or balsamic syrup, each one ounce;
White sugar, two drachms.
Mix and make them into a lohoch.

Here is a recipe for rose tablets found in Edinburgh in the late eighteenth century, clearly the ancestor of the rosebud confections I had purchased at I Love Candy.

TABELLAE ROSACEAE

Take:
Conserve of red roses, four ounces;
White sugar, in powder, one pound.
If any moisture is required, take of syrup of dry roses a sufficient
*   quantity for forming them into troches, which are to be dried,*
*   with a gentle heat.*

How were these sugary concoctions perceived by the public at large? According to William Lewis, in his book *The New Dispensatory*, published in 1785:

These preparations are chiefly valued for their agreeableness to the eye and palate. Some likewise esteem them, medicinally, as light restringents; and look upon them, not undeservedly, as an excellent addition to milk in phthisical and hectic cafes.

In other words, they looked good, and they tasted better.

But the recipe that caught my attention was the following:

TROCHISCI BECHICI NIGRI

Take of
Extract of licorice,
Double refined sugar, each ten ounces;
Gum tragacanth, half a pound.
Drop upon these ingredients so much water as will make the mass
soft enough to be formed into troches

This is the recipe for black licorice. One of the people responsible for this was George Dunhill, an apothecary from Pontefract. It was not until 1760 that he hit upon the idea of adding sugar to the apothecary's licorice recipe and began to produce Pomfret cakes commercially as a sweet. Within a few years, Dunhill's became one of the most well-known English manufacturers of licorice, and Pontefract (as well as Pomfret) would become inextricably linked with the product. So if you're a black licorice hater, and you're looking for someone to blame, George Dunhill is your man.

Licorice root is one of those herbs that have been around since ancient times. It was used by the pharaohs of ancient Egypt, the Brahmans of India, as well as the Hindus, the Greeks, the Romans, the Babylonians, and the Chinese. Not surprisingly, it became a part of several medicinal applications throughout the world. The Chinese believed it could cure coughs. Indians used it as a laxative. The ancient Hindus believed it would increase sexual vigor.

The Scythians taught the use of the herb to the Greeks. Theophrastus, a botanist from ancient Greece, called it Scythian root. He wrote of the plant in the third century BC, stating that the Scythians were able to survive in the desert for a week or so without drinking water because they chewed on licorice root.

Our old friend Dioscorides gave the plant its botanical name *Glycyrrhiza* (from the Greek: glykys, "sweet" and rhiza, "root"). It was also Dioscorides who told the troops of Alexander the Great to carry and chew licorice root in order to temper their thirst when water was unavailable. He also claimed that it would give them stamina and endurance during their long marches and that it was good for stomach trouble, throat trouble, and liver and kidney disorders. Dioscorides generally felt that the root was nothing short of miraculous and deserved a place in all medicines.

By the Middle Ages, licorice was just another go-to ingredient when it came to medications. Its status as a "wonder drug" allowed it to be used as an after-dinner item, something to be chewed upon in order to alleviate the bad effects of highly spiced or overcooked food. It had a value similar to that of sugar, and as such, imported licorice was taxed in order to aid in providing funds to repair London Bridge during the reign of Edward I in 1305. By the fifteenth century, licorice's ubiquity was such that it was often found in the inventory of Italian apothecaries, and it was documented in a list of medicines, written about the year 1450, submitted to the city council of Frankfurt. By the time it started taking off in popularity in Pontefract in the 1600s, licorice was not only important medicinally but was used as a flavoring agent in tobacco and ales and as a foaming agent in fire extinguishers.

But one question is how the licorice plant ended up in Yorkshire, which served as the center of licorice cultivation in England for many centuries. Clearly licorice isn't native to England.

Religious orders, specifically the Cluniac monks, are reputed to have brought licorice to Pontefract. Robert de Lacy, along with three other monks sent from La Charité-sur-Loire in France, founded the Pontefract Priory in about 1090, very soon after the building of Pontefract Castle, a central fortification dating from 1070 AD.

Sure, the monks' primary tasks were prayer and providing a daily round of masses and other church services. But the priory, like most aspects of the Catholic Church, served as a large-scale business combined with social services. To ensure that they and their families would go to heaven, people gave the priory properties all over Yorkshire. These properties had to be farmed in order to pay for the priory's upkeep and cover its operating costs. In return for these tithes, the monks served the community by providing not only prayer for the salvation of their flock but also education, care, and, lo and behold, medicine. Being wise in the ways of the medicine of the Middle Ages, the monks made licorice part of their repertoire.

What the monks likely knew was that the licorice plant needed deep soil to grow, what with the roots running as long as four feet. What they soon found out was that the soft, mineral-laden, and quite deep topsoil of Pontefract was more than ideal. Sure, the plants didn't flower in the colder English climate, but that didn't matter because the root provided what was needed. Soon the sap was being extracted from the roots of the plant and used medicinally by the monks along with all the other herbs that were used for easing coughs, taking care of rashes, and soothing stomach complaints.

By 1614, extract of licorice was being applied to the standard confectionery techniques of the day and added into the sweetened sugar lozenges that had become a standard part of the apothecaries' trade. It is said that Sir George Savile himself had applied a small stamp to each of these round "cakes" in order to make them easily discernable from other, presumably less authentic, licorice cakes of the early 1600s. Again, this is more likely legend than fact.

The popularity of the medicine took off, and soon large areas of the town and surrounding regions were growing licorice. After Pontefract Castle was razed to the ground in 1649 during the English civil war, the yard inside was used for market gardens, and records show licorice was grown there.

In fact, licorice was being grown in the region on a large scale by the mid-seventeenth century. Siege plans show a licorice garth (field) between the castle and the siege works, and by 1750 there were forty-seven licorice growers in Pontefract. Included among these growers was the Dunhill family, who in 1720 had rented land in this region to grow licorice. George Dunhill—again, the person I blame for all of this—got his licorice from this yard.

But I was in Pontefract to answer a much more personal question. Namely, is there possibly a piece of black licorice that I can get down without my gag reflex kicking in?

Yes, I am one of *those* people—the type who believes that eating black licorice is only marginally preferable to gnawing on frog's skin wrapped in tree bark and topped with sugar.

As a child, I spat out Good & Plentys. There were Halloweens when I cried because someone had put a packet of black licorice Twizzlers in my trick-or-treat bag. I am one of but a handful of people in the world who believes that the Nordic tradition of adding salt (actually, ammonium chloride) to black licorice is actually a viable option for making it palatable.

After my conversation with Kelly at that dinner party, I realized that perhaps, just perhaps, I'd been sampling versions of black licorice that weren't representative of its true quality. Pontefract, home of the black licorice Pontefract cakes, seemed like the perfect place to put this matter to rest once and for all.

Pontefract itself is an interesting little town to the west of Leeds. This is an area of England that the locals lovingly refer to as "the North." To get an idea of how the North is perceived in England, it helps to remember that ancient Rome called this area of northern England "Britannia Inferior." Today, many people in the southern parts of England consider this a bit of an understatement, while those who reside here take it as a badge of honor.

To put it another way, I had once talked to an Englishman about visiting London, and he shook his head upon hearing the news. "No, no, no," he admonished. "If you want to visit England—real England—you need to get to the North. Manchester, York, Leeds. These are the places you needs to see if you want to see England. *Real* England."

So here I was, in Pontefract, in real England. With the gray skies and a great majority of the area peppered with sandstone rock, the town appeared to me as if it was trying to paint itself in its most romantic light. What I didn't know was that the area's golden age of licorice was long gone.

Ponteract's history with licorice was the perfect example of a cottage industry, one where families contracted to sweet firms. They would gather the licorice roots, soak them in hot water in their homes, and then boil the resulting liquor on the kitchen cooking range until the concoction was suitably reduced.

The problem was that demand for the root outweighed the region's ability to provide it. As more licorice factories opened in the nineteenth century, a shortage of the locally grown raw material was inevitable. Soon licorice root had to be imported from Spain and Turkey in order to produce the confections. By the end of the nineteenth century, most of the licorice fields had gone, replaced in the market by regions of the world that could grow the root cheaper and more effectively. The last licorice harvest in Pontefract took place sometime in the 1960s or early 1970s.

At one time there were thirteen licorice factories in the town, but owing to the cost of importing ingredients, as well as the rise in wages, these candy companies were doomed. By 1960, several of the factories had either joined forces, been sold to other larger companies, or simply gone out of business. By the time I entered the city, there were only two licorice companies left: one owned by the British company Tangerine Confectionery and the other by worldwide candy conglomerate Haribo, a German confection company known around the world for its extensive gummy variations. Haribo has an outlet store of sorts in Pontefract. This was my first stop.

An electric "bing-bong" went off as I pushed open the door, and a lone woman, her black hair encased in a hairnet, gave me a brief nod of acknowledgment as she looked out from the back room. Otherwise, the only things in the room were several dozen types of Haribo products and an eerie silence that was broken every time I picked up a rustling cellophane bag full of gummies.

"Can I help you?" the young woman from the back eventually said. Her black hair contrasted against her pale skin, and her bright red lipstick made it appear as if she had been taking beauty lessons from movie stars from the 1940s.

"I . . . uh . . . ," I stumbled over my words, not really knowing how to broach the subject. Admitting one's ignorance is never an easy process. "I know this is going to sound odd, but I was wondering if you could recommend some licorice."

"What you have in your hand is a good start."

I looked down, noticed the bag of Pontefract cakes that I had picked up and tried to act like I knew that I had intended this purchase all along.

"Right, that. This." I lifted up the bag and studied it as I tried to explain myself. "I know very little about licorice. I have no idea what's good and what's not."

She looked at me suspiciously, as if I was going to run off with this bag of candy without paying.

Very much aware of my role as a lonely American in the heart of England, I reached for anything that could be interpreted as relevant to this conversation.

"Why is licorice so horrible?" I asked, unable to stop the words as they came out of my mouth.

Oh. That. Was. Just. Perfect. I had just insulted one of the major icons of her city. I would have been less conspicuous if had called Queen Elizabeth a rambling she-monkey.

The young woman looked at me with a combination of pity and amusement, walked toward a different shelf, and picked up a bag.

"If you don't like licorice, I recommend you start out on these instead." She showed me the bag of candy in her hands: licorice allsorts.

She moved behind the counter and began to ring up my order as I agreed to her suggestion. "It's not black licorice you hate, by the way," she said, sounding as if she'd mentioned this ten times a day, every day, for the past year. "It's the aniseed oil that's added to it that makes it taste that way. Some companies add way too much."

I think it's safe to say that I was a tad annoyed at this new bit of information. I've gone forty-some years of my life with a particular worldview, only to discover that this perspective is not only wrong, but had I taken even the littlest of initiative, I would have uncovered this information years ago.

The news? Licorice doesn't actually taste like licorice.

Okay, okay, okay. Of course it tastes like licorice . . . because that's what it is. What the shopkeeper was saying was that licorice

Kate's Candy Bag

BLACK LICORICE JELLY BEANS

Before Jelly Bellys, jelly beans used to be the dull, boring candies offered only at Easter and in flavors that could, at best, be called interesting. Some flavors were specific, like cherry. Others were a little more ambiguous, like those called "spice."

And then there were the black ones. While all other jelly beans may have been passable to the palate of a child, finding a black jelly bean among them was akin to finding a dead fly in your pack of raisins. I knew of several friends who felt their Easters had been ruined when they found black jelly beans in their Easter baskets.

What made our disgust for these beans even worse were the two or three children in our class who actually liked them. These were the children who first made us question our sanity. These kids were either aliens or just plain weird.

Candy Exchange Rate:
1,645 black jelly beans = 1 York Peppermint Pattie

doesn't taste like anise, which is that deep, sweet-savory-herbal component that most of us equate with black licorice. So now I look back to all the times my friends and I have tasted fennel, or absinthe, and said it has a licoriceness about it; we've been flat out wrong.

All of you long-term licorice fans can feel free to mock the rest of us.

I paid for the allsorts as well as the Pontefract cakes, thanked the young lady for her help, and walked out into the streets of the town from which the cakes took their name. I was dizzy from this new bit of information and subconsciously berated myself for making an incorrect assumption based on absolutely no evidence at all. As I walked toward the center of town, I decided then and there to get up to speed on licorice as quickly as I could.

First, I visited a Holland & Barrett, a national health food chain, and picked up some licorice root tea and a selection of chewable licorice root.

Next, I walked to the shopping district and found a local pub called the Licorice Bush. I walked in, sat down at a table by myself, and ordered a pint and a cup of hot water, into which I placed a bit of the licorice tea.

As I waited for the tea to brew, I reviewed the candies I had purchased. In each, aniseed was a listed ingredient. I sighed to myself, acknowledging my incompetence.

When the tea finished brewing, I looked at it, and then took a sip.

I could say that the tea tasted of a lot of things. It was a bit woodsy, had a deep finish, and tasted like I had licked the side of a tree. Which was to be expected, as the tea itself mostly consisted of root.

But what licorice root mostly tastes of is sweetness. This new knowledge was even more embarrassing considering that the word "licorice" means, literally, "sweet root." It's exactly what it says on the tin. And here I was thinking that *Glycyrrhiza glabra* was some sort of incantation created by H. P. Lovecraft.

What is notable is what it did not taste like. Namely, black licorice. Or, as the young lady at the Haribo outlet noted, aniseed oil.

This new knowledge came with new questions: specifically, why do some licorice makers seem to go overboard on anise oil? I understand why it's there to begin with (mostly a cross between tradition and pharmacological reasons), but at some point, when the medical benefits of licorice candies came into doubt, somebody somewhere said, "Oh, what the hell," and decided what licorice really needed was an overdose of anise oil. Of course, there are also the folks who decided to add salt to the mix, so perhaps trying to find a logical reasoning for licorice ingredients is simply a lost cause.

I took a swig of my beer and then ordered dinner—a simple hamburger, purchased mostly to assuage my own guilt as I was using a public dining space to conduct taste tests on products not purchased there.

I opened the bag of Haribo Pontefract Cakes. A whiff of the dark spice permeated the air around me, and I looked at the black disks with the Haribo stamps with unease. I placed one in my mouth and bit down.

It wasn't a pleasing taste, but it wasn't horrible either. It had a texture that was sort of a cross between that of fondant and a gummy. The aniseed oil wasn't overpowering, but it certainly made itself known, much like the kid in first grade who knows the answer to every question the teacher poses. And much like I did in first grade, I wanted to move as far away as I could from it. I eyed the bag of allsorts, deciding then and there to rip the bag open.

Allsorts are not too well known in the States. They are licorice candies that have been wrapped in another nonlicorice candy. In any given bag you may find licorice surrounded by coconut marshmallow, layered with pieces of fruit-flavored gelatin or fondant, or enrobed in gelatin and then coated with tiny flavored dragées.

Bassett, an industrial confectioner owned by Cadbury, claims that it invented allsorts when, in 1899, a sales representative named Charlie Thompson supposedly dropped a tray of samples he was showing a client, mixing up the various sweets. He scrambled to rearrange them, and the client was intrigued by the new creation. Quickly the company began to mass-produce the allsorts, and they became very popular.

Personally, I think their story is yet another urban legend. I'd be more prone to swallow it if the Brits weren't so keen on Dolly Mix, a collection of sweets similar to allsorts, except that they use fondant in place of the licorice.

I opened the bag and picked up a bright yellow piece and gave it a quick sniff. Coconut. A voice in the back of my head said, "I'm intrigued. Let's investigate further."

I put the piece of candy in my mouth and the sweetness of the coconut marshmallow flooded in. Suddenly, the small bit of licorice made its way to my tongue, and I began to chew.

And I didn't hate it.

In fact, I liked it. I liked it a lot. There was a certain consistency to all of this, both in the texture of the candy and in the logic. The way to make licorice candy palatable is to overwhelm it with other, nonlicorice, candy. This was the confectionery equivalent of hiding liver in a pool of ketchup. A licorice that didn't taste like licorice—I mean anised. This was a licorice I could get behind.

I had learned something new this day. What the woman behind the counter was innocently pointing out was that we Americans have a fairly large misconception when it comes to candy; namely, we believe that black licorice is a flavor. When I have gone to fancy dinners with friends and the chef has used fennel or anise in the dish, someone will invariably state that "this tastes like licorice." This is akin to eating a sprig of mint and stating that it tastes like a Life Saver.

Instead, aniseed is nothing more than a flavor, and one that can be paired with another, to the point where the anise flavoring complements the other flavors instead of dominating them. This was an approach to licorice that I not only could respect, I could wholeheartedly support, even if that meant restricting my licorice input to sweets that didn't taste like licorice. Some may quibble that this isn't really eating black licorice at all. To them I say, "What are you complaining about? That just means more for you!"

Chapter 11

The British Get Sugar

● ● ● ● ● ● ● ● ●

London is, quite possibly, my favorite city on the planet. There's an energy, a vibrancy, to it that is quite unlike any other. At a young age, while sitting underneath the covers with a flashlight (while I was supposed to be sleeping), I read the stories of Charles Dickens and created in my mind an image of what London was and what it should be. As I read various tracts and treatises on the history of Europe, I found my mind wondering what the city must have looked like during the civil war and, later, the Reformation. London is an entity unto itself in history, a character far greater than any individual, including William Shakespeare, Samuel Pepys, or Henry VIII. Here was a city that has affected more lives than any other city on the planet, with the possible exception of Beijing.

Every time I get into London, there is one park that I strive to visit at least once. The Victoria Tower Gardens sit directly south of Westminster Palace, nearly in the shadow of Big Ben and Westminster Abbey. For reasons I have yet to fathom, I have never run into any large crowds at this park, even though a mere two hundred yards to the north are several of the most popular tourist attractions in Europe and quite possibly the world.

But quiet it has been for me, which is perfectly acceptable. The park is smallish, at least when compared to the massive Hyde Park that is a mile or so away. Its intimacy is made all the more comforting as it sits cozied up next to the Thames. If one finds the right park bench, one can get an excellent view of the London Eye about a quarter of a mile up the river.

It is from this bench that I contemplate London. When I am in a more cynical mood, I think about the choices that those in Parliament have made over the past centuries. I think of the role they played in sugar, confection, and, as we shall see soon enough, chocolate. But before that, we have to go to back to the late sixteenth century in order to get a read on the political situation of the day.

Back in 1588, Spain was still the empire to beat in Europe. Its expansion into the Western Hemisphere had been successful; of this there is little doubt. But their arrogance and lust for power got the better of the Spaniards. Their goal of punishing the heretical Protestants of England now seems like an overreach, but at the time they had an excess of both money and guns and they had ample political cover for the action, as Elizabeth I had supported the Dutch revolt against the Spaniards. The Spanish must have thought it would be a cakewalk to invade England because they believed their actions were ordained by God.

As I sat on the bench, I imagined how the news of the subsequent events must have been received here at Westminster. Most were likely hoping to simply repel the invasion, and to gain a little dignity within the European courts. Imagine how they must have reacted when they learned that the British navy had not only defeated the mighty Spanish armada, but that Spain had lost almost 65 percent of its ships.

During this time England was a country looking to expand, but it was having difficulty establishing colonies. This was especially true in the Caribbean, where the Spaniards had established their empire, and the recently independent Dutch had started following in the footsteps of their old rulers. The paths established by these two trading giants would soon be followed by the British as they developed a sugar "utopia."

For a country that was seeing an increase in the demands for sugar by the upper class, wealthy housewives, and the apothecary guilds, these events could not have happened at a better time. The wealth created by the trade from the Caribbean would help pay for not only the British navy, but ultimately a fair amount of the British army and the infrastructure needed to support such forces.

And the decisions that would guide these forces had been made only a few feet from where I was sitting.

My mind was officially boggled.

For me to fully understand just exactly what had happened, I needed to jump back two generations or so in history.

Prior to Columbus's journeys, sugar had slowly but effectively been moved out of the Mediterranean and into the Atlantic islands off the west coast of Africa. The Portuguese, under Henry the Navigator, had planted sugarcane on Madeira because they were looking to create colonies and ports of call for their fleet as they sought a way to put a dent in the Venetian spice route monopoly. Sugar was planted on Madeira about ten years after the arrival of the Portuguese in 1425, and by the mid-1450s, enough was being produced to export back to the Continent. By 1456, sugar from Madeira was reaching Bristol. This new source of sugar helped increase the supply, which in turn helped lower its price. As sugar was now traded through not only Venice but Lisbon, Amsterdam, and Antwerp in the north, prices fell throughout the latter half of the fifteenth century.

Benefiting from the success of Madeira, the Portuguese then looked to replicate it elsewhere. Soon afterward, they planted sugar on the tropical island of São Tome, then in the Azores, and then they hit the jackpot when they made it to what is present-day Brazil.

Spain followed Portugal's lead and began refining sugar-cane in the Canary Islands. Columbus, as mentioned previously, planted sugar in Hispaniola during his second trip across the Atlantic in 1493. There are also records of the Spanish planting sugarcane nearly everywhere they landed, including Mexico, Cuba, Jamaica, and Puerto Rico.

In the years after Columbus "discovered" the Caribbean, thousands of Spanish, seeking their fortune and the freedom that the New World provided from the distant eyes of the Catholic Church, went to this New World. Many of these settlers were eager to claim land and work it as their own. Others, sensing an opportunity of profit, looked to export the resources of the land. The sugar crop, always at the back of many entrepreneurial minds, soon found its way into the islands.

By the early sixteenth century, the sugar industry started to thrive. As money began to be made in Santo Domingo, then in Cuba, and soon after in Puerto Rico, people back in Europe noticed. And while the development of this industry was hampered by the large labor force needed to grow the crop and produce the sugar, many people soon realized that the long-term investment in the sugar industry held a far more reliable return than a short-term quest for silver and gold.

There was inherent tension throughout these years as various countries vied for the right to colonize and exploit the resources of the Caribbean Islands. The first issues occurred between Europeans and the native peoples. The Dutch, furthering the practice started by the Portuguese, established a slavery monopoly during their war with Spain and Portugal. The British saw their opportunity to open a third front and attacked various Dutch strongholds. The French, also seeing this as an opportunity, soon stepped in. Several of the islands switched hands many times, but by the end of the seventeenth century, the Caribbean islands were, for the most part, divided between France and Britain, with Spain and the Netherlands occupying a few areas and Portugal even fewer. England and France then took advantage of the region's sugar industry. They looked toward the aboriginals, and afterward indentured servants, to work the sugarcane fields and the processing houses.

Brazil, rather than the Spanish Caribbean, offered the first example of the wealth to be made from large-scale plantations worked by black slave labor. At first Portugal didn't promote serious colonization in Brazil, and their outposts remained thinly settled. It wasn't until the 1540s, after reports of the French looking to land and acquire a few new colonies in the region, that the government back in Lisbon looked to establish some measure of infrastructure for their colonies. The Brazilian northeast was well suited to the growing of sugarcane, so several full-blown plantations were created and production on a large scale was started.

Providing labor for these plantations was difficult. The environment was as close to a natural hell on earth as one can imagine. The heat and humidity required to grow sugarcane meant that the more productive the growing region, the less habitable it was for humans. The work needed to convert the cane into granulated sugar was arduous, from the harvesting of the sinewy cane with machetes, to the carrying of hundreds of pounds of cane to the crushing houses where the sugar juice was extracted, to the extreme heat required to repeatedly crystallize the sugar. Danger lurked in every aspect of the job, and soon it became apparent that this was not the sort of work that people volunteered for, especially when it required a journey across the Atlantic to a foreign land. Soon plantations turned to the cheapest form of labor—slavery.

This wasn't a new approach to solving the labor problem in sugar production. Slavery was well established in the medieval sugar industry of the Middle East and the Mediterranean, although not to the extent that later occurred in the Caribbean. While Muslims and Catholics had been enslaving one another for ages, they soon found that those slaves who had no recourse to escape were able to be retained for longer periods of time. This meant that they looked farther south, in Africa, where trade routes and interactions with central African cultures were limited. Under an edict from Pope Nicolas I, who had established the church's position that pagans could be used as slaves without violating Catholic doctrine, the slave trade began in earnest. Soon, a black African slave workforce could be found in many of the sugar plantations of the fourteenth- and fifteenth-century Mediterranean.

Back in Brazil, Portuguese plantation owners found that aboriginal labor was problematic. Those few who did not die from smallpox or other new diseases that had been brought to the Western Hemisphere found it easy to escape. Knowing the lands and having the ability to communicate with other tribes in the area made it easy for the locals to simply vanish from the plantation. Indentured servants from Europe were equally problematic, as they simply refused to sign up for such work. In order to fulfill their labor requirements, the Portuguese turned to the labor they had relied upon in the Mediterranean—African slaves.

With this unfortunate model, money soon came rolling in. The Portuguese found themselves in a region of the world that seemed made for sugarcane growth, and they were able to produce the sugar on site at minimal cost. On the backs of African slaves, the Portuguese soon dominated the sugar market. In 1522, there was 1 sugar refinery; by 1550, there were 5 sugar plants in Brazil; and by 1623, there were 350. Sugar, once a luxury commodity, soon began to glut the market. Ports throughout western Europe soon had refineries of their own when it was determined it would be cheaper to further refine sugar on the Continent. By the mid-1560s, several cities were refining more sugar in two weeks than Venice ever had in a single year. The profits being made financed more expeditions to the New World, where more sugar plantations could be created. These plantations essentially led to the collapse of the sugar plantations in the Mediterranean. But a new industry would fill the void: the slave trade. For with each new plantation created in the New World by the Portuguese, more labor was needed. And this need for cheap labor would soon grow exponentially.

The Dutch West India Company seized the Brazilian settlement of Pernambuco from the Portuguese in the 1630s, and soon the reason for the Portuguese's amazing profits became fully known by the Dutch. Rather than shutting down the slave trade, they expanded upon it, and when the Portuguese eventually kicked the Dutch out of Brazil in 1640, the Dutch took their knowledge of the Portuguese plantations throughout the New World and saw for themselves the profit to be made by trading human lives. Many Dutch merchants soon were making their living in the slave trade and were happy to provide the highest bidders with workers for their fields and refineries.

The Spanish and Portuguese enjoyed a monopoly on the importation of sugar from the Americas throughout the 1500s, but this was about to change. The English, French, and Dutch sought several means to disrupt the Spanish and Portuguese hold over sugar. The British, a generation removed from their victory over the Spanish armada, looked toward the Caribbean with envy and determination. They settled an island that had been conquered and then deserted by both the Portuguese and the Spanish: Barbados.

In the 1640s and 1650s, Barbados would provide the model for the sugar plantation and set the trend that would be followed for generations to come.

The first English ship touched the island on May 14, 1625, and claimed the land on behalf of King James I. On February 17, 1627, a party of eighty settlers and ten slaves sought to occupy and settle the island. In the mid-1630s, sugarcane, cotton, and tobacco were introduced and production took off.

The production of sugar, tobacco, and cotton on Barbados during these startup years was heavily reliant on indentured servants. White civilians who wanted to emigrate overseas to start a new life could do so by signing an agreement to serve a planter in Barbados for a period of five or seven years. But this wasn't sufficient labor to meet the demands of a plantation.

As sugar became the staple crop of the island, the drawbacks of dependence upon indentured labor became quite clear to the planters. Not only did white servants prove unruly and rebellious when they found themselves condemned to effective servitude on the sugar plantations, but they were reluctant to continue to stay on as wage earners when their period of indenture expired. Plantation owners turned to the British government, who offered them criminals to work their land. When that didn't work out owing to the frequent pardons and escapes, kidnappers filled the void. They were then followed by Dutch slave traders.

The slaves came from Sierra Leone, Ghana, the Ivory Coast, Cameroon, Nigeria, and Guinea. Many slaves did not survive the journey from Africa, but many thousands still reached their destination. As the demand for sugar soared, so too did the numbers of African slaves. By 1660, out of a total population of 40,000, there were as many blacks as whites on Barbados. By 1724, the number of slaves on the island was pushing 55,000, constituting nearly three-quarters of the entire island's population.

The Barbadians dominated the Caribbean sugar industry during this time. But, for the British, this wasn't enough. With money from taxes now rolling into the government coffers, they learned just how much was to be made in the sugar industry. They turned their eyes to the third largest island in the Caribbean—Jamaica. The problem was, it was still under Spanish control.

No matter. In 1655, General-at-Sea William Penn seized Jamaica, without orders, in the name of England's Lord Protector, Oliver Cromwell. Spain never succeeded in retaking the island, and within a few years, Jamaica became another British colony. Sugar and coffee would make Jamaica one of the most valuable possessions in the world for the next 150 years.

By the 1660s, the Anglo-Caribe system of large plantations worked by African slaves was proving more profitable than the Portuguese model used in Brazil. It was this model that was used in the tobacco and cotton plantations of the Americas. This was the primary point of the triangle trade of the 1700s. If we are to expand upon this point further, the dynamics of American politics, even today, find their roots here at this point of Caribbean history, where the English, Portuguese, Spanish, and Dutch all looked to find a way to fill their coffers from the demand of sugar. This demand first came from confection, and later from rum.

The English sugar industry spread wherever it went in the Caribbean. It brought with it social, economic, and political transformations so vast and rapid that many historians have called it the Sugar Revolution. "England fought the most, conquered the most colonies, imported the most slaves and went furthest and fastest in creating a plantation system," wrote Sidney Mintz in *Sweetness and Power*. After England had conquered Jamaica—an island nearly thirty times the size of Barbados—in 1655, it became the de facto power in the European sugar trade. By 1763, five of the ten most profitable sugar islands in the world were owned by Britain. Notes Conrad Goodwin, an anthropologist who has spent more than a decade excavating and studying sugar plantations on Antigua and the neighboring island of Montserrat, "Barbados, in one period, and Antigua, in another, were producing more wealth than the entire North American continent—most of this on the backs of those who had been stolen from their homelands or had grown up without basic liberties." During the 1600s, the British shipped about 250,000 African slaves in total to the Caribbean. By the 1700s the average number was 45,000 *per year.*

As confectionery has an innocent, nearly juvenile quality about it, it would be easy for us to separate the actions of man from candy itself. But to do so would be disingenuous. There was a demand for sugar, specifically cheap sugar. Confectionery, whether for medicine or for pleasure, was a large part of that demand. It is not difficult to draw a line from the subtleties of the European banquet table to the humid plantations of Barbados. As we will see later on, this problem still exists today with regard to the trade in chocolate.

To say that these new sugar colonies and trading routes helped Britain's confectionery industry would be akin to stating that the auto industry helped Detroit. Such proclamations are an understatement. The fact of the matter is plain: the confectionery industry we know today in the United States would not exist without Britain's commitment to sugar in the seventeenth and eighteenth centuries. And that commitment came at a devastating price.

I looked out at the Thames from my park bench next to the Houses of Parliament and contemplated all of this. I had come to England to engage my inner child, and instead I had tumbled headlong into the history of a trade that had taken millions of lives, both directly and indirectly. From my laptop bag, I took out a piece of candy: a Soor Ploom I had left over from Edinburgh.

I had in my hand a piece of the puzzle, of this horrific picture, and I tried to reconcile it with memories of my youth.

I couldn't. Rationally, I knew I shouldn't. As a child of the 1970s, I had no influence upon the past. Rationally, I knew this.

I flicked the candy over the cement railing and into the river, picked up my bag, and headed back to my hotel. It was an empty gesture, at best.

Even worse? Deep in the back of my mind, I was thinking where I could go to find more.

Chapter 12

London: City of Candy

• • • • • • • • • • •

$\mathcal{S}$ugar consumption in Europe steadily rose through the six-teenth and seventeenth centuries as the prices fell and the product became more widely available. Abraham Ortelius remarked in his *Theatrum Orbis Terrarum* of 1572: "Whereas before, sugar was only obtainable in the shops of apothecaries, who kept it exclusively for invalids, today people devour it out of gluttony. . . . What used to be a medicine is nowadays eaten as food." By 1700, sugar was flooding in from the Caribbean. The price of the commodity dropped, which opened up new retail markets, and over the next one hundred years sugar consumption increased dramatically.

This, along with the start of the Industrial Revolution, fur-thered the market for candy in eighteenth-century Britain. Sugar, and products made with sugar, became affordable to the lower classes. This made possible a viable trade in confection-ery and the emergence of professional confectioners. These new entrepreneurs could tap into two different markets: apothecaries looking to have someone else assume the cost of making their medicines and individuals seeking confection for its own wonderful taste, regardless of its health properties. In the early 1700s we start to see sweet shops, often partnered with or part of pastry shops. Many patisseries of the day were required to know and sell items that we would recognize today as candy.

None other than Daniel Defoe, better known to us now as the author of *Robinson Crusoe,* documented these shops in 1724 in *The Complete English Tradesman,* where he tells us of the expense of running and outfitting a proper pastry shop, details what a proper shop could look like, and states that the expense for the showroom could run almost six times the cost of the equipment needed to produce the confections.

This runs counter to how we view candy shops today, which, for the most part, end up as retailers for other candy makers. Even the sellers of some brands of high-end chocolate rarely make the chocolates themselves, relying on various brands of couverture, which they then outsource to other companies to melt and reconstitute into their own confections.

Once again, the publishing industry was there to help the confection industry along. But instead of confections made for the homes of the upper class and providing hints on how one may become a better "huswife," by the mid-1700s, books began appearing on the scene that promoted confectionery and sweets as their own culinary art. Books such as *The Court and the Country Confectioner, The Compleat Confectioner,* and *The Art of Confectionery* all provided recipes to those in the candy trade.

What did one see when one came across such a shop in eighteenth-century London? Laura Mason, in her book *Sugar-Plums and Sherbet,* digs into our stereotype of such shops, compares it against the books of the day, and extrapolates the following:

Flash and glitter is still expected of a sweet shop. The use of salvers reflected eighteenth-century desserts where biscuits, marzipan and preserved fruit were piled in high pyramids on shallow china or silver dishes. As more glass jars were used, filled with transparent jellies, fruit preserves, little candies and comfits, so they were placed in the window to glint in the light streaming through those expensive glass planes. Inside, candlelight reflected in the mirrors sparkled among glass and gilding. The sweet shop was a grotto.

This is the ideal that has been sold to consumers of the twentieth and twenty-first centuries. Very few candy shops of today can meet this ideal, and most don't even try. But so strong is this ideal that it is what had drawn me to London. Somewhere in this city of seven and a half million people there was such a grotto, or at least a reasonable facsimile of one. I was sure I could find a candy shop that could satiate this need for sweets I had within, and one that would open doors to my youth.

There are those who head to Harrods department store when they are able to make it to London. This is understandable, as the food courts are famous, the toy store is a must-see, and the throngs of crowds that enter the store make it one of many retail outlets in London that is a tourist destination. As far as brand recognition is concerned, it is one of the few department stores that American travelers recognize by name.

While I have a healthy respect for Harrods (I did mention the food courts, didn't I?), my department store of choice in London is Fortnum & Mason. It is a department store that is so high end that it makes Harrods look like Sears, and makes Sears look like a dollar store.

Much like Harrods, Fortnum & Mason has its own food

courts, and when you enter the store, both the basement and ground floors deal almost exclusively with consumables of some sort. But instead of harsh linoleum and hard incandescent lighting, the store is decorated with a soft, sea-foam blue carpeting, with lighting that provides an almost ethereal glow—a hint to what is being sold.

On the first floor, next to the chocolate counter, where boxes of chocolate selections can go for as much as $75, is a counter that deals exclusively in sugar confectionery. This fact delights me no end. Here, in possibly one of the most exclusive department stores on the planet, is a food counter that sells boiled sweets and marshmallows. Such a place couldn't seem more out of place if it had been set in the middle of Tiffany's in Manhattan. As customers swirled around me, either looking for the rare blend of tea that Fortnum's sells, or seeing whether their favorite bottle of champagne was currently available, I was crouched down rather uncouthly, my nose nearly pressing the glass of the display, trying to determine whether I wanted 100 grams of either rhubarb custards or Jordan almonds.

This was not the candy shop of my dreams, nor one of Laura Mason's description. But it was a great place to start. Seeing a candy counter here in the midst of posh central London gave me faith that candy still reaches across class boundaries. These sugary treats should know no income levels, and they could and should easily transcend status.

Later, when I remarked to a friend about this scene, I was reminded that our department stores here in the States used to carry confections as well. This was a memory that I had completely forgotten—the trips to Montgomery Ward and Sears, and the stops by Brach's bin o' delights. But at some point over the past generation, someone, somewhere, decided that candy was not a department store product, and soon they were all systematically removed. I find it interesting that on the ground floor of

Kate's Candy Bag

JORDAN ALMONDS

These were the candies that adults said "are not for children. They are for company!" The status afforded these candy-coated nuts seemed callous. There's a candy not for children? How dare they!

After company arrived, we were allowed to have two or three, and then found out that, while tasty, they were nothing compared to peanut M&M's. They could keep their Jordan almonds. We kids would keep our M&M's.

Candy Exchange Rate:
two 8-ounce bags of Jordan almonds = 1 York Peppermint Pattie

the major department stores in London, one can find candy, chocolate, and tea, whereas in Manhattan, on the ground floor of major department stores one will find makeup counters and perfumeries. From my own perspective, this is yet another example of our American culture that demonstrates our predilection for image over substance.

Of course, the fact that I found myself in orbit around the candy and chocolate counters rather than, say, the tea or fruit displays, is another American tradition, but we'll just set that fact aside for the moment.

After purchasing a bag of rhubarb custards and a small sack of Jordan almonds, I headed through heavily congested Piccadilly Circus to find a smaller shop located just to the north. In one of the many narrow side streets one finds in greater metropolitan London sits a shop seemingly no bigger than the office of a midlevel manager. The walls are lined with glass jar after glass jar, each filled to varying capacities with brightly colored joy. I had entered Mrs Kibble's Olde Sweet Shoppe, and it had about as much to do with eighteenth-century sweet shops as Disney's Animal Kingdom has to do with the savannas of Africa.

There are several key clues that reveal "shoppes" such as these to be modern re-creations of the stores of two hundred plus years ago. Some of them are readily apparent, such as the prevalence of sugar-free sweets, candies that are designed to appeal to our twentieth-century health consciousness.

Other aspects are far more nuanced. The clue here is the size of the shop. Because rents are high for stores located so close to Piccadilly Circus, the smaller the shop, the lower the rent. There is clearly no room for these places to be making confectionery of their own. All the candies that decorate the shelves are made elsewhere, likely in an industrial environment of one sort or another.

These "shoppes" (there are several throughout London, and even more throughout the United Kingdom) are designed to re-create the experience of the eighteenth century. But they don't have the heavy financial overhead of production and the slim profit margins that come with them.

So the question becomes, "Does it matter? Does it matter that these stores are re-creations?" Well, yes, but the reason differs depending on one's perspective.

From a confection maker's point of view, candy stores such as these aren't a priority. Sure, they'll supply them, as every revenue stream matters. But there are other sellers that have larger product turnover. In talking with Chris Marshall, managing director of Tangerine Confectionery, the largest sugar confectionery producer in the United Kingdom, places such as Mrs

Kibble's are quaint, but the big money comes from the Tescos and the Costcos of the world. More effort is put into ensuring their products are on the shelves of large-scale franchised grocery stores. A generation ago, children would get their candy fix by heading to the local newsagent. Today, they're more likely to get it when walking down the grocery aisle with their parents.

From an individual perspective, the experience of walking into a candy shop changes the type of experience one is having with the candy. Typically when one makes a candy purchase at a grocery store, it's done by happenstance, by impulse (in fact, many sellers refer to candy today as "impulse purchases").

But those who enter candy shops have already decided that they want candy the moment they go into the shop. They aren't there by happenstance. They are there with specific intent. Their relationship with candy is one of both a re-creation of one's innocent past and the joyful anxiety of making the best possible decision with such a diversity of options. In a candy shop, there is as much fun in making the decision of whether one wants a lemon sherbet or an Everton Mint as there is in consuming the result of that decision.

Back in the eighteenth and nineteenth centuries, consumers of confections could only get their fix through their interactions with the sweet shop or, if they had the skills, by making sweets at home. In the twenty-first century, we see candy everywhere, and with its ubiquity we have lost the concept of how special sweets once were. Candy shops, even modern "sweet shoppes," give us a swift kick in our nostalgia, reminding us of candy's specialness—or at the very least, of how special it should be today.

I wanted to make a risky purchase, one that would subject my taste buds to a candy that I typically would not consume. Considering my recent victory at Pontefract, I purchased a small bag of Stockley's Army & Navy candies, a hard-boiled sweet flavored with aniseed. Taking my risky purchase, I walked throughout Soho and Covent Garden, continuing on my visits to London candy shops of note. I avoided walking into newsagents or grocery stores, instead looking for a kick start to my innocence that only candy shops can bring.

Lucky for me, Covent Garden is full of such shops. A few steps from the Theatre Royal in Drury Lane, there is Hope and Greenwood, another modern sweet shop. A few blocks to the west sits Cybercandy, a shop that takes a more modern approach to candy by providing sweets from other countries—from Japan, Australia, even America. Around the corner from Cybercandy is yet another sweet shop. In fact, finding shops that deal exclusively in candy is not a difficult task at all.

One thing becomes quickly apparent in these locations. Although each store may have a diverse selection of sweets, they have mostly the same diverse selection. This too differs from the sweet shops of the eighteenth century. Back then, many shops had a type of confectionery in which they specialized, so that if you craved one specific type, your options for shopping were somewhat limited.

Not so today. In each of the stores around London, I found sherbets, bonbons, mint cakes, mint balls, rocks, custards, butterscotches, toffees, and caramels. This ready access bothered me not at all.

Butterscotches, toffees, and caramels hold an odd place in the confectionery universe as they are all relative newcomers, each tracing their candy lineage to the late eighteenth and early nineteenth centuries. They also hold a special spot in my heart because evidence shows that they are creations not of candy shops but of home cooks. Toffees seem to have been of particular interest to these cooks.

Laura Mason, once again in her book *Sugar-Plums and Sherbet*, hypothesizes that when sugar became affordable to the lower classes, they created a treat that would be consumed to celebrate All Soul's Day, observed on November 1. Whereas those with greater resources would create cakes and pastries to celebrate the day, families in the lower classes relied upon sugar, honey, flour, and butter to create a confection to bring to the churches and festivals. This would have occurred in the early 1800s. Etymological evidence demonstrates that a sweet known as "taffie," a confection made of treacle and flour, was known in Scotland around 1825. Mason points to a specific recipe written by one Mrs. Ann Hailstone of Bradford, an area in northern England around Yorkshire, sometime between 1808 and 1833:

TOFFY

One lb of brown sugar 2 tablespoonful of treacle dissolved in a gill of water on the fire, and then add 8 ounces of fresh butter boil the whole till it will drop crisp. You may add a few drops of essence of lemon.

The flavor of toffee (and butterscotch and caramels) is created by a reaction that takes place during boiling. Proteins, such as those contained in dairy products such as butter, combine with the sugar in a process known to chemists as the Maillard reaction. This particular piece of culinary magic produces a rich-looking brown color and creates attractive smells and flavors. For example, that inviting deep bronze crust and that fresh aroma of newly baked bread? That's the result of the Maillard reaction. Toast is the most obvious product of this process. When applied to sugar, it is sometimes known as caramelization.

Toffee became popular in the early 1800s when sugar, and specifically treacle (a sugar syrup like molasses), had become cheap enough to be an everyday commodity. The earliest references to toffee all come from the north of England, and most

Kate's Candy Bag

HEATH BAR

Every child seems to have one candy bar that she likes that the rest of her peers find odd. Mine was the Heath bar, a bit of hardened toffee coated in milk chocolate. When the rest of the neighborhood would trade off for Snickers or Reese's Peanut Butter Cups, I would consider it a win if I could get two or three Heath bars for a Hershey bar or two.

While the kids in my neighborhood may not have cottoned to the Heath bar, it was clear that many other people around the country did. The demand for the Heath bar was so great that the Hershey Company felt it could provide a viable alternative and get a bit of the Heath bar fans converted to their new candy bar called Skor. Alas, when Skor didn't sell as well as Hershey had anticipated, and failed in its attempt to knock the Heath bar off of its toffee perch, Hershey ended up buying the rights to the Heath bar, leaving them with two hardened toffee bars covered in milk chocolate.

Candy Exchange Rate:
1 Heath bar = 2 York Peppermint Patties

mention friends getting together to boil treacle with flour in order to make a sticky treat that was to be shared among the participants of the get-together. Here again, we see home candy making as a means of socialization.

Improvements were soon made to this basic mixture, and

recipes started to add cream or butter. The end result was a bold-flavored confection, sweet as sugar but with a richer character.

Buttery toffee is often called butterscotch, which suggests it was invented in Scotland, but this is simply not true. The word was first recorded in the Yorkshire town of Doncaster, where Samuel Parkinson began making this sort of toffee around 1817. It is suggested that the "scotch" part of its name derives from "scorch," but even this is a tenuous tie. Better is the word "scotch" as a verb, which means "to cut or score"; this is more in line with how butter is added to the toffee—instead of one big lump of butter, various cut pieces are periodically tossed into the boiling sugar.

One point here needs to be stated clearly to us Americans. What we know of as butterscotch isn't what one might claim to be true or authentic butterscotch. Instead, those bright yellowish-orangeish boiled sweets we find in typical Brach's mixes and the golden syrups we pour onto our scoops of ice cream are artificially flavored re-creations of the more traditional toffee-flavored treats of years gone by. But the flavor we know as butterscotch is so ensconced in our culture that it's never likely to change. But know this—American butterscotch is a pretender to the throne. In the late 1800s and early 1900s, our idea of butterscotch was more in line with the traditional British version, with various of the ear including ingredients such as brown sugar, white sugar, or molasses, and techniques similar to those used to make toffee.

Toffee is one of the easiest sweets to make. It is historically significant, not for any great invention or technique that helped change the industry, but for the role it has played in how accessible candy making had become to the homemaker. While it is surprising that butter showed up in confectionery relatively recently, it is more significant that using molasses, butter, and acids such as vinegar (to prevent sugar graining) became widely grasped at a basic level to the point where even home cooks could make it.

This didn't change the fact that making confectionery, toffees or otherwise, was a labor-intensive affair. To this day, it is still an advantage to have someone share the work when it comes to sugar boiling. Back at the start of the nineteenth century, professional confectioners who were making candies on a day-to-day basis had their families, journeymen, and apprentices to help. But home candy makers used this need for labor as an excuse for a social event. F. Marian McNeill, in her book *The Scots Kitchen*, published in 1929, describes candy making as an evening's entertainment.

We see this throughout the nineteenth century. In north Wales toffee pulls around Christmas or New Year were traditional, with friends and family joining in. Toffee-boiling nights as an excuse for gathering were also recorded in Yorkshire. Taffy pulls or candy pulls became a custom in North America, too.

By the time the music hall, and then later cinema, provided alternative entertainment, taffy pulls had become a quaint custom on both sides of the Atlantic. The point is that the tradition has become ensconced enough in both British and American cultures that home candy making is still practiced to this day, albeit not to the extent it once was. And demand for the toffee was enough that local confectioneries had no problem filling that void and improving upon the recipes that had established the candies.

So where do caramels fit into all of this? This is where we see the first American influence on the candy scene, as caramels appear very much to be an American invention. But care is needed here to differentiate the act of caramelizing sugar (which is bringing sugar to a specific temperature) and caramel candy. The two are quite different beasts, and one should not think that caramel candies are made by ensuring that sugar reaches a specific temperature. Caramel candies have a specific recipe, similar to that of toffee, but with milk added in place of water. One late nineteenth-century English confectioner by the name of E. Skuse mentions in the book *Skuse's Complete Confectioner* that caramels were brought over from America and were received very well at first, but the marketplace came in and . . . well, it's a story that one could easily apply to many products:

> Caramels. When first brought over from America, these goods were certainly a treat. They were rather dear, but they were good; the public appreciated them. Very soon the demand was universal, then competition stepped in with the usual result—the prices lowered, the quality suffered, until anything cut into the shape were called caramels. Consequently, the demand lessened; still they were forced on the market cheaper and cheaper, worse and worse, until only those who liked plenty of money bought the vile concoctions. The very name has almost become a synonym for rubbish. (pp. 60–61)

Caramels play a huge part in American chocolate history, but I'm getting a tad ahead of myself. Suffice it to say that by the late 1800s, caramels, toffee, and butterscotch had firmly placed themselves into the candy lexicon.

One of the things that strikes me about toffee and its counterparts, caramel and butterscotch, is that their creation and invention happened so recently. These candies seem so basic, so primal, that it's difficult for me to believe that someone, somewhere, hadn't thought to mix sugar, water, and honey together with a bit of butter and bring it to a boil. Either the recipe was so simple that no one had previously bothered to write it down, or sugar was previously such a revered and expensive commodity that confectioners simply didn't think to apply such a luxurious ingredient to a recipe so unsophisticated. Either way, the questions surrounding these candies make them all the more special in my eyes. For if indeed toffee, caramels, and butterscotches are candies of the lower class, it demonstrates just how much sugar had infiltrated everyday life for all classes in England, not just the aristocrats, landed gentry, or apothecary entrepreneurs. It means that the candy world, as we know it today, was the result of the work across the classes of all of England, not just a select few.

I considered this for a moment. Sugar from the Caribbean came into England, where it could find itself in the hands of the wealthy or the poor. It could have ended up in chocolate or in a toffee made around Everton. The crop that was initially a curiosity to the Greeks and a luxury to the Italians had made it into the hands of the British working class.

Candy and sweets had played a distinct part in that growth. Yes, for the longest time it had camouflaged itself as medicine. But by the beginning of the nineteenth century, such approaches were no longer needed. We could now have candy for candy's sake.

Chapter 13

And Along Comes Chocolate

• • • • • • • • • • • • • •

hose of you keen of sight and aware of history will note a candy that I have not covered in great detail, one that is so ubiquitous today that we take it for granted—chocolate. Sure, I talked about the bean as Columbus found it, but not chocolate confectionery. There is a reason for this: chocolate in its candy form did not come into being until the 1800s. London, however, plays an integral role in chocolate's history. This is what clicked when I further explored the development of candy.

It's easy to get swept up by London's energy. There are monuments, churches, and plaques everywhere to remind you of its history, but it's hard to focus on a single aspect of that history because you're constantly pulled in another direction by more monuments, churches, and plaques. Add to this the general hubbub of today's city, with people everywhere and the focus on tourists, restaurateurs vying for diners and shopkeepers plying their goods, and London quickly becomes a city in which one can lose track of time and distance. Soon I found myself near St. Paul's Cathedral, tracking northeast, where I stumbled on a street that I remembered from my notes about chocolate: Bishopsgate.

Not far from Bishopsgate is one of the shops set up by Paul A. Young, one of the many celebrities in the chocolate world. Are you surprised to learn that there's an entire subculture related to chocolate with its own celebrities? So was I.

Paul Young's shop is just a stone's throw from the Bank of England, which is fitting, as both have influenced their own world. Paul's mere presence in England demonstrates just how far chocolate has come in this country.

There's a bit of a problem here, however. Mr. Young and other high-end chocolatiers are reluctant to call their products candy. Chocolates, absolutely. Confections, undoubtedly. But candy? Um, er, uh . . . could they, perhaps, interest you in a sea-salted rocher made with 64 percent Madagascan dark chocolate?

In the interest of fairness, I should probably cop to my own problems with high-end chocolates. I find chocolatiers both intimidating and borderline pretentious. Let me also acknowledge that this is my own issue, and every artisan of chocolate confections whom I have met has been a stand-up, passionate person willing to give of himself or herself at a moment's notice for the promotion of chocolate as so much more than a simple Hershey bar.

Therein lays the issue. For if we are to accept their premise that there is chocolate, and then there is *chocolate*, ipso facto, we have enjoyed chocolate incorrectly, or, more specifically, we have had bad chocolate and have enjoyed it anyway.

The second part of this problem is that chocolatiers go to great lengths to describe their creations in floral prose, telling us of chocolate truffles filled with a gentle nougat, topped with salted caramel and crushed roasted peanuts. But then they will hem and haw for a moment or two when asked, "How does this confection differ from a Snickers bar?"

The secret here, the one that these confectioners don't really talk about all that much, is that the products that they sell at their high-end shops and the cheap, mass-produced chocolate in the grocery store are actually two sides of the same coin. You cannot have one without the other, and their histories are tied from the very beginning, from the time when the cacao bean was first harvested, up through its introduction to the West and its integration into the Industrial Age, to the mass-market reach of chocolate in our day and the artisanal revolution that has occurred in response. Paul A. Young would not exist without Hershey, Cadbury, or Mars; and Hershey, Cadbury, and Mars would not exist without the hundreds of chocolate artisans that existed in the eighteenth and nineteenth centuries.

I returned to my hotel room and checked for a reference in my notes: a copy of a notice in *The Public Advertiser* from June 16, 1657, which signaled the appearance of a chocolate house in London, perhaps the first. The notice read: "In Bishopsgate Street, in Queen Head Alley at a Frenchman's House is an excellent West Indian drink, called chocolate, to be sold, where you may have it ready at any time, and also unmade at reasonable rates."

This is ironic considering the curmudgeon that was running England at the time, one Oliver Cromwell. Not that he or many of the other puritanical Roundheads would have known the pleasure to be found in the cacao bean. The commodity of chocolate was very much a product of colonialism and arrived in England at the beginning of the British Empire. But chocolate is not chocolate candy. Chocolate bars are a by-product of the Industrial Revolution. Explaining how the bean evolved into a mass-produced product is a story unto itself.

Legend has it that chocolate arrived into the royal French court around 1615, the result of a double royal marriage, and thus a diplomatic tie, between France and Spain. Chocolate was said to be served at the festivities, a political friendship was sealed, and a new luxury drink was established.

Except this is not quite the entire story. The Spaniards didn't take to the drink immediately, and there were many missives sent back to Spain from Mexico during this era in which someone or another is complaining about the bitter drink, usually noting how nasty the concoction was. The method of preparation that was taught to the Spaniards by the Aztecs involved smashing the beans, adding hot water, and then whipping furiously until the residual cocoa butter turned frothy. There's no record of sweeteners, sugar or otherwise, being used, although it's likely that some other flavorings, such as chili peppers, were added.

It took a while for the Spaniards to see the value of chocolate. There was no "Aha!" moment that ensured a get-rich-quick scheme was soon to follow. Instead, what likely happened was a cross-pollination of culture. The Spaniards only took to chocolate once they began marrying or mingling with the native women of the New World, and the women introduced them to the bean. As Sophie and Michael Coe write in their book *The True History of Chocolate:*

It was not long before an entire generation of Spanish Creoles was to be born in the old Aztec realm, never to set foot in the old country from which their parents had come. Thus, an entirely new, creolized culture was taking form that partook of elements of both cultures, but was different from both. This was the context in which chocolate was taken into the Colonial cuisine of New Spain, and was eventually transplanted to Old Spain and the rest of Europe. (p. 113)

How was chocolate consumed? By the end of the sixteenth century, almost exclusively as a room-temperature, unsweetened drink. Chocolate as a hot beverage was a rare but not unheard of drink, one that the Europeans helped popularize back in the old world.

So, where did the idea of chocolate candy come from? Before getting into that question, it's best to understand the makeup of chocolate.

Chocolate comes from the seeds of the fruit of *Theobroma cacao,* also known as the cacao tree. The tree is relatively small, peaking anywhere between fifteen and twenty-five feet tall, and it is native to the tropical regions of the Americas. A cacao pod or bean has a leathery rind about an inch thick and is filled with sweet, mucilaginous pulp called *baba de cacao.*

I know what you're thinking. "Mmmm. Mucilaginous pulp. Sounds delish!"

Surprisingly, this pulp is quite edible, being sweet and tangy when ripe, unlike the beans, which are bitter and rough. However, it's not the pulp that attracts the chocolate fiend, but the beans. These beans are fatty, and it is from them that cocoa solids and cocoa butter are extracted. But at first no one knew how to do this.

When chocolate drinks were created with these beans, a layer of fat would develop on top. As José de Acosta, naturalist and Spanish missionary, wrote in the late sixteenth century:

> The main benefit of this cacao is a beverage which they make called Chocolate, which is a crazy thing valued in that country. It disgusts those who are not used to it, for it has a foam on top, or a scum-like bubbling.

Regardless of one's approach to adventurous eating, anything described as having a "scum-like bubbling" would likely be a tough sell to the more picky eaters out there. The fat, which likely was a primary component of this scum, was made more palatable by creating an emulsion with the rest of the ingredients of the beverage by using a *molinillo,* what we would recognize today as a wooden whisk or beater. The first *molinillo,* created by sixteenth-century Spanish colonists, was made to fit into a container with the handle extending out of the top. The *molinillo* was then rotated between the user's two hands with the palm sides placed together. The twisting motion frothed the fat, the beans, and the liquid within the drink, creating a foam that was not only palatable, but quite tasty. The quality of the drink would then not only be affected by the quality of the ingredients, but also by the skill of the person preparing the drink. It's no wonder that the many descriptions of the quality of the drink are so varied.

The trick was in the whipping of the drink in order to get an emulsion that would make the cocoa butter, creating a sort of a cocoa butter version of whipped cream, albeit runnier. Whip the drink with the appropriate amount of talent, and you'll have a delightful drink. But if the whipper lacked the requisite talent or knowledge of sweeteners, one could end up with a bitter drink with a thick layer of scum upon it, which was likely as appetizing as it sounds. My guess is that this is why we see some references to chocolate in the 1500s similar to what Girolamo Benzoni wrote in his book *A History of the New World,* published in 1575: "[Chocolate] seemed more a drink more for pigs, than a drink for humanity."

The Spanish eventually did become quite enamored of the flavor of chocolate, and they took it back to Spain; from Spain it traveled to the rest of Europe, typically through the various royal courts. Except for England, whose subjects apparently first heard of chocolate through pirates. (That's a long story involving privateers and the British insistence on pissing off the

Spaniards during the time before the defeat of the Spanish armada.)

So which Europeans had the best access to the correct whip to whip up a cup of cocoa? There are two suspects to look at. First, you have the lower classes of the Spanish colonials who were the first to marry and intermingle with the natives. It is this group in which we see the cross-pollination of cultures, including an appreciation of cocoa.

Second would be the missionaries who had gone to the New World to spread the word of Christ. Many of these monks, in their quest to convert the locals, would have seen this ritual up close and personal, and many would have acquired a taste for the drink once it had been made for them properly. Many of these same monks, and those who learned the ritual from them, would have returned to Europe and spread this information wherever they came upon chocolate. Traveling monks are said to have introduced the proper way to drink cocoa in France and Germany, and by the turn of the seventeenth century, the Spaniards were the de facto experts on chocolate. By 1613, Antonio de Ledesma Colmenero wrote a treatise on chocolate in Spanish, entitled, *Chocolata Inda, Opusculum De Qualitate Et Natura Chocolatae* ("A Curious Treatise of the Quality and Nature of Chocolate"). During the next decade, his book was so popular that it was translated into English, French, and Latin.

Not surprisingly, cocoa was exalted not just for its taste but for its supposed medical benefits. The Spanish king Philip II sent his royal physician, Francisco Hernandez, to the New World in 1570, to find and classify new plants and animals and relate them to the humoristic approach of medicine. Not surprisingly, Hernandez came across chocolate and found it "temperate," but leaning toward "cold and humid," good for "[warming] the stomach, perfuming the breath," and "combating poisons, and alleviating intestinal pains and colic." This would not be the first or the last time that health benefits would be ascribed to the bean.

By the start of the 1600s, the cocoa drink started to take off among the upper classes, who were convinced of both its exotic nature and its health benefits. There were, however, two problems. First was the time needed to create the drink to make it palatable. Other beverage commodities of the era needed little to no time to create. Both tea and coffee, now finding their ways to the tables of the Europeans, took little time and less skill to make. Cocoa had a learning curve and required a skilled hand. Second, the chocolate that was being drunk during this era had to be extremely rich, because of the excessive amount of cocoa butter that was part of the bean. No one had yet figured out how to remove the fat from the bean, and this would have made the drink difficult for some to digest.

This comparison of cocoa and coffee is notable, for when cocoa became more popular, more accessible, and thus, cheaper, it migrated from the sitting rooms of castles and noble houses into the coffeehouses in the more cosmopolitan cities of the Continent, where entrepreneurs soon turned to cocoa to help supplement their incomes.

The first coffeehouse that we know of in London was opened in St. Michael's Alley, Cornhill, in 1652, and it was a mere five years later that we see the ad for chocolate at Bishopsgate. Both drinks took off. The English diarist Samuel Pepys noted in November of 1664 that he had been "to a coffee house to drink jocolatte, very good." The popularity of such houses was such that by 1722, a continental traveler named John Macky described the Pall Mall area of London as the ordinary place of residence of all strangers "because of its vicinity to the King's Palace, the parks, the Parliament House, the theatres and the chocolate and coffee houses where the best company frequent." Coffee and chocolate houses were the places to be seen.

And the English were now able to get a regular supply of cocoa. For by the time they conquered Jamaica and kicked out the Spanish, not only were sugar plantations thriving on the island, but cocoa plantations were as well.

The two problems with cocoa still existed—it took time and skill to make, and the excessive fat content of cocoa made it inedible to some. And the more cocoa makers rushed to make a drink, the less chance they had to make it well. There had to be a way to address these issues. There had to be a way to provide cocoa in a quick and easy manner for the shopkeepers. The answer would be provided by the suppliers of chocolate.

It is not known whether manufactured chocolate was being produced in England at the beginning of the eighteenth century. All we have to get a picture of the chocolate world at this time is circumstantial evidence. There's no evidence that the English government at the time, which never met a tax that it didn't like, was levying duties on raw cacao beans. This suggests that few if any were imported at the time. However, duty *was* imposed at 8 shillings per gallon on manufactured chocolate. And as with any tax, the cost of this was ultimately placed upon the consumer. From this evidence, it seems probable that the proprietors of the chocolate houses were importing manufactured chocolate, likely coming from France or Spain, to use in their drinks. It is possible that these chocolate manufacturers were importing the beans from Mexico and the Caribbean, including the cocoa plantations owned by the British.

It's important to note that manufactured chocolate at this point was not the smooth, silky, solid chocolate bars that we see today. Instead, it was more like a thick paste. In *The Accomplish'd Female Instructor,* published in London in 1704, we find this recipe for a cup of cocoa:

TO MAKE CHOCOLATE THE BEST WAY

Take an equal Proportion of Water and Milk, let them well incorporate in Boylin, but continually stir them, lest they burn to the Bottom; so having grated or beaten your Chocolate Cakes fine, put to a Quart of the Liquor an Ounce and a half or two Ounces, if you would have it rich, then take it off the Fire, and put to it two Yolks of new lay'd Eggs well beaten up with as much fin Sugar dissolved in Rose-Water, as will sweeten it; then mill it with a Milling-stick, till it becomes tick, and so pour it into dishes.

There are all sorts of clues here as to what chocolate consisted of to the well-off populace of Britain. Manufactured chocolate came in a simple cake form that was little more than roasted cocoa beans that had been ground to a fine paste and allowed to solidify by adding any number of fillers that were available to the artisan who had produced them. These cakes were very rich, due to the high fat content from the cocoa butter, and likely quite unpalatable without milk, water, sugar, and various other spices being added to them.

This isn't the only evidence we have, either. Throughout the evolution of chocolate from drink to confection, we see several examples of solid chocolate being used in order to make the chocolate drink. In 1685 Philippe S. Dufour, a Frenchman, wrote a seminal book about coffee, tea, and chocolate, in which he dismissed the typical English way of making a cocoa drink and instead offered up this recipe:

Take a cake of chocolate, and either pound it in a mortar or grate it into a fine powder. Mix this with sugar, and pour it into a little pot in which water is boiling. Then, take the pot from the fire and work it well with your little Mill; if you don't have a mill, pour it a score of times from one pot into another [shades of classic Maya!], but this is not as good. Finally, let it be drunk without separating the "scum" from it.

There are two things of note here from Dufour's recipe. One, it provides evidence that the chocolate connoisseurs of the day preferred their drink with scum instead of without it. Second, he is making the chocolate drink from a chocolate cake. It's unlikely that he's referring to a cake in its pastry definition, but rather to a more condensed solid.

What does this mean in the big picture? Europeans likely acquired their taste for chocolate from the drink, but eventually were able to get their chocolate fix from the cakes that were initially used to make these drinks.

More importantly, these cakes were unrefined, to the point where one could still grate or beat them and have residual cocoa liquor to which one could add boiling milk and water. These cakes had to come from somewhere, and because of the political instability of the era, it was only a matter of time before some Englishman would replicate the products that the French or Spanish were providing to the English coffeehouses.

Walter Churchman appears to be that first chocolate manufacturer in Britain. There is evidence that he had premises in Bristol in 1728 where he manufactured chocolate. He also had a warehouse in St. Paul's Churchyard, London, from which he may have supplied some of the more fashionable coffee and chocolate houses.

Looking for a way to improve his business, Walter Churchman invested in a water engine that enabled him to grind his chocolate more finely, and in 1729 he was granted letters of patent by George II. This event was noted in *Farley's Bristol Newspaper* in June 1731:

His Majesty, having been pleased to grant to Walter Church-man Letters Patent for his new invention of making choco-late without fire, to greater perfection in all respects, than will appear on Trial, by its immediate dissolving, full flavour, smoothness on the palate and intimate union with Liquids; and as it is so much finer than any other sort, so it will go much further and be less offensive to weak digestions, being by this method made free of grit and gross particles so much disliked which is referred to the fair and impartial experi-ment.

NB. The curious may be supplied with his superfine choco-late which is as many degrees finer than the above Standard, as that exceeds the finest sold by other makers, plain at six shil-lings per pound; with vanello, seven shillings per pound.

To be sold for ready money only at Mr. Churchman's choc-olate Warehouse at Mr. John Young's in St. Paul's Churchyard, London.

This product that Walter Churchman had made, this cake for cocoa that was purported to be easier to dissolve in liquids and finer to the palate, was the forebear of chocolate candy. From this product stems the multibillion-dollar industry.

Walter Churchman didn't live much longer after his patent was granted, but his son, Charles, carried on the business while continuing to practice as a solicitor.

Meanwhile, also in Bristol, one Joseph Fry was establishing his trade as an apothecary, and he began competing with the Churchmans in the chocolate trade. In 1738, an announcement appeared in the local press stating "the best sorts of chocolate, made and sold wholesale and retail by Joseph Fry, Apothecary, in Small Street, Bristol."

When Charles Churchman died in 1761, he left the patent

Kate's Candy Bag

TAZA CHOCOLATE MEXICANO DISCS

This is an odd chocolate bar, having about as much to do with Mexican chocolate as Taco Bell has to do with Mexican cuisine. First off, Taza is based in Massachusetts, and second, it only started making chocolate in 2006. And, in truth, the result of its production techniques seems to have more in common with chocolate cakes of the seventeenth and eighteenth centuries.

But I love them. They seek to grind the beans more coarsely, and the result is akin to listening to the Sex Pistols for the first time. While many upscale chocolate companies want you to hear Vivaldi in your mind when you take a bite of their candies, Taza wants you to hear power chords from a tuned-down guitar that's been plugged into a distorted amplifier.

And it doesn't hurt that the chocolate is quite delicious.

Candy Exchange Rate:
1 Taza Chocolate Mexicano Disc = 3 York Peppermint Patties

for the water engine and his chocolate business to his executor, John Vaughan. Fry, seeing an opportunity, purchased the patent and advertised the fact in the local paper: "Churchman's patent chocolate is now made by Joseph Fry and John Vaughan Jnr, the said Churchman's executor, the present sole proprietors of the famous water engine at Castle Mills." While competition surely existed, it was Fry's business that prospered, and soon a warehouse was established in London under the supervision of the founder's brother, John.

By the middle of the eighteenth century, chocolate was being made throughout Europe and in the colonies, but all the better-known manufacturers postdate Fry and Vaughan. Lombard of France, which claims to be *la plus ancienne chocolaterie de France*, started business in 1766; von Lippe of Germany started the previous year, as did Dr. James Baker of the United States. Large-scale chocolate manufacturing has its roots in the western British port of Bristol, and the popularity of manufactured chocolate began to increase throughout the world.

Seeing Fry's success, others tried to duplicate it, many by infringing upon the patent for the water engine. Competition was such that soon Fry had to find other ways to differentiate his product from those of lesser quality. Announcements stated "only chocolate with a stamp of an oval form . . . affixed to each half pound and quarter pound," with the words "Churchman's Patent Chocolate, made only by Joseph Fry of Bristol" were placed in newspapers both in Bristol and London. This started two traditions still in use today—branding the chocolate with logos and a regular commitment to advertising. Fry had developed a reputation for a high-quality product, and the branding, together with the fact that he was a Quaker (generally believed to be honest traders), ensured and cemented Fry's success.

When Joseph passed away, the business was left to his wife, Anna Fry, and his son, Joseph Storrs Fry I. They changed the name to Anna Fry and Son, and the business soon flourished even more as Anna invested in advertising. Proclamations of the healthful properties of chocolate began to pop up throughout England, and advertisements stated that Anna Fry's cocoa was recommended by "the most eminent of the Faculty, in preference to every other kind of Breakfast, to such who have tender

Habits, decayed Health, weak Lungs or scorbutic Tendancies, being easy of Digestion, affording a fine and light nourishment, and greatly correction the sharp Humours in the Constitution."

Instructions for making cocoa were helpfully added to these announcements:

> Take an ounce of cocoa, (which is about a common Tea Cupful) boil it in a Pint and a Half of Water for Ten or Fifteen minutes, then keep it near the fire to settle and become fine, after that, decant it off into another Pot for immediate Use. It is drunk as Coffee, sweetened with a fine moist sugar, and a little cream or milk should be added.

As chocolate became cheaper to make, it became cheaper for the general public. By the start of the 1800s, it was no longer a luxury for the well-to-do. Instead it paralleled the same trajectory as sugar, albeit in a condensed time line—discovery, intellectual curiosity, early adoption by the upper class supported by health proclamations, technological improvements in production and distribution, adoption by the middle class, and finally ubiquity. But whereas sugar took nearly two thousand years to travel this path, chocolate had taken a mere three centuries. By the start of the 1800s, per capita consumption of chocolate, which had been fairly low for centuries, shot up dramatically. Not coincidentally, this occurred at the same time as the increase in consumption of sugar, as sugared products had transitioned from medicine to treats. Candy had developed into a commodity separate from that of medicine, and soon chocolate would be making the same journey.

This demand helped foster the innovation for chocolate. The process of boiling and skimming off the excess fat was still an issue for many people, more so now that drinking chocolate was becoming readily available to many in the middle class.

In 1825, a Dutch chemist named Coenraad Johannes Van Houten was looking for a method that would finally deal with this notable characteristic of chocolate. His goal was to remove any excess cocoa butter from the chocolate. Typically, before Van Houten, chocolate liquor contained about 53 percent cocoa butter.

What Van Houten concocted was a hydraulic press, one that would separate much of that cocoa butter from the pulverized powder, leaving a cake that was down to 27 percent cocoa butter.

This added another problem. This cake didn't mix as well with water or milk. His solution? Treat the cake with alkaline salts (potassium or sodium carbonates). This is what we now know as cocoa.

This addition of alkaline salts to the cocoa was henceforth termed "dutching," and the benefits were such that it improved cocoa powder's miscibility (not, as some believed, its solubility) in warm liquid. It also had the side effect of making the chocolate darker in color and, more important, milder in flavor.

This was the game changer, and soon further developments to his press saw the percentage of fat in the cocoa drop even lower. From this point on, the fat-laden foamy drink of the upper class was now accessible to all, and it required as much time to prepare as one would take to make tea or coffee. More importantly, Van Houten's invention of the defatting and alkalizing processes resulted in a cheap cocoa powder, from which the modern-day chocolate bar was born.

Fry and Son took full advantage of this technological breakthrough. In 1847, the company was under the leadership of the founder's grandson, Francis, and great-grandson, Joseph Storrs Fry. They figured out that cocoa butter could be removed from the bean and mixed back into the powder, albeit at a lower fat-to-chocolate ratio. By mixing a blend of cocoa powder and sugar with melted cocoa butter instead of with warm water, they

Kate's Candy Bag

CADBURY DAIRY BAR

Cadbury dairy bar is to Great Britain as the Hershey bar is to the United States. Keeping that in mind will grant you a measure of perspective on the quality of the chocolate, and the marketing machine behind it.

However, I was not afforded this perspective the first time I had the chocolate bar. It was given to me by a relative and upsold to me by telling me "It's English." At the age of ten, I thought this meant that it was exotic, and when I tasted it, I would be transformed into a chocolate sophisticate.

What I soon discovered was that Cadbury's chocolate didn't make me any different from what I was ten minutes prior. Cadbury makes a sweeter version of chocolate and tastes different from my vaunted Hershey bar. Different. Not better.

Candy Exchange Rate:
1 Cadbury dairy bar = 1 York Peppermint Pattie

found that they could create a chocolate "paste" that could be molded into appealing shapes. They named these chocolate bars Chocolat Délicieux à Manger, hoping that the French name would give them an air of class, and they exhibited the product in Birmingham in 1849. This was the world's first *eating* chocolate. Yes, it was likely that people had nibbled upon the chocolate cakes from time to time, but the intent of those manufactured cakes was to prepare a drink.

By the latter half of the 1800s, J. S. Fry & Sons was the largest chocolate manufacturer in the world. It was the sole supplier of chocolate and cocoa to the Royal Navy. It introduced dozens if not hundreds of types of chocolate candy over the course of the next fifty years. In 1896 the firm became a registered private company run by the Fry family, with Joseph Storrs Fry II, grandson of the first Joseph Storrs Fry, as the chairman. J. S. Fry & Sons paved the way for other national chocolate companies, including Nestlé, Lindt, and eventually Hershey and Mars.

Yet very few of us in the United States are aware of Fry's influence on the history of chocolate. There's a reason for this: in 1919, the company merged with, and then was swallowed up entirely by, one of its largest competitors in England: Cadbury.

Chapter 14

A Death in the Family

• • • • • • • • • •

$\mathcal{I}$f we were to plant a marker in history to demonstrate that the effect of the Industrial Revolution was not only here to stay, but would be the driving factor of the world until the Silicon Age in the late twentieth century, then the Great Exhibition held in London in 1851 would be a great place to mark the era.

It was one of the first, if not *the* first, international exhibitions on a grand scale. Britain, at the time, was at the top of its empire. The British were self-motivated, they were all-powerful, and they believed that their empire made them self-reliant, willfully ignoring the fact that a fair amount of resources that they garnered from their colonies came on the backs of those who were definitely not British. They were living fully in the industrial era, an era that had started in England. And they were reaping the benefits from it.

In March 1850, Prince Albert, an ardent supporter of the

Great Exhibition, gave a speech at a banquet to recruit support for the event. He reflected on Britain's place in the world at the middle of the nineteenth century and its future direction:

> Nobody . . . who has paid any attention to the peculiar fea
> tures of our present era, will doubt for a moment that we are
> living at a period of most wonderful transition, which tends
> rapidly to accomplish that great end, to which, indeed, all
> history points—the realization of the unity of mankind. . . .
> The distances which separated the different nations and
> parts of the globe are rapidly vanishing before the achieve-
> ments of modern invention, and we can traverse them with
> incredible ease; . . . thought is communicated with the rapid-
> ity, and even by the power, of lightning.

The intent of the exhibition was to demonstrate the current level of industrial design in Britain, to show how much any given industry could produce (and, by implication, how much it could profit), and then either to sell this technology to the highest bidder or acquire new and larger markets. By every marker, the exhibition was a success. It was open in Hyde Park for five months and fifteen days. In that time, over six million visitors came to see some fourteen thousand exhibits.

Confectionery, both of the chocolate and the sugar variety, were well represented at this grand event. Fry & Sons displayed the trunk of a cocoa tree and showed various displays of flowers, pods, and nuts from the West Indies, as well as the manufactured goods made from their cocoa and chocolate. Gatti & Bolla, partners from Holborn Hill, showed a model of a steam engine that was designed for the manufacture of French and Italian chocolate. Queen Victoria was reported to have been greatly impressed by the chocolate-making machine belonging to the Ticinese owners of a café in Charing Cross, which they displayed at the Great Exhibition. With various companies demonstrating new and efficient means for creating confections, the industrial age was showing that candy could be made cheaper and more quickly, and that the days of the independent confectioners were numbered.

It's not difficult to see the results of the industrial age. From the viewpoint of the consumer, we're still living with its results, and one needs to go no further than the checkout lane of most grocery or convenience stores to see its evidence. All the candy and chocolate one finds in the grocery stores come from industrial producers. Rare is the sugar or chocolate confection that is made in the back of the store. As the Great Exhibition foretold, it is simply cheaper to make candy in bulk off-site and sell to dozens of wholesalers, who in turn sell to hundreds of retailers. The lesson of the exhibition was that a market of millions was far more lucrative than a market of dozens.

From a romantic's point of view, this is a dreadful result, as the candy maker is now at least four steps away from the person who buys the wares. That intimacy that once existed between candy maker and child is now gone, if it even existed at all. The conclusion of this path of the Industrial Revolution was now sitting in front of me, in a small town just outside of Bristol.

In the course of researching and writing a book on candy, the last thing I expected was to look upon a dying body. Unfortunately, that's where I found myself—or more specifically, that's how I felt when I saw the half-empty shell of a factory, one where chocolate, until the past few months, had been made for several generations.

I was in a field just outside of Keynsham, a small town of roughly fifteen thousand people located about halfway between Bristol and Bath, some 120 miles to the west of London. In front of me was the Somerdale Factory, home of Fry's chocolate creams, Dairy Milk, and Cadbury creme eggs. Although the factory was still in operation, the workers inside were on borrowed time. In 2011, the factory was closed, the various lines moved to factories in Poland. As I stood there, I felt as if I had lost an associate or coworker. I wasn't exactly sad, but I could not help but think that something here was being lost, aside from the jobs of four hundred people who would have to look for other sources of income. I felt I needed answers, but I was unsure of the questions.

In fact, this feeling was common throughout my stay in the Bristol region of England. When I planned my trips for this book, Bristol was an obvious place to put on my itinerary. In the late eighteenth century it was one of the major ports of Great Britain, and as such, it was a place where trade thrived. For all the products that ended up on the shelves of London merchants were most likely to have entered England through Bristol, then up the Thames to London. The Fry company was in Bristol at a time when chocolate began entering England in earnest from this location. Sugar had made many a Bristol trader quite wealthy. And the fates of the slaves used to produce these products were decided upon in rooms of this city throughout the eighteenth century.

There is evidence of the sugar trade and the slave trade that it created in many places in Bristol. Whether it's the Three Sugar Loaves Pub, named after a nearby sugar refinery that burned down in 1859, or Jamaica Street, named after the West Indian island were slaves were kept to grow sugar, there are many places in Bristol that recall both industries.

By 1730, Britain had become the biggest slave-trading country in the world, and seven years later Bristol had overtaken London as England's number one slaving port. As the center of the British slave trade, it was also soon to become the center of the British abolitionist movement.

Most of the slave trade was there to support the sugar industry. It is said that, by 1760, twenty sugar refineries were operating in Bristol, processing over 831,600 pounds of sugarcane per year in order to supply the British demand for the sweet. Much of the sugar went to produce rum, but much of it also went to support the burgeoning candy makers of London and the rest of Great Britain.

The Quakers helped lead the way for the abolition of slavery, although their power and influence were only made possible by their initial investment in the trade. In Bristol during the 1700s, there were several Quaker ship owners and merchants. The Goldney family made their money by making brass and iron goods that were traded in West Africa to buy slaves. Charles and John Scandrett were Bristol Quakers who owned slave ships. But by the 1760s, the Quakers had adopted the policy that slavery was morally wrong. They approached the topic with a zeal that spoke to their commitment to the cause, and they began to actively campaign against the trade. Soon, the Quakers became some of the more vocal leaders of the abolitionist movement.

By 1787, with help from Quaker antislavery campaigner Thomas Clarkson, Bristol became the first city outside of London to set up a committee for the abolition of the slave trade.

One year later, eight hundred people volunteered to sign the first Bristol petition against the slave trade, with signatures including dozens of women, making this one of the first times in England that an organization of women got involved in politics. Bristol newspapers were full of poems and letters condemning the slave trade. The Bristol poets Robert Southey, William Wordsworth, Hannah More, Anne Yearsley, and Samuel Coleridge all wrote against the trade. Southey wrote about tea drinkers: "Oh ye who at your ease Sip the blood-sweeten'd beverage!" Leaflets were published and passed about, spoofing advertisements found in the newspapers trying to sell articles surrounding the slave trade. Boycotts were organized against the companies that used slave labor in their sugar production. The residents of Bristol, particularly the Quakers, soon found themselves at the forefront of the movement to dismantle the industry that had helped support the sugar industry since the era of the first plantations in the Mediterranean.

While all of this was going on, Joseph Fry—himself a Quaker—was making and experimenting with chocolate. The sugar he was using in his concoctions was most likely coming from these plantations and, as a Quaker, he would have been aware of the origin of his products. Whether or not he scrutinized the origins of his chocolate or sugar is unknown. The point is this: not only did milk chocolate and the chocolate industry evolve from the shop of Joseph Fry; the wares that came from his shop were made possible by the shipping industry of Bristol and the slave labor that Bristol initially embraced and then later rejected.

While there is evidence of the sugar and slave trade of the eighteenth century all throughout Bristol, there's very little one can find with regard to the role Bristol played in the evolution of chocolate. The old Keynsham factory, the factory that Cadbury acquired after it acquired Fry's, was the last major landmark in the area that could trace its roots directly into the eighteenth century.

The reverberations of this factory closing barely raised a ripple in the chocolate industry. Business is business after all, and closing up a shop because a product could be made cheaper elsewhere is a standard business practice. I don't like this fact, but I recognize that, much like the venom in a scorpion, it is part of a corporation's intrinsic nature.

But here's the thing—without the influence of the innovation and the expansion of Fry's in the eighteenth and nineteenth century, the landscape of today's chocolate industry would look markedly different. There are not many areas of the world that can make that claim. Looking upon the half-empty Keynsham factory made me realize that this important piece of history in chocolate's development was fast becoming nothing more than a bit of trivia right before my eyes.

Something else unsettling was fluttering through my mind. With Kraft's purchase of Cadbury, the major providers of mass-produced chocolates in the United Kingdom were based in other countries: Kraft and Mars are American and Nestlé is Swiss; there is no longer a British company influencing chocolate's direction. For a country with such a deep history with the commodity, this somehow felt wrong.

I jumped in my rental car to see how, exactly, Kraft was presenting its new British acquisition to the world, hoping that it knew of the piece of history it was purchasing. I was off to Bourneville, just outside of Birmingham. This was the home of Cadbury and, by inference, Cadbury World.

As I was driving up the M32, I considered Cadbury's place in today's chocolate world. It is certainly one of the world's most popular brands, of this there is little doubt. But its reputation of late has been a little less than stellar. If it's not the quality of Cadbury's chocolate that's being lambasted by various world aficionados, then it's the company's business dealings that get put under the microscope. And, as many large corporations have done in order to promote their brand and massage their less-than-stellar reputation, Cadbury continues to put a smiling face on its public persona. Nowhere is this more evident than at Cadbury World.

Cadbury World is Cadbury's attempt to show its fans a chocolate factory without having to give an actual tour in their factory. There is a benefit to this. It costs less, there's no risk of tourists getting hurt, and it keeps industrial spies at bay (a seemingly silly but very real concern). Chocolate production can now proceed unimpeded and curious fans can get a glimpse of what a chocolate factory looks like.

Kate's Candy Bag

CADBURY EGG

Cadbury's foray into the Easter candy business, the Egg, is little more than an albumin and yolk-colored fondant covered with an overly sweet chocolate. Here in the United States, Cadbury Creme Eggs are distributed by the Hershey Company. Of course, they aren't really Cadbury Eggs. They started out as Fry's Creme Eggs back in the early 1920s.

Cadbury Eggs are one of the few sweets that have a cult following. Although I used to be a member of said cult, I have since renounced my membership when the U.S. version of the treat became mysteriously smaller between 2005 and 2007. That being said, I wouldn't turn one down if offered.

Candy Exchange Rate:
1 Cadbury Egg = 1 York Peppermint Pattie

There is another downside to factory tours. Chocolate made on an industrial scale has all the romance and charm of an accountant's spreadsheet, which is sort of the antithesis of a tourist destination. While a few visitors might be interested in the true inner workings of a factory, the majority of people get bored after fifteen minutes and will never visit again.

This does not make for an effective business plan.

A much better plan is one that appeals to all comers. Enough information should be provided to satisfy those who appreciate the historical and engineering aspects of chocolate production, yet the tour should contain enough charm and personality that it doesn't spoil the Willy Wonka–type fantasies that the majority of us hold dear. Finally, it should make money, either immediately or through payoff in something called "brand loyalty." This translates into ticket sales, encouraging visitors to shop in their gift shop, topped off with enough advertising that it would kill a lesser species from sensory overload.

And as a bonus? Cadbury gets to keep the families there long enough that parents have to buy their children lunch in the on-premises cafeteria instead of looking for a local restaurant.

As a means of making money, this plan holds a tremendous amount of potential, so much so that Cadbury World averages half a million visitors per year, or roughly 1,500 people per day.

What this means is that Cadbury is under no obligation whatsoever to be historically accurate or to acknowledge its competitors at all. Why mention Nestlé or Mars when you want visitors to spend money on Cadbury products in the gift shop?

All of this I suspected before even setting foot in Bourneville. Having been to more than my fair share of corporate tourist destinations, I was well acquainted with their basic philosophy. I had expected to be given the hard sell and to be told just how awesome Cadbury was.

What I did not expect was the £14.30 entrance fee. I had expected some sort of cost to enter their premises. I looked at the menu board again. Children had to pay £10.40. That would mean an average entrance fee of £12.35, meaning that Cadbury World makes over £6 million per year, and this is before one single parent opens up his or her wallet in the gift shop or cafeteria.

I was a bit taken aback by this. The implication, at least from a perspective on value, is that my visit here, and the experience offered, would be worth more than a visit to the local cinema.

The start of the visit was eerily similar to that of a trip to the movies, in that I had to wait in line among hordes of schoolchildren doing their best to contain their excitement and failing wonderfully. Yeah, okay. I may be a bit cynical in my older age, but seeing a child's joy surrounding a promise of candy is sometimes enough to melt even the coldest of hearts.

The tour started out simply enough, with the mob of people who had paid for their tickets herded into a staging area, better known as purgatory, where one must wait with an uncomfortable amount of people until deemed worthy of moving on. After a wait, we were placed in a group of thirty people. Each of the thirty people had their tickets checked, were handed a Curly Wurly, and were then shoved into the tour.

From there it was clear that the tour guide we were assigned was far more interested in ensuring that we met our schedule. We were warned that we had to be out of certain areas of the tour in an appropriate amount of time or subsequent groups of thirty would end up as part of our group, and from there it was only three steps until chaos, rioting, and anarchy would break out. I'm paraphrasing here, but the tour guide requested of the children's school chaperone, "For the love of all that is dear and holy, please keep the children in line!"

Soon we found ourselves whisked, Curly Wurlys in hand, into the rain forest, in a dramatic re-creation of European explorers meeting the Aztecs of Central America. And if I could read the subtext of the mannequins' expressions, everyone was jovial, and no one had to be concerned with smallpox or accidentally having too much gold. It was here that the re-created Maya gladly told the re-created Spaniards about chocolate: "Please, why don't you have some, as there is plenty to go around."

Two minutes later, we were herded into a multimedia room, where we learned, in a lavish 3-D spectacle, how cocoa beans crossed the ocean on a Spanish galleon and ended up as the drink of choice for high society.

Five minutes later, we were invited into a re-creation of Birmingham in the nineteenth century, where John Cadbury magically had access to chocolate as well as the technique for making chocolate bars.

The children ate this up, transfixed by the power of suggestion. The adults, at least those aware of the larger realities of history, worked to ensure that the children didn't go into diabetic comas and didn't cross-pollinate with other groups.

It wasn't that the history being told was wrong. Rather, it was incomplete. Massively incomplete. Imagine the reality of chocolate history being represented by a one-hundred-thousand-seat stadium. Cadbury's truth would take up about a dozen seats, while the rest of the stadium sat empty.

This is the problem with corporate tourist destinations. They will, by definition, make themselves out to be the arbiter of all things related to their industry. They can pick and choose pieces of history that make them more relevant to their audience, while glossing over the more uncomfortable truths. For example, that Cadbury had once sued to enforce a trademark on the color purple, or that its recipe for chocolate recently included palm oil instead of cocoa butter, likely under the auspices of lowering its cost and/or increasing the product's profit margin, were conveniently left out.

The rest of the tour went by in a haze of pseudo re-creations of the manufacturing process, and an all too real dose of advertising, including one section where they ever so kindly showed everyone the history of Cadbury's advertising. When I saw the animatronic DJ spinning some "Mad Tracks" of past and current Cadbury jingles at a decibel level that would stun a moose, with a light display that would make Nikola Tesla weep, I decided I had had enough. It was an Ecstasy trip gone horribly wrong. Some things were too much to bear. I had paid over $20 to have Cadbury not only advertise to me for an hour, but do so LOUDLY, and I needed to retreat.

When I walked out I realized that the Keynsham factory was going away, and that it was likely that Bristol's last tie to its place in the history of chocolate was going with it.

As I got into the car to head back to London, I contemplated why it mattered to me and whether it should matter to anyone else. I didn't have a good answer then, and still don't to this day. I could make an argument for community, but factories in other industries close all the time with barely a flicker of significance crossing my mind when I read of them. I could make an argument for maintaining the nostalgia of youth, but children don't care about where candy comes from, only that they can have some.

There's definitely a historical argument to be made, but Bristol's involvement in the sugar and slave trades means that chocolate would take a backseat to any events surrounding these institutions.

There was another thing that was bothering me. Throughout Britain, one can find dozens of re-creations of old timey confectionery shoppes. Heck, even Bristol had its own, called Treasure Island Sweets, found in St. Nicholas Market, a small shop that even had front-window displays.

But these shops are few and far between. More prevalent, at least in the big cities, were the newsagents and tobacconists. British children of the past seventy years or so would more likely get their candy from a small corner store that sold cigarettes than head out to an upscale candy shop. The British candy shoppe fantasy that I had in my head no longer existed, and hadn't in several generations. In the end, Roald Dahl got it right. Willy Wonka wasn't the proprietor of a candy shop; he was the CEO of an industrial giant.

And now, even that was slowly being erased from the British economy. Cadbury now belonged to the Americans. Up north in York, Rowntree's had been bought by Nestlé in order to own the rights to produce Kit Kat and Aero bars. Maynards and Bassetts, major sugar confectioners in Britain, had been bought by Cadbury and now also belonged to Kraft.

What Keynsham is representative of, at least to me, is the slow evolution of sweets and candy from luxuries that once tied adults and children alike to a community into a cold, global commodity. While Italy embraced its confection culture, Britain seemingly had its own packaged up, branded, and sold to the highest bidder. The lessons of the Great Exhibition of 1851 were still being learned.

Perhaps I was being too romantic. Thinking back to my childhood, it mattered not whether the candy I had eaten had been made locally (although locally made candy did have a novelty about it). What mattered to me was the person who supplied the candy, whether it was my parents or grandparents or the shopkeeper who had taken the time to ensure that I had spent my allowance wisely. In the end, isn't that all that matters?

I parked the rental car at the hotel outside Heathrow where I was to stay one last night in the United Kingdom before heading back to the States. Hopefully there I could find an answer to the questions I had uncovered. There's a distinct line between nostalgia and history. My problem, as far as I could tell, was that I was beginning to mistake the loss of a chocolate factory, and all of its historical significance, for the loss of my youth. The fact that this was the exact opposite of what I wanted to accomplish with this trip was duly noted over a Mars bar and a sip of milk.

Chapter 15

The Rock of Gibralter

• • • • • • • • • •

*I*t's unsurprising that colonial America gets its sweet tooth from England, as many of the shops predating the American Revolution tried to follow the same basic paths as those across the Atlantic. The ultimate goal, of course, was to make the colonists who had arrived from Europe feel a bit closer to home.

This wasn't a process that happened overnight; in fact quite the opposite. From the landing of the *Mayflower* to the mid-eighteenth century, shipping goods across the ocean was a costly affair, and the luxuries of the day often had to be set aside for simple necessities. As such, luxuries were, for the most part, not part of the culinary equation. American cuisine was rudimentary and farm-based. Coffeehouses, with their chocolate, and apothecaries, with their confectionery, were part of the urban landscape. The American colonies were decidedly rural. There was one long-term goal when it came to food: establish colonies that could feed themselves. Life in the Americas was rural, agrarian, and limited in the amount of snacks and sweets one could take for the sheer joy of it.

So if the colonists weren't going to stores for their sweets, what were they doing?

Making them at home, of course, much like they did back in England one hundred years prior. The educated and wealthy brought with them books, like *The English Hus-wife,* the purpose of which was to provide recipes and techniques that would allow for "medicines" to be made at home. In the New World, such a book would be valuable, and would be referred to when a family member got ill. Today, while you or I can go to the local pharmacy and purchase over-the-counter medicines when we get a bit of a cold, such luxuries were unheard of back then, and even a trip to a knowledgeable apothecary would have been rare, if not outright impossible in colonial America.

One of the more informative books on sweetmeats in America started out not as a book at all but rather as a collection of confectionery recipes handed down from generation to generation. That the matriarch of the family was none other than Martha Washington imbues the document with history, not just from a culinary perspective but also from that of early American politics.

To understand American cooking in the eighteenth century, it is necessary to start with English cooking in the seventeenth century, the cuisine that was brought over by the early settlers. The Puritans who settled on the stony soil of New England, the Quakers who settled in the richer lands of Pennsylvania, and the landed gentry (largely younger sons of younger sons whose families had run out of land in England), and assorted others who came to the tidelands of Virginia all brought essentially the same idea of cuisine with them. All seem to have used the same cookbooks and recipes from England.

While back in England, new cookbooks and new books on

confectionery were being introduced, in America, many of the collections of the recipes floating around were derivations of those from one hundred years past, with personal alterations made in order to accommodate the resources of the local region. Martha Washington's recipes were no exception.

Her collection starts with the several stages of sugar cooking, from the process of clarifying the sugar, to knowing when the sugar "is at candy height," educating any first-time home manager on the foundations of candy making.

From there, recipes evolve into everything from preserving quinces and making marmalade, to making rock candy and marzipan (still called "marchepane" back then). A typical recipe looked like this:

TO CANDY ANY FLOWERS FRUITS OR SPICES WITH YE ROCK CANDY

Take two pound of barbary sugar, great grayned, and clarefy it with ye whites of 2 eggs. and boyle it almoste to the height of Manus Christi.* then put it in A pipkin that is not very rough, then put it in your flowers, fruits, or spices. & then put your pipkin into A still, and make A little fire of small cole or charcole under it. and in the space of 12 days your fruit, flowers, or spice will be rock candid.

Several things jump out at me surrounding these instructions, mostly the fact that a family would have no problems and great patience to wait for twelve days in order to see the result of this recipe.

---

* Manus Christi height indicated a degree of sugar boiling, a temperature which one would suppose to be the right degree for making manus Christi, itself a confection roughly similar to that of a lozenge that had been flavored with rose water, with gold leaf and bits of pearl added both for decoration and in a mistaken belief in its health benefits.

While these recipes of the first first lady were not published as a collection until recently, they do seem indicative of recipes of the day, at least for the wealthy. Note that the first ingredient listed in the instructions above—two pounds of barbary sugar— would have been expensive and the first of two indications of wealth for a family.

The second, literacy, would also be a factor in candy development, but it should be noted that illiteracy was not a complete handicap in learning how to cook. For while literacy allowed for a home cook to learn on his or her own, it did not indicate whether one could or could not follow a recipe. Oral learning and first-hand experience were, back then as well as today, the most efficient means of learning how to cook. Once learned, many a homemaker would have her own variation of recipes that would evolve in similar patterns to those of the wealthy. The difference? The resources available to them. And when it came to sweeteners, the wealthy were able to purchase barbary sugar, while the lower classes used either sorghum in the south, maple syrup in the north, or molasses or honey elsewhere, if they could procure it.

Maple syrup gives us evidence of the first candy makers in North America—Native Americans. They used it as a flavoring for breads, stews, beverages, and vegetables. Once the colonists appeared, Native Americans realized they could trade maple sugar for other products they needed. Soon, the French and English learned the process of making it and applying the techniques used to make sugar, and they found they could make a variation that we know of today as maple sugar. In this form, it was easier to store and transport and could easily be reconstituted to syrup by adding water. When cane sugar was finally available in the American colonies, New Englanders still preferred maple sugar because it was cheaper.

The process of making maple candy was far more simple than making many sugar confections: heat maple syrup to the desired temperature and then cool it with or without stirring. Soon those with ready access to maple syrup were making maple candies in their homes.

But getting access to the sweetener, whether sugar or syrup, was always a difficult affair, and sweeteners often fell into the "nice to have, but not a necessity" category for most residents of colonial America. Sugar and all of the products that result from this commodity were still a luxury.

So imagine the delight of those in Philadelphia when, in 1730, Evan Morgan, a corsetiere who also made children's clothing, began to advertise in the local gazette "very good Chocolate, Wine, Rum, Melasses, Sugar" at "reasonable prices." Or when Nicholas Bayard, in the same year, opened the first sugar refinery in the American colonies and offered four different kinds of refined sugar and "Sugar-Candy." While sugar itself would have been available, and most certainly molasses (which was cheaper than sugar, because of its lack of refinement), both chocolate and sugar candy would have brought with them an air of sophistication.

The evolution of American candy paralleled that of Europe, but in a much smaller time frame. Sugar was initially used to help preserve imported fruit and soon found its way into other confections. In 1775, as the colonies began their search for independence, a shopkeeper in Philadelphia by the name of Patrick Wright was offering various comfits, boiled sweets, rock candy, fruits, jellies, and preserves, as well as macaroons and biscuits. While the number of confectioners in colonial America would have paled in comparison to the number in Britain, their selection of sweets would have been similar.

I was in Salem, Massachusetts, in order to get a feel for what these confection shops would have been like. Salem is home to quite possibly the oldest candy company in North America.

I had arrived in Massachusetts the day before, at the tail end of the third major snowstorm to hit New England in the course of a week. My hotel in Boston was nearly empty as the city worked its way out of the blankets of snow that had pushed the boundaries of their patience, if not their infrastructure. As I walked into the lobby, I greeted the doorman with a passive "Good evening," to which the doorman responded with a direct "Nothing good about it." He opened the door absentmindedly as he continued to stare out at the snow still coming down.

The next morning, the sun greeted us all in the Athens of America, letting the city know that it hadn't gone away. Looking out my window, I watched the plows move the snow off to the sidewalks and the shopkeepers swear at the plows as they worked to shovel and salt a pathway for the pedestrians.

I had concerns of my own with regard to the snow. How was I to get out of the city? I had briefly toyed with the idea of renting a car, undaunted by my friends' gales of laughter. Bad traffic I could handle—but bad traffic after a snowstorm? No, thank you. I had to find another way. A quick review on the Internet indicated that, unlike Seattle, Boston had a healthy train system, with a robust subway system, and marginally efficient commuter rail routes, one of which would drop me off a mere mile from my destination. This was a mile I could, theoretically, walk with ease. Ninety minutes later, I found myself stepping off that train, the sun shining and the winter wind whipping about.

Three steps later, I stood in an icy puddle, setting a pattern that would repeat itself several times during my visit to this fair town.

Salem, Massachusetts, as most American tenth graders could tell you, was the location of the Salem witch trials of 1692, forever associating this city with necromancy and the supernatural. However, it is the twenty-first century, so this has manifested itself in Salem as both a means to capture the dollar of any tourist who comes wandering into the town and a drawing card for half the new-age businesses in New England. For every wax museum and "historical" house, there were businesses selling tarot cards, books on magick (it's the k that lets you know it's authentic magic), and crystal skulls. As I counted the last of these, I decided that while one such store was cute, three was overkill, and seven was nothing more than a blatant move to separate tourists from their dollars.

After a mile of counting witch stores and avoiding every third slush puddle, I was able to make my way to Ye Olde Pepper Candy Companie, just off of Derby Street, a block northwest from the House of the Seven Gables, which purports to have influenced Nathaniel Hawthorne's novel of the same name, though more than likely the reverse is true.

This cynicism in tourist centers puts me on alert, and as I entered the candy shop, I was expecting to be let down.

What I was greeted with instead was a smallish woman pleading with a contractor to get the snow and ice off the building, or else the old building would collapse. I stopped in my tracks.

When she hung up the phone, I offered a meek, "I, uh, could come back."

A smile spread across the woman's face. "No, no, no. You're perfectly safe." Her New England accent coated her voice like sugar on a donut. She laughed, apparently at the joke regarding our mortal peril. As I began to look about the store, she explained the ice placed an excessive burden upon one wall, and this was affecting the pipes and electrical system.

"So, aside from the plumbing, the electricity, and the fact that a wall might collapse, we're perfectly safe," I said.

The woman chuckled and responded, "Yeah, I think that about sums it up. Let me know if you have any questions." She turned her back and left me to peruse the shop and its goodies.

And what a shop it was. Smallish, to be sure, but the candies inside were, for the most part, classic candies, without any signs of major brands. Looking around, I found sassafras slugs, butterscotch drops, Boston beans, and molasses cuts. They all looked as if they were made on site.

"Were these made here?" I asked the woman.

"Oh yes. They're made in the back. We use a machine similar to the one you see by the door there."

I looked over to where she pointed. There, sitting on a display next to the door, were two well-worn rolling machines, each looking as if they were, at minimum, one hundred years old. Both had the same basic principle—two metal cylinders, each with its own distinct pattern, were laid lengthwise on top of each other. Presumably a sheet of pulled sugar or boiled sugar would be fed into one side, and someone would turn the crank attached to said cylinder, forcing the heated candy through where it would be flattened except for the space allowed by the patterns that had been inlaid within the metal. Out the other side would pop either the drops, slugs, or cuts, and likely a fair bit of scrap that could be reheated and then fed through the process again.

These machines looked both ingenious and exhausting. The engineering principle behind them was dead simple. The labor needed to run the machine looked as if it would result in the operator having one arm with the biceps of a body builder and the other like those of a ninety-eight-pound weakling.

Further exploration of the shop uncovered another ancient item, this time a piece of candy that was 177 years old. Called a gibralter, the piece of candy in question was there to represent one thing—that the candy, and by inference the store that sold it, had been around a very long time.

A gibralter is made of sugar, water, cream of tartar (an emulsifier), and either oil of lemon or oil of peppermint. The batch is then pulled like a taffy in order to aerate it and give it a chalky-white color. A small portion is left unpulled and stays clear and shiny; this is used to make a stripe across the center of the candy. It is then stretched across a long table and cut with large scissors into fairly substantial diamond-shaped pieces. One piece of gibralter will not fit easily into one's mouth. For those of you who were paying attention earlier in the book, it is a rock candy, a near relative to the Edinburgh Rock.

As delicious as this candy is, it isn't what makes the shop intriguing. Posted on the walls of this smallish shop with its red carpeting and pinkish brocaded wallpaper were newspaper clippings from generations ago, detailing the life of the founder of the oldest U.S. candy company—Mary Spencer.

In March 1805, the *Jupiter,* a ship based in London, set sail for New York City. Aboard this ship was a family of fifteen, which included one thirty-something woman who went by the name of Mary Spencer. There is anecdotal evidence that "Spencer" was her married name and that her maiden name may have been "Smith" but proof of this, and other aspects of her life in Britain, is sketchy at best.

Mary Spencer did leave something quite valuable behind in London: Her thirteen-year-old son, Thomas Spencer, whose role in the candy shop would be of some importance two decades later.

On April 6, 1805, the *Jupiter* struck an iceberg off the coast of Newfoundland and sank in less than half an hour. Nine of the fifteen members of Mary's family drowned. The others, including Mary, were rescued by another ship. Two weeks later, they were put ashore at Marblehead, Massachusetts.

The six remaining members of the family moved on from Marblehead to Newburyport, and then to Salem. With all of their possessions lost, they had to turn to local church congregations for help in settling in. The story goes that Mary told them that she knew how to make confections, and they offered her a barrel of sugar to help her get started. A brochure at Ye Olde Pepper Candy Companie explains what happened after that bit of generosity.

> Little did they know that this single act of kindness would produce the "Salem Gibralter," said to be the first candy made and sold commercially in America and carried around the world by sea captains and their crew.
>
> She first sold her candies from wood firkins on the steps of the First Church; however, the candies became so popular that she purchased a horse and wagon (displayed in the Peabody Essex Museum) to peddle her confections. Dressed in the long attire of the day with sunbonnet to shield her eyes, she sat proud and straight in the open wagon guiding the horse to neighboring towns, thus our horse and wagon logo.
>
> When Mrs. Spencer died her son carried on the business until about 1830, when he decided to return to England. The company was then sold to a John William Pepper, under whose leadership the company prospered for many years, adding items to its catalogue such as the Black Jack (an all-natural stick candy made from black strap molasses).

The truth seems to be a little more interesting. Mary Spencer was a bit of a firebrand, a member of the independent Congregationalists, a sect with the same religious beliefs that the Pilgrims held. In the period of time between the landing at Plymouth Rock and the time the *Jupiter* sank, Congregational churches had spread throughout New England. With their independent philosophies and focus on concerns affecting the immediate congregation rather than the national, the Congregationalists found themselves at the forefront of many grassroots movements of their time, including abolition of slavery as well as women's suffrage.

This was the world that Mary Spencer was now a part of and

soon participated in fully. She left her mark upon members of the Salem congregation and the rest of the small town. She sold the candies she made in order to support herself and the causes that she and the church supported. Business must have been brisk, for in 1816 she sent for her son Thomas, and soon he found himself not only helping his mother but working with members of the local congregation on the cause of abolition. By 1820, Mary Spencer had made enough to purchase a bark-seller's cart. She became so familiar a public figure that by 1822 engravings were circulating depicting her driving the cart. These items can be seen today in the Peabody Essex Museum in Salem.

By 1830, the business had been sold to one John William Pepper. Both Thomas Spencer and his mother were deep into the abolitionist movement, and much evidence exists that they were around for years afterward (which runs in contradiction to the Pepper Company brochure). Within a year, Thomas was working with William Lloyd Garrison, the prominent American abolitionist and journalist, and rumor has it that Spencer's home was one of the final stops of the Underground Railroad.

As I walked about the candy shop, trying to determine which bits of candy I wanted to try and take home, I tried to connect the dots. If the business was popular enough that Mary was able to purchase a cart with the profits, and she was so recognizable that local silversmiths had made engravings of her selling her wares, why sell?

The answer may likely concern where they had to buy their sugar from. They may have found out at some point that the sugar they were purchasing was coming from a plantation that was using slave labor; or they could not verify that the sugar was produced with free labor. Although possible, it seems unlikely that either Mary or Thomas would have been unaware of the blood and tears involved in the sugar industry.

I rolled various scenarios around in my head as I looked over trays of fudge and turtles. Here we are in the twenty-first century, where race relations still form a part of our national character, which was shaped in large part by the institution of slavery. Here I was, standing in the showroom of what is likely the oldest candy company in the United States, one that is also defined by the issue of slavery.

I picked up two packages of gibralters, one package of Black Jacks, some maple walnut fudge, and a package of pecan caramel turtles topped with milk chocolate. I paid for my purchase, and for the first time in a while on this trip, I walked out of the store with

 Kate's Candy Bag

FUDGE

Fudge isn't a flavor, it's a candy style, a variant of fondant, created by mixing sugar, butter, and milk (or condensed milk) into the soft-ball stage. What makes fudge special is how adaptable it is to different flavors and ingredients, with chocolate being many folks' top choice.

As it is quite easy to make, and so adaptable, there are hundreds, if not thousands of fudge recipes out there. In our family alone, several recipes were trotted out at Christmastime, with each being happily sampled by children and adults alike. Nowadays, one is likely to find fudge at rustic tourist stops throughout the States and England.

Candy Exchange Rate:
one 8-ounce package of fudge = 2 York Peppermint Patties

a smile. I had finally stumbled across evidence of someone in the candy supply chain who seemed to have some ethical convictions, someone who made a choice that put the well-being of our society over that of profit and power. Mary Spencer may not have altered the course of history in regard to slavery, but as an entrepreneur, she decided she had responsibility to know the source of her ingredients and all that that entailed. The use of money in any transaction, whether for service or product, gave tacit approval of the methods and means used to create said service or product. And we, as individuals, have the ability, the responsibility, and the moral obligation to not spend money on items that we feel were produced via means detrimental to our society.

As I walked back to the train station with one cold foot and one arm laden with confectionery, a cynical thought formed in the recesses of my mind. "It's a nice story you're telling yourself. You do realize that the evidence supporting it is merely circumstantial." I rationalized to the cynic within, "At this point, I'll take what I can get. To me, the Spencers will always represent what candy should lead to."

"Which is?" replied my dark self.

"The ability to see the truth behind the most innocent of topics and make moral decisions based on that truth, regardless of the possible outcomes."

"Could you do that?"

I hemmed and hawed as I rolled that question about my brain. That was the real question, wasn't it?

Chapter 16

Olde-Time Candy

• • • • • • • •

The next morning I looked at my bounty with the same look that binge drinkers give to the slew of empty beer bottles they find strewn about their apartment. I had spent $40 on candy at Ye Olde Pepper Candy Company. Granted, it was done under the auspices of "research" and "gift giving," but somewhere deep within the recesses of my heart, I knew that I was satisfying some base, reptilian need. Sure, I could rationalize it, but the truth? If I had no impulse control or gag reflex, I would likely eat enough candy to kill a small cat.

There are several reasons why I do have some measure of impulse control. Candy, here at the start of the twenty-first century, is a ubiquitous product. Sugar and sugar products, exponentially more so. How would I have acted in the beginning of the nineteenth century, when sugar was rare in this country, and confectionery even rarer? Probably like the Philadelphian gentle-man who, in 1826, was reported to have owed nearly $190 to his local candy maker, an amount equal to an average blue-collar man's annual salary. We may be astonished by such a number, but there are a handful of us out there who likely understand how one could accrue such debt, all in the name of a sweet tooth.

As in Britain fifty years earlier, confection and sugar were luxury items until 1830, and those who made confections sold their wares strictly to the upper class. Those who had money and power (and accessibility) had the ability to get refined sugar. For everyone else, molasses was the primary sugarcane option avail-able, with honey and maple syrup filling in the void when neces-sary. So when people walked into an American confectionery at the beginning of the nineteenth century, they were demonstrat-ing their power. This led to an odd gender stereotype surround-ing confectionery. Wendy Woloson noted in her book *Refined Tastes: Sugar, Confectionery, and Consumers in Nineteenth-Century America* that it was mostly men who bought candies. This dif-fered from Britain, where the ability to purchase sweets was seen as class-specific, but not gender-specific.

Two generations later, that perception had been flipped on its ear. Not only had the perception of confectionery changed, so had the clientele. By 1890, children were the primary consumers of candy, and penny candy was their confection of choice.

Why the change? The same reason sweets became cheap in England—sugar became cheaper, as did the cost of candy pro-duction.

For many historians, Chicago is the center of the universe when it comes to candy in America. Their perspective is not un-founded. Chicago is where the Mars candy company made its name. It is where Frederick William Rueckheim and his brother Louis refined a recipe for Cracker Jacks. On the north side, there is the mecca of hapless baseball fans, Wrigley Field, named after William Wrigley Jr., the man who made his millions selling chewing gum. It was in Chicago where, at the World's Columbian Exposition of 1893, one Milton Hershey saw the machinery for chocolate making that would change his life, and later, the world of confection.

 Kate's Candy Bag

WRIGLEY JUICY FRUIT

Juicy Fruit has, quite possibly, the most pleasant aroma on the planet. Candy aficionados have been known to come to near blows when trying to determine the exact makeup of the gum's flavor. Is it banana? Peach? Pineapple? Personally, the aroma reminds me a little bit of banana and a little bit of bergamot.

What makes Juicy Fruit notable for me is that it was the first candy to teach me disappointment. For all of the deliciousness that the aroma promises, the reality is that the flavor lasts about as long as a commercial. As gum is known for lasting a long time in the mouth, I was under the impression as a youth that the flavor of the gum should last just as long as the gum itself. Instead what we got was thirty seconds of joy, and then forty minutes of chewing rubber.

Candy Exchange Rate:
5 packs of Juicy Fruit = 1 York Peppermint Pattie

Yes, when it comes to candy, Chicago has played a major role. But its role is a very industrial role. It did not occur in a vacuum. It is the result of a confectionery culture that had developed elsewhere.

That "elsewhere"? Every small town and city in the northern United States, best epitomized by the city where I was currently staying, Boston, and the New England Confectionery Company, better known to you and me as Necco.

As with nearly every other aspect of history, the story of Necco starts in the world of the apothecary, roughly fifty years prior to Milton Hershey's visit to the World's Columbian Exposition.

The story began with one Oliver Chase, who had worked his way into a career where he was to provide product to Boston's druggists by making lozenges of gum arabic, peppermint oil, and unrefined sugar.

At this time, lozenges were still made the same way the Arab druggists had made them seven hundred years before. The unrefined sugar was clarified with egg whites, and then the mixture was pulverized in a mortar with a pestle. In a different pan, the peppermint oil was mixed with the gum arabic, and then the sugar and gum were combined into a doughlike paste, which was worked, kneaded, rolled out thin, and cut into small round discs. The work was tedious and labor-intensive.

Oliver Chase decided to look for a different method of production, one that was easier and less time consuming. Taking his cues from the industrial development going on in Britain at the time, he developed a lozenge cutter that "looked like a clothes wringer with a series of holes cut for the lozenges." Once the paste had been worked out, it could be fed into one side of the machine, and after a few minutes of cranking, a slew of lozenges would emerge out the other side of the machine. So it was in Boston, not Chicago, that American confectionery makers entered the industrial era. With his brother, Silas Edwin,

Oliver founded Chase and Company, which would eventually become Necco.

After focusing on the end of the process, Chase looked at ways to make the beginning of the process easier. In 1851, he patented a mill for powdering sugar, and with a few alterations, he could make the unrefined sugar into different grades of granularity. With this invention, Chase and Company now had three revenue streams—selling the lozenge maker to various candy operations on the East Coast, selling the sugar mill in the same area, and selling lozenges. The company was taking off.

Oliver's brother, Daniel, also a part of Chase and Company, wondered whether they could print phrases directly upon the candies. Working with a felt roller dyed with vegetable-based food coloring, he devised a way for a die to print words on the mint while it was being cut. Daniel Chase had just developed Conversation Hearts, known to us today as the heart-shaped candies with phrases such as WHO ME? or LUV U printed on them. The difference was that Daniel's mints were larger and could hold longer phrases. MARRIED IN WHITE, YOU HAVE CHOSEN RIGHT and the wordy WHY IS A STYLISH GIRL LIKE A THRIFTY HOUSEKEEPER? Printed on the other side was the answer: BECAUSE SHE MAKES A BIG BUSTLE ABOUT A LITTLE WAIST.

With the dawn of the twentieth century, a get-together impulse began to manifest itself in American business. Firms that had been active rivals finally saw the wisdom of pooling their resources and working together for larger markets. Chase and Company; Fobes and Hayward, owners of a local and popular chocolate company; and Wright and Moody, a company known for its gumdrops and jujubes, got together to discuss the methods for competing with Hershey and Wrigley. Their conclusion? Combine forces and consolidate. In 1901, they came together under the trade name of Necco with a combined capital of just over $1 million. By 1903, they had moved into a manufacturing plant at Summer and Melcher streets in Boston. At the time it was the largest establishment in the United States devoted to the production of confectionery, with each of its four large buildings standing five stories tall, for a total of five acres of space. By 1905, Necco products were being sold in every state in the union, as well as several countries in Europe, Australia, and South America. Its most popular item, the Necco Wafers, were direct descendants of the lozenges that Oliver Chase had rolled off of his machine sixty years prior. Necco had found itself at the heart of the penny candy revolution going on in the United States at the turn of the twentieth century.

During the fifty-odd years that Oliver Chase developed his business into the biggest U.S candy company, the industrial age was affecting another aspect of American culture. Children, either those of the working class (usually working themselves) or of the expanding middle class, which now had disposable income, were purchasing candy themselves, at stores similar to those in Britain.

It is unclear whether the idea of the candy store had been transported from England or simply evolved more organically. What is known is that at the beginning of the 1800s, confections were quite the adult product, sold primarily as medicines. By the time of the Civil War, candy had exploded upon the scene, and was available in most major cities of the nation. By the 1880s, retail candy could even be purchased in the more remote areas of the United States. But unlike in Britain, American children were buying candy directly, with the parent nowhere to be seen.

This was due, in part, to the nature of the era. By the 1870s, children were active in the workplace, in both industry and the service sectors. By 1880, one in every three male children between ten and fifteen years old was part of the U.S. labor force. Although most of this money likely went back to the head of the household, some measure of it would have remained in the child's pocket, to do with as he wished. And what many of them wished for were sweets.

Candy shops became the place for children to socialize, often away from parental control. And what did they do there? Invariably they began to act as proto-adults. Certainly there were instances when the children were excitable, immature, and, well, children. We have evidence of this with a report of a candy shop owner in rural Pennsylvania forbidding loitering. But there's also evidence of adult-style decisions, typified by evidence of an effective boycott of the aforementioned shop owner, organized by those children he had subjected to his loitering rules.

Most candy producers of the time knew exactly who was buttering their bread and would not have dared to cut access to their product from their most profitable consumers. In fact, just the opposite. By this time, most shop owners either supplemented their own confections with those made by the larger confection companies, or they stopped candy production altogether and relied on these producers. These producers soon had the power to market their products to the shop owners, and in turn to children.

As a result, these confectioners found themselves competing against each other and developing ways to differentiate themselves from one another. They tried new flavors, new shapes, different levels of quality. The late nineteenth century saw the evolution of marketing these candies to children. Many molded their candies into recognizable shapes, mimicking the toys either owned or coveted by children. Candies in the shapes of dolls, flowers, marbles, bears, and dogs all made their way onto the scene.

And if they didn't mimic toys, they mimicked tools and vices of adults. It is in this era that candy cigars, cigarettes, and even guns appeared, establishing a precedent that still exists today—most obviously by Big League Chew, a bubble gum that

Kate's Candy Bag

CANDY CIGARETTES

Even back when I was young, now over a generation past, there was concern that candy cigarettes were a corrupting influence on our lives. Parents were sure that eating candy cigarettes would lead us down the path to the evil nicotine.

I don't recall feeling more adult when we puffed on these sugar sticks. Yes, it was cool that these faux Pall Malls did puff, what with the excessive sugar that gave the illusion of smoke. But these were second-rate candies at best. At worst, they were props in our inadvertent re-creations of Who's Afraid of Virginia Woolf? *when we tried to emulate our parents.*

Candy Exchange Rate:

2 packs of candy cigarettes = 1 York Peppermint Pattie

clearly mimics the action of chewing tobacco. Whether it's to encourage chewing tobacco or to offer a viable alternative is often in the eye of the beholder.

It wasn't long until real toys were introduced as prizes for purchasing certain candies; in some cases even money was added, all with the intent of getting the child's money out of his pocket, into the shop owner's, and ultimately into the pocket of the industrial confectioner.

There was a dark side to all of this. Some producers took to increasing their profit margin by using inferior and sometimes dangerous ingredients. Items such as lead or gypsum were used as coloring ingredients. Sawdust was used as filler, and ground soapstone was used to give texture. Items that we classify as drugs today, such as cocaine and opium, were added to some candies. Anything that could be used to keep costs low and profit margins high was tried, and deaths resulted throughout the United States. This inevitably led to government oversight in the form of the Pure Food and Drug Act of 1906, which itself helped lead to the formation of the Food and Drug Administration.

This was the environment that Necco found itself in, and by offering quality candy made with quality ingredients, they began the twentieth century as one of the preeminent American confection houses. Although they have since been surpassed by Hershey and Mars, Necco was there first, having blazed the trail that the chocolate companies would follow.

I had spent the night before wondering how to pay tribute to the Necco wafer. If I am to be truthful, I hadn't sampled the candy since I was in elementary school, and even then I felt as if Neccos were the white linoleum of the candy world. They were dull. They were . . . not chocolate. No one noticed them unless someone specifically pointed them out. My recollections were that they were sweet but bland, and nothing in the past thirty-odd years had compelled me to search them out again. I mean really, it takes a special sort of talent to make the confectionery equivalent to chartered accountancy.

And now, here I was in Boston, home to the treats and quite possibly the oldest industrialized candy company in the country, and I had to work myself up to find something, anything to do that would pay proper homage to these flavored lozenges.

My first plan was to head over to where the Necco plant *used* to be. I quickly scrubbed this idea as being needlessly sentimental. Necco hadn't closed. They moved five miles up the road to Revere, Massachusetts, and were, as far as I was aware, still a distinctive part of the Boston landscape.

"Oh, this is ridiculous," I said to myself. The first thing I should do was give them a break. I hadn't eaten the candy in ages, and my vehement indifference to their product was clouding my judgment. I needed to start from the beginning and see if I liked their product *as an adult*. I grabbed my coat, headed down to the lobby, and asked the concierge for the nearest candy store.

"There's Sugar Heaven, right on the next block. You can't miss it. It's right next to the dentist." He laughed at the irony.

I thanked him and went out into the cold.

A mere two hundred yards away, right next to a dentist's office, was indeed, Sugar Heaven.

The candy store was an exercise in sensory overload. The music, playing Boston's own Aerosmith, was at a level that might cause internal bleeding. And the store itself had a decor that suggested what would happen if one were to tie a brick of C-4 to Bozo the Clown, hit the detonate button, and then turn a rack of high-luminescence fluorescent lighting on the result. "Please, make it stop," my mind repeated several times over the course of my visit. All I wanted was some Necco Wafers, and suddenly I found myself thrust into a shop that was the bastard child of Romper Room and the Whisky a Go Go circa 1979.

"Canihlpyoufndsmthing?" a voice said behind me.

I turned, and yelled, "WHAT??" at a nineteen-year-old woman who clearly had realized a week earlier that she had made a horrible career move going into candy retailing and had decided to communicate her discomfort through indifference and annoyance. She rolled her eyes with such efficiency that it said two distinct things: (1) It acknowledged my inability to hear over the rousing rendition of "Don't Wanna Miss a Thing"; and (2) she didn't give a shit.

"CAN I HELP YOU WITH SOMETHING?!?" she said again.

Clever person that I am, I responded the only way I knew how. "DO YOU HAVE ANY CANDY?"

I had not only called her on her passive aggressiveness, I had doubled down by acting like a moron.

Stunned by the sheer stupidity of my question, she looked at me as if to say, "YOU'RE IN A GOD-DAMNED CANDY STORE." Then she blinked, unable to respond to my move.

"OH, LOOK!" I said, feigning delight, "NECCO WAFERS!" I pointed to an area where I hoped Boston's culinary addition to the confection world would be stashed. I added, for no reason other than to be an ass, "THANKS!"

I walked past several displays and indeed found not only a roll of the Necco Wafer assortment pack but also a roll of their chocolate wafers. I had hit pay dirt. I placed the two rolls into my basket.

I turned to head for the counter and instead came across a wall of gummy products. I'm not sure what compelled me to do so (other than the fact that, up until that moment, I hadn't really paid much attention to these candies), but I stopped, looked, and contemplated the *idea* of the gummy. That Aerosmith had moved on to "Sweet Emotion" only added to the surreal aspect of the moment.

I looked up and down the rows and rows of gummy products available. In front of me there were gummy worms, sour apples, gummy spiders, cola bottles, gummy sharks, and peach slices. And of course, there were the ever-popular gummy bears.

Where did these candies come from? The story starts with a tree that was domesticated in India about eleven thousand years ago, the *Ziziphus jujuba*, better known today as the jujube tree. What made the jujube tree particularly interesting was its fruit, technically a drupe that had a sweet taste but a mucilaginous texture, one that had a propensity to coat the throat when consumed. As with sugar, this berry became associated not only with treats but with medicines, particularly that of syrups and lozenges. Its popularity became so great that soon attempts were made to replicate the qualities of the fruit. Our friends the apothecaries found several ways to replicate the jujube berry, often by simply mixing sugar with an excessive amount of gum arabic. By 1820, we find a recipe for jujube paste, which included gum oriental, sugar, and orange flower water.

The results of this recipe were iffy at best, with some commenting that the texture was similar to that of rubber. But there was enough popularity to the confection, at least as a medicine, to maintain substantial sales in Britain and Europe throughout the nineteenth century. By the turn of the twentieth century, Rowntree, in England, had developed a clear gum and jelly that we can find today in the fruit gums and fruit pastille lines.

By the time that Necco was ruling the American market and Hershey was just starting up, various confectioners in Europe were beginning to reap the benefits of the new industrial technologies that were being developed and implemented. They were providing new results to traditional ingredients such as pectins, gelatins, and new ingredients that included various vegetable starches that had begun entering the market in force.

By 1920, the tools and ingredients were in place for the creation of the *Gummibär* (literally, "rubber bear"). Its German inventor, Hans Riegel, at the age of twenty-seven, decided to enter the candy market himself by starting his own candy company. Naming it Haribo (the *ha* came from Hans, the *ri* came from Riegel, and *bo* came from Bonn, where he had located his company), Riegel and his wife used the recipes for spice gums and fruit pastilles that were on the market, altering them a bit to allow for more citric acid and then shaping them into a familiar and appealing toy—the teddy bear.

The candy took off immediately, but the company nearly fell apart during World War II. Riegel's sons took over the company after the war, and they quickly found themselves running one of the more successful sugar confectioneries in all of Europe. By

1950, they employed over one thousand people and soon were large enough to leverage their success into takeovers of other companies, one of which included the licorice factories of Pontefract.

For many years, gummy bears were imported into the United States. Perhaps not so strangely, high school students studying the German language were among the first Americans introduced to the Haribo Gold-Bear, learning about the candy from their German teachers who brought samples of the "dancing bears" for students to try. Elsewhere, families of servicemen who had served in the U.S. Armed Forces in Germany after World War II also began to develop a taste for the squishy candy and looked for it when they returned to the States. Slowly, demand for the bears began growing in the United States.

The first American-made gummy bears were produced by the Herman Goelitz Candy Company in 1981, which later renamed itself the Jelly Belly Candy Company, after purchasing the trademark from Jelly Belly creator David Klein. Also in 1981, a company called Trolli introduced the gummy worm, which quickly became one of the more popular gummy products on the market. Haribo had initially sold its gummys through a variety of U.S. distributors, but seeing the market slowly slipping into their competitors' hands, it created its own distribution center in Baltimore, Maryland, in 1982.

By the middle of the 1980s, the gummy phenomenon had hit its stride. Because of the huge popularity of the little bears in the United States, soon numerous other candy companies were making some variety of the gummy bear. Some companies, in order to differentiate their gummy products from others, invented new shapes and added new flavors. Slices, sharks, and spiders all found their way into the candy bins, each flavored with differing amounts of citric acid mixed with ingredients meant to replicate raspberries, colas, peaches, and apples. At

Kate's Candy Bag

SWEDISH FISH

A small corner store in Arnold, Pennsylvania, in the year 1979, saw the first introduction of a small, red, gelatin candy in the shape of a fish. These fish were from Sweden, which gave them an air of exoticness, likely the first time that any food from this Nordic country had been given this compliment.

My friends and I loved them, and during the summer of 1979, they became our candy of choice. It was something new, something different from the everyday options available to us. Swedish Fish set the stage for the rest of my life when it came to candy. For it was this gummy fish that made me want to try each new and different candy that crossed my path.

Candy Exchange Rate:
1 bag of Swedish Fish = 2 York Peppermint Patties

one point, even the Disney Company got into the gummy game by producing an animated television series entitled *Disney's Adventures of the Gummi Bears,* a show about bouncing bears who were exiled by humans to Gummi Glen in the Kingdom of Dunwyn. This new confection industry had become popular, riding the rise of the popularity of the bulk bins that were returning to grocery stores throughout the Western countries of the world.

I looked at the bins in front of me, the Necco Wafers suddenly a secondary priority. The selection was vast, the colors were bright, and the prices were cheap. For a brief moment, I connected with the kids of the late nineteenth century who would stare and consider their purchases carefully. I settled on a handful of peach slices and a small amount of gummy bears, for the sake of tradition.

I checked my basket. Overall, not a bad haul, I thought to myself. I went to the counter, and checked out my purchases with the indifferent countergirl. We both said nothing, acknowledging the adversarial aspect of our brief relationship. We had reached a truce of sorts. She wouldn't act like she was annoyed at my presence, and I wouldn't provoke her further by acting like a moron. I left, shutting the door on Steven Tyler screaming "Dream On."

I rushed back to my hotel room, clutching to my chest my second bag of candy in two days. This was starting to seem like a problem. But in that two hundred yards from the candy store to the hotel, I felt as close to my youth as I had since the start of my journey. It wasn't based on much—nothing more than indulging in gummy products for the first time in years. Perhaps it was helped by acting like an immature fool or perhaps it was a true amount of excitement for a piece of candy. I can't say for sure. But in the brief time it took me to get to my room, I felt a thrill.

Too brief, as it turned out. By the time I opened the bag in my hotel room, whatever magic there was had dissipated. And what was in the candy bag wasn't the representation of my youth. Instead there were gummys supplied by god knows who, and Necco Wafers that brought back memories of Halloweens where the wafers sat in the bottom of my trick-or-treat bag all the way past Election Day and straight into Thanksgiving. These were the candies that were unloved by every child. Unable to be traded, and unable to compete with the chocolate goodness of Hershey's or Snickers bars, Neccos seemed to be to candy what the Osmond Brothers were to rock and roll—dull, prefabricated, and devoid of meaning.

I opened the variety pack roll and tried to be objective. Sugar dust fell from the package. Several of the candies had cracked or fallen apart completely. I picked up a white disc dusted with a white powder, either sugar or cornstarch. I hoped for the best.

It wasn't bad. Certainly not as bad as I'd anticipated, nor as I remembered. It was sweet, to be sure, but there was enough flavor to be more than that. Clove permeated across my palate and complemented the sugar quite nicely.

But what made the wafer interesting was not just the flavor. It was the crunch. Theoretically, each candy was designed to dissolve in the mouth. Practically, I got a charge from the crunch when I bit down.

I looked at the Necco Wafers and picked up another. Peppermint? CRUNCH. Soon, several more pieces entered my mouth, each providing a brief bit of flavor before I brought my teeth down. Orange, CRUNCH. Cinnamon, CRUNCH. Lemon, CRUNCH. Chocolate, CRUNCH.

Before long I had eaten the entire roll of Necco Wafers. I had intended to try to connect with the children of the late nineteenth century, but I barely had a moment to come up for a breath. Upon reflection, I felt as if I finally understood not just the appeal of Necco, but the reasons why candy doesn't have to be of the highest quality to become popular. Sweets can, at times, create a near primal desire. There's some measure of rational thought involved, but it's easy, almost too easy, to get wrapped up in both the desire for the candy and the reaction that the candy elicits in the body. The crunch was fun, and the sweetness let me want to continue on with each wafer, unabated.

I was wrong about Necco. They weren't dull or devoid of

meaning. Candy had exploded upon the American landscape in the late 1800s. Much of it was local, but some of it was national. Necco had created a trail that the Hershey Company would follow.

Chapter 17

The Chocolate Kingdom

● ● ● ● ● ● ● ● ● ● ●

Growing up in western Pennsylvania, I always had a special interest in Hershey. Here, in my own state, was a city dedicated to candy. A candy city! The rest of the United States could have their fantasy surrounding Gene Wilder's Willy Wonka. We had a real live candy park.

Not only did they have chocolate, they had a Hersheypark as well—an amusement park combined with all things candy! Imagine the joy you would have as an adult if you had a stock portfolio that returned 15 percent annually *and* automatically paid your mortgage. This was the equivalent joy that Pennsylvanian children held with regard to Hershey. It was the living manifestation of Christmas and Halloween on the same day.

Alas, my parents did not have the same view of the place as my siblings and I had. To my father, amusement parks in Pittsburgh could provide the same excitement as Hersheypark. And if we wanted chocolate? Well, our $3 allowance should cover that with no problem.

To my mother, Hershey represented an indulgent fantasy that detracted from the real culture of south central Pennsylvania, namely, the Amish and all things Gettysburg. Any journeys to the region had to deal with these two topics only.

So I grew up never going to Hersheypark, and instead let the town percolate in my imagination. I became more cynical as I became older, and when I tasted higher-end chocolate, I abandoned Hershey completely. When I drove into the town early on a Saturday afternoon over Labor Day weekend, I was prepared to hate the place.

Milton Hershey was born on September 13, 1857, on a farm near Derry Church, a small town about twenty miles east of Harrisburg. A child of Fannie and Henry Hershey, Milton was raised primarily by his mother, as his father was a bit of a bohemian, or at least as close to a bohemian as a nineteenth-century Mennonite could get. Herself a child of a Mennonite minister, Fannie raised Milton in the strict discipline of her faith, and the community supported them. Later, this same community would support Milton both morally and financially as he embarked on his life in the candy industry (something he had to do early in life, as parental philosophies, family needs, and frequent family moves left him with a limited formal education).

Milton started with a four-year apprenticeship with a Lancaster candy maker. After learning the basics, he attempted his first candy-making business in Philadelphia, which failed. So did his next two attempts at confectionery in Chicago and New York. Returning to Lancaster in 1883, Hershey created the Lancaster Caramel Company. It was caramels, and not chocolate, that brought Milton his initial success, and ultimately to the national stage. The recipe was dead simple, relying upon sugar and milk boiled together slowly to provide a deep, rich sweet taste, heavily influenced by the Maillard effect. The genius that Hershey provided, or perhaps the people who worked for him, was not in the caramel recipe, but in its marketing and expansion.

By all indications, Hershey was unexcited by the business aspect of his company. Its size and sales meant that it could not take a chance with its core recipe. The Lancaster Caramel Company would sell only caramels, and its board of trustees would not allow anything that might risk that million-dollar income.

Hershey, being a candy maker at heart, found himself with nothing to do. With his new wealth, and perhaps bored by it, he found himself traveling the world trying to find ways to occupy himself. At the World's Columbian Exposition in Chicago in 1893, he came across a working chocolate-making machine from Dresden, Germany. Hershey immediately fell in love with the idea of chocolate making. He purchased the entire display, cutting a check to the owners of the equipment, and had it shipped to Lancaster after the exposition had closed. He set up his chocolate equipment on the third floor of his caramel factory, and in 1894 he created the Hershey Chocolate Company.

His initial successes were limited, providing chocolate coating for the caramel company at first, and then manufacturing baking chocolate and powdered cocoa. By the turn of the century, Hershey, buoyed by massive advertising, had a catalog of more than one hundred chocolate products.

What happened next? According to the Hershey legend, in 1900, Milton saw the future of candy and saw that it contained not caramel but chocolate. With this insight, he sold his caramel company for $1 million. This is too pat of an answer and the real story is likely far too complex to go into here. The important fact is that in 1900 Milton Hershey had $1 million in his pocket, a fully equipped chocolate company (although he now needed a new location), and a stellar reputation among both his

customers and his peers in the business world. Whatever moti-
vated him to get to this point is moot, but what happened next
changed the candy landscape in the United States.

In 1902, he bought 1,200 acres a mere mile from where he was
born, smack dab in dairy country. In this region of Pennsylvania,
Milton Hershey would not only build his factory, but create a
company town that would support his vision—a confectionery
utopia where he could not only be a business success but a positive influence on the lives of those who supported him and his
company. In this dairy valley Hershey, Pennsylvania, was born.
The path to the future, Hershey had decided, was paved in milk
chocolate.

Milk chocolate was a recent product, relatively speaking, a
creation of Swiss cocoa pioneer Daniel Peter and baby formula
maker Henri Nestlé. They altered the process of making solid
chocolate by removing the water. Water in the chocolate increased
the rate at which mildew would form. Peter and Nestlé thought
that using either powdered or condensed milk would reduce this
possibility and worked together to find a solution that would give
chocolate a longer shelf life without adversely affecting its taste.
They were successful in 1875, and by 1879 Peter began his own
chocolate company and met with instant success. His company
ended up in the Nestlé domain by 1929, ten years after Peter's
death.

So how is milk chocolate made? All chocolate begins with the
harvest of the cocoa beans, which are fermented and then dried.
The beans are then cleaned, roasted, cooled, and cracked open.
The resulting nibs are ground, to form a chocolate liquor. This
liquor is then heated and compressed, a process that removes the
fat, as Van Houten had discovered at the beginning of the 1800s.
The result is two products: cocoa powder and cocoa butter.

Dark chocolate is a recombination of cocoa powder, cocoa
butter, some amount of sugar, and possibly other ingredients

(which differ from country to country, depending upon various laws). Milk chocolate mixes precise amounts of cocoa powder, cocoa butter, sugar, milk powder (or condensed milk), and vanilla (and other flavorings).

This is what Hershey wanted to sell. His problem? He had no documentation on how milk chocolate was made. He had to resort to trial and error, eventually coming across a recipe that is either a delicious take on accessible chocolate or a heaping pile of rubbish, depending on whom you ask. What he had done was create a chocolate that looked beautiful, coming out of production with a brown satiny appearance. Its taste, however, was distinctive, and to some it was soured, or "off." What Hershey had done, with limited formal education and no experience in chemistry, was to create a viable alternative to the milk chocolate coming out of Europe.

It's a taste that is its own, and many a chocolate expert will tell you of the lack of quality within a Hershey bar. While I'm of the mind that any product put into the marketplace is ripe for critiquing, it is worth acknowledging that, regardless of one's opinion of Hershey's chocolate, the company has sold billions of dollars' worth of the stuff. By 1907, benefiting from his unique position as the only national distributor of chocolate, Hershey's company was achieving close to $2 million in sales. Someone out there—many someones out there—clearly liked his product.

And the money that came in from the chocolate, along with the seed money from his sale of the caramel company, allowed Milton to create a company town to help supply his factory with workers. His goal was to create a workers' utopia, and his town eventually came to be recognized as such. The town had its own gymnasium, public pool, and large park. Workers could buy cheap housing and place their savings in the local bank, also owned by Hershey. The success of the chocolate town created a cottage tourist industry, bringing with it one hundred thousand visitors per year very soon after its inception and establishing a side industry in the town that survives to this day. Hershey, Pennsylvania, was the town that chocolate built, an industrial paradise with a happy workforce and a benevolent philanthropist at the helm.

Or at least, that's what many of the historians would like us to believe. Historically speaking, company towns were rarely success stories for anyone save management. Having grown up a stone's throw from Braddock, Pennsylvania, a city made possible by Andrew Carnegie's steel dreams, I've seen firsthand the long decline of company towns. Almost always, these towns were meant to benefit the company rather than the inhabitants. I wanted to see if Hershey lived up to the hype.

Of course, there was a side benefit to this trip as well. I could finally answer my inner child's questions about the town. I was as excited about visiting Hershey as I had been about visiting Venice and London.

As I drove down Chocolate Avenue, all concern about corporate politics and civic history went out the window. Suddenly, I was a seven-year-old again, albeit one with knowledge of how to drive a car.

When Chocolate Avenue crossed with Cocoa Street, I giggled with joy. As I passed the streetlamps, I opened up the windows and stuck my head out in order to get a better view of the Hershey Kisses that adorned their tops. And once the windows opened, I could inhale the aroma of cocoa that permeated the air. I smiled and laughed. It had taken me nearly a generation, but I had finally made it to Hershey.

The sky was blue, the temperature was in the mid-60s, and the Saturday promised to carry with it a return to childhood. I bought a breakfast of an omelet and scrapple at the Hershey Pantry, a local diner aimed a bit at both the locals and the tourists. As I downed the last swallow of my diner-grade coffee, I

Kate's Candy Bag

HERSHEY BAR

Let's face it. The Hershey bar is an American icon, regardless of whether we enjoy the chocolate or not. And for those of us who grew up in Pennsylvania, Hershey bars were evidence that Willy Wonka could exist in real life. When we were given a Hershey bar, there wasn't the pure joy that a Snickers bar would elicit. Instead, there was something more akin to awe. To us, the thought was always along the lines of "Milton Hershey made his own chocolate bar, and then made an amusement park. He is a god."

To this day, even knowing what I know about the Hershey Company of today, I still get wistful when I hold a Hershey bar in my hands. For the Hershey bar has a direct link to the hands of Milton Hershey. And in the end, what I know for certain about him is that he was one of us—he was a candy fanatic. He loved candy more than he loved money. I'm not sure that in this age of corporations we will ever see anyone like him again.

Candy Exchange Rate:
1 Hershey bar = 3 York Peppermint Patties

looked at my itinerary for the day. Hit Hershey's Chocolate World first, follow up with a quick visit to Hersheypark, and then end the day at the Milton Hershey Museum. By the end of the day, I hoped to have had the full Hershey experience.

I drove over to the tourist attractions, parked the car, and walked to the line for Hershey's Chocolate World, where I was greeted by a trio of anthropomorphic mascots. One was shaped like a Hershey's Kiss, another like a Reese's Peanut Butter Cup, and the third looked like the classic Hershey bar; they each had their own eyes, nose, arms, legs, and smile that seemed to indicate that they knew you were about to eat their kin and they didn't mind in the least. My mind wandered back to the Bassett's allsorts mascot, which was also presented as a living, breathing, sentient piece of candy. I shuddered at the uncomfortable thoughts that arose from this macabre portrayal.

It used to be that anyone off the street could walk into the Hershey Company during working hours and take part in the tour that took them through the actual production facilities. But those days have been gone for nearly a generation now. With Chocolate World designed to replace the tours, the production facilities could now pay lower insurance premiums and prevent prying eyes from rival companies seeing what was going on. Chocolate World opened for business in 1973 and millions of visitors have walked through its doors.

While at Chocolate World, one can take a trolley ride around the city. The guide points out key aspects of the history of Hershey, both the town and the company. If an hour-long trip around the town doesn't sound appealing, parents can take their children to an area where they can make their own candy bar.

Or, visitors can see a 3-D movie where the aforementioned creepy, anthropomorphic mascots "come to life as never before" and resident chocolate historian Professor D. P. Quigley takes the viewer "on a magical journey through HERSHEY'S entertaining history." For children, the movie is a bright and shiny object that kept them entertained through sugary jingles, clever computer animation, and bells and whistles such as seat ticklers, butt kickers, fog, bubbles, snow, spritzers, confetti air cannons, and a chocolate smell that reminded me of Kellogg's Cocoa Krispies. For adults, it is the closest they could get to a bad acid trip sponsored by a candy corporation—and all for just $6.

There are two other major aspects to Chocolate World, and the respective importance of each is determined by one's perspective. If you're a tourist, that centerpiece is bound to be the Chocolate Tour. Visitors wait in line for up to thirty minutes (depending on the time of day they visit) before being whisked away in a cart through a bizarre re-creation of a chocolate factory, where animatronic cows sing the virtue of using the right kind of milk in milk chocolate through the use of the Motown motif, while chocolate candies are made in sheets that whisk over one's head at thirty-five miles per hour. At the end, visitors purchase a picture of their visit for a mere $9.95.

If I sound cynical about this enterprise, it's because I am an adult, and such a ride was not made with me in mind. The ride was clearly made for the kiddies and should never be considered an authentic re-creation of the chocolate-making process. I did note, however, the attention to detail on this trip, as faux bird poo had been painted upon the various wooden stumps meant to re-create the nineteenth-century shipping docks of whatever tropical paradise the cocoa bean was coming from. Somewhere in this town a discussion was held that covered the merits of the verisimilitude of re-created bird poo. This was oddly satisfying on some level.

After purchasing said picture, visitors are handed a bite-sized piece of Hershey's chocolate, unless there's an unveiling of a new product, in which case visitors may get a full-sized candy bar. From there, visitors head into the area that Hershey's management believes is the most important part of the tour—the gift shop.

I've been to many a corporate gift shop before, for companies both popular and not, and I can say without hesitation that

Hershey's gift shop exists on a scale that is not often matched. It is the first gift shop that I've been to that has its own food court.

But I was here for one thing only, the thing that I had been dreaming of since I was seven—the candy. Hershey bars were everywhere, in sizes ranging from forty-three grams to one that was close to five pounds (only $39.95!). You could buy Hershey Kisses in a souvenir coffee mug or in a twenty-five-pound case (yours for only $95!).

The shelves were packed with variations of Twizzlers (in black licorice, strawberry, cherry, and chocolate), Jolly Rancher (in classic flavors, the more recent sours, and the new fruit smoothies), and America's favorite comfit, Good & Plenty, which sat next to the Good & Fruity, and the rarer Hot & Plenty. After scouring the shelves, I found myself next to Hershey's Rally bar, a popular chocolate-covered nut bar that I thought had been retired years before. Yet here it sat before me, with its funky, 1970s era logo staring at me, daring me to purchase it.

Memories of my youth came flooding back, with Heath bars to the left, PayDay bars to the right, and Almond Joys directly in front. Then I saw it. Off to the side, and buried next to the ZERO bar was the western Pennsylvanian candy bar Zagnut. My poor, poor Zagnut bar, shunted off to the side like a Charlie-in-a-Box. Hershey owned Zagnut? Who knew?

In western Pennsylvania, there were two candy bars that we could proudly call our own. There was the Clark bar, a chocolate-covered peanut butter crunch bar, and the Zagnut bar, a peanut butter crunch bar coated with roasted coconut. When the owners of these two brands, the Pittsburgh Food and Beverage Company, entered bankruptcy in 1995, both properties were sold. The Clark bar went to the Necco, but I had no idea what happened to the Zagnut. And here it was, sitting lonely on the shelf, treated like an unwanted stepchild. I grabbed a bar and put it into my shopping basket.

Suddenly I remembered all the reasons why Hershey was having a bit of a public relations problem of late. It started when it committed to competing with the Mars Corporation, took stock of its catalog of candies, and found it wanting. From there Hershey went on a spending spree, looking to diversify its product.

The result? A catalog of candies that had their roots in other regions of the United States and the world. Kit Kat bars? York, England. Heath bars? Robinson, Illinois. PayDay bars? Hollywood, Minnesota. Looking at the various brands in the gift shop—5th Avenue, Almond Joy, Bubble Yum, Good & Plenty, Good & Fruity, Heath bar, Ice Breakers, Jolly Rancher, Krackel, Milk Duds, Mounds, Oh Henry!, PayDay, Twizzlers, Whoppers, York Peppermint Pattie, Zagnut, ZERO—all were created by companies not named Hershey, yet sit on Hershey shelves, allowing Hershey to reap the benefits of somebody else's work. As I was looking up and down the shelves it became apparent to me that Hershey's recent definition of innovation primarily involved buying out the companies that had actually done the innovating.

The problem with this approach is that the company will play favorites with its catalog. Some candies will get more attention than others. While this behavior is likely determined by sales reports and marketing response, some of the brands eventually fall through the cracks.

Much like my beloved Zagnut, a brand that warranted only one slice of one shelf in a gift shop that is larger than many grocery stores. My inner voice wondered whether Milton would have approved of this approach to candy-making success. For someone who supposedly loved candy as much as the historians indicate, would Mr. Hershey think that restricting access to regional favorites would be endearing to consumers?

Of course, asking Mr. Hershey these questions in my mind is nothing more than me asking these questions of myself, as I have

Kate's Candy Bag

REESE'S PEANUT BUTTER CUP

The Reese's Peanut Butter Cup was the second most appreciated candy bar from my youth, sitting only behind the Snickers bar in terms of popularity. This is the candy that is able to integrate the taste of salt (found ever so slightly in the peanut butter) with the sweet. The result is a recipe that is so perfect, not even the use of cheap ingredients detracts from it. Even the cup aspect of the candy is spot on, giving the consumer the perfect serving size.

For years I did not realize that the possessive in the brand name indicated that the peanut butter cup belonged to some person who went by the name of Reese. It turns out that Reese was a real person, and that the peanut butter cup later sold by Hershey was, indeed, Reese's idea. Harry Burnett Reese came from a big family and he himself had many children. He had worked as a dairy manager for the Hershey Company for a bit but lost his job when the farm was later closed.

It was his desire to give his children a better life and feed his growing family that encouraged him to try his hand at making candy. He created the peanut butter cup in 1928; it quickly became his most popular item. The Hershey Company later bought the brand and owns it to this day.

Candy Exchange Rate:
1 Reese's Peanut Butter Cup = 3 York Peppermint Patties

no idea what a man who has been dead for three generations could think about these developments.

But there are other questions being asked today that seem to run counter to the Hershey philosophy that is heavily marketed by both the local tourist board and the company itself. Behind the scenes there is a different story, one where Hershey is acting less like a Willy Wonka company and more like an industry that has to appeal to stockholders and make the gurus on Wall Street feel at ease. It starts with the Hershey School Trust.

The school was (and is) a philanthropic endeavor, started by Milton Hershey in 1909 to provide an education to boys (and, since 1977, to girls) who would otherwise not have access to high-quality schools. The trust was developed to oversee the school.

It was a tremendous success. Children who otherwise had limited options in life found themselves in an environment where they were encouraged to reach their potential, and they were given the skills and tools to do so. The trust, supported by its stock in a world-renowned confectionery company, had the resources to do what it believed best for the children. By most metrics, it worked.

The trust's finances are tied to Hershey's. As of 2008, the trust was sitting on a $7.8 billion endowment, most of it coming from shares of Hershey stock. With this leverage, the trust uses its control of the company to provide high-quality education to 1,700 children. What is apparent is that the executors of the trust don't wish to risk this endowment. They determined that in order to ensure adequate funding for the Milton Hershey School, they needed to diversify.

The problem? The trust fund owned close to 77 percent of the controlling stake of the Hershey corporation's stock. Diversifying their portfolio would put the company at risk, so much so that when the trust approached then CEO Richard Lenny, he opposed the idea vehemently and looked for other solutions. The executors of the trust rejected every one of them and planned to proceed with diversification.

The Hershey Company wants (and some would argue needs) to act like the corporate giant it is. It doesn't wish to cede market share to its competitors. In order to remain competitive, the company board wants to squeeze every last bit of profit they can out of their margin, up to and including finding cheap labor outside of Hershey, Pennsylvania. This has led to a conflict between Hershey, the corporate chocolate giant, and Hershey, the philanthropist, and has resulted in some very public disputes, culminating in 2007 when the trust used its stock ownership to oust Hershey's board of directors and force the retirement of Richard Lenny.

Meanwhile, the citizens of Hershey, a place where the median income is $43,000 per year, are stuck in the middle, waiting to see how these billion-dollar institutions settle their dispute. The citizens have asked for transparency of the trust, demanded to know how their endowment is being spent, and questioned whether the trust is still meeting Milton Hershey's initial intent.

Regardless of one's position on this matter, it's clear that this mess, this conflict of philosophies, runs counter to the world of innocence that Hershey markets. At its core, it's a battle between profit and identity. Both the company and the trust are looking to ensure their missions and have decided that the best way to do so is to pursue the almighty dollar.

Many of the Hershey locals view this conflict as a risk to their livelihood and identity. Having a billion-dollar company leave the small town could be devastating. For those who have dedicated their lives to the ideal of Hershey, whether working for the corporation or for the many supporting companies that exist as the result of Hershey, the mere thought of the company rejecting the civic institution of Hershey, the city, is the ultimate betrayal. That the trust seemingly isn't looking out for the city is just another dagger in the back.

The current conflict in Hershey boils down to this: when the wolves attack, do you blame the wolves? Or the guards who let wolves into the city? The problem that the citizens of Hershey understand is that once the wolves are at your door, asking who to blame is essentially moot.

Note: There are times when timing can be everything. Shortly before this book was to go to press, Hershey issued a press release that spelled out their plans to institute a long-term commitment to west Africa by investing $10 million in the Ivory Coast and Ghana over five years, in order to reduce child labor and improve the cocoa supply. Two million dollars each year doesn't break down to a lot of money on a per-farmer basis, nor does Hershey's pledge come anywhere close to meeting all of the articles established in the Cocoa Protocol, but their offer is a good first step.

Chapter 18

Candy Day

● ● ● ● ●

T left the Hershey complex, with its Chocolate World, its mega-sized gift shop selling nothing but candy and items that helped promote said candy, and its amusement park, which had evolved into a vehicle to promote the Hershey brand (and had the added benefit of making some money, well, a lot of money, on the side). I was not jaded, but rather, more clear of mind. Business is business after all, and that means that sometimes companies have to create marketing devices that are more than a little like a four-year-old child screaming, "Look at me! Look at me!" The corporate world is one where cynicism isn't a recognizable trait. At least not unless there is money to be made in it.

Okay, I *was* jaded. But it wasn't Hershey that made me this way. It was a culmination of information that caused me to look on the candy industry this way. Nearly everywhere I turned on this trip, I had run into a fact or an instance that reminded me of the fallibility of man. For some reason, sugar and chocolate brings out the seamier sides of our collective personality.

I headed to downtown Hershey to get away from the shouting apparatus that repeatedly declared how awesome the company was. I wondered what the odds were that I could find candy in this city that had *not* been made by Hershey. I parked the car in a lot right across the street from the factory on Chocolate Avenue and then headed west. My goal? The same it had been since the start of the trip—to connect to the innocent part of me, the one that I last remember seeing back around the age of eleven.

It didn't take long for me to realize that Hershey, as a town, was quite nice—beautiful even, at least within its own aesthetic. The streets were clean and lined with trees, graffiti nowhere to be seen. Traffic was minimal (surprisingly, for a tourist town), and it seemed as if a sense of civic pride permeated the air. Of course, the air smelled of cocoa, and I realized that, for many here, civic pride and chocolate likely went hand in hand. Hershey was exactly what my mind believed a small town should look like. That this civic pride was being exhibited and exploited by the company with all the subtlety of . . . well, an amusement park, that was little more than an unfortunate side effect. About a mile into my walk, I started believing that the magic of Hershey came not from the chocolate being made by the company, but rather from its place in history. Yes, that history is and always will be tied to the company, but it wasn't difficult for me to come to the conclusion that the town and the people in it would rather be tied to Milton Hershey, the man.

It wasn't long until I came across a Rite-Aid, a drugstore right off Chocolate Avenue. If there was any place in Hershey that would sell non-Hershey products, it would be here. I stepped into the store and was blinded by the fluorescent lights. I headed to the candy aisle, and soon it became apparent that

the way this drugstore was celebrating Labor Day was by selling Halloween candy.

I find it remarkable, and perhaps a bit coincidental, that here
in the twenty-first century, one of the better places that Americans can get their candy fix is not in candy stores that deal exclusively in confectionery, but in drugstores throughout the
land. And it is here that one can find the true legacy of Milton
Hershey.

What Milton Hershey kicked off at the start of the twentieth
century was the golden age of candy—industrial candy, if one
wishes to get particular. The Hershey's success brought to the
national stage a host of imitators and innovators, each looking
for a way into the candy world. From 1907 until about the end
of World War II, candy production migrated from the local re-
tailer in the back room of the candy store, to the regional supplier,
to a national distribution model. It took more than a generation
to occur, but the end result is the candy scene recognizable to
every one of us today.

I looked at the variety of candy in the aisle and did a quick history in my mind. Necco wafers? 1901. Hershey Kisses? 1906. Peppermint Life Savers? They were created by a Cleveland chocolatier
in 1912, as a summer alternative to chocolate. Baby Ruth bars?
Started life in Chicago in 1900 as Kandy Kake and were renamed
Baby Ruth in 1921. Snickers? 1930. Tootsie Roll Pops? 1931. 3 Musketeers? 1932.

These were the brands that made it. For every one that still
exists today from this era, there are likely dozens, if not hundreds, that have been lost to time or takeover. Names include
the Red Grange bar, the Seven Up bar, the Chicken Dinner bar,
and the Vegetable Sandwich bar. The last two brands may
sound odd to us today, what with their connotations of meal
replacements and food substitutions, but considering the close
associations to health and medicine that candy had had through-

Kate's Candy Bag

3 MUSKETEERS BAR

There's a mystery behind the 3 Musketeers bar. As a point of fact, there is only one musketeer found within any Musketeer bar. So what happened?

When the bar was first introduced back in 1932, it had three flavors of nougat: strawberry, vanilla, and chocolate. Each nougat was coated in chocolate, and there were three pieces of candy in each bar. When rationing occurred during World War II, and ingredients became more difficult to obtain (and thus more expensive), Mars, seeking to save money, cut two of the Musketeers, leaving only chocolate.

Of course, we didn't know this history when I was a child, but I do know that the extra varieties would have been a welcome addition to an already excellent candy bar.

Candy Exchange Rate:
one 3 Musketeers bar = 2 York Peppermint Patties

out its history, it's difficult for me to consider these brands too much of a novelty.

Starting a candy company must have seemed like a decent way to make a buck or two. After all, who hates candy? By this era, there was only one group of folks who were turning a careful eye on the industry, and it came from the most unlikely of places—the medical community that helped establish the commodity of confectionery in the first place.

This shift was gradual, starting back in the Age of Reason with the introduction of the modern scientific method. By the 1800s, Galen's theory of humorism had been mostly rejected in the Western world and replaced by the beginnings of medicine and surgery that we see today. Biochemistry is the science that, hypothetically, oversees our philosophy of nutrition, and it is from this branch that we approach candy with tentative steps.

Here's the weird thing: as of today, there is only one confirmed disease that comes from eating candy on a regular basis: tooth decay, something people were aware of as far back as the time of Queen Elizabeth I. Sugar ferments into lactic acid in the mouth; that acid goes to town on tooth enamel if the pH of the saliva falls beneath 5.5. Additionally, for people who have a problem with spiking in blood sugar, for example, diabetics, candy may be something that needs to be avoided.

Every other medical problem associated with sugar comes with a qualifying phrase: *for some people*. For some people, sugar may lead to or assist in a metabolic decrease. For some people, sugar may lead to obesity. For some people, sugar may cause acid reflux.

The problem with that phrase indicates that the cause may be sugar, but then again, it may be something else. For the most part, the evidence to support these claims is either incomplete or completely unjustified.

This isn't me saying, "Yay, candy! Eat all you want!" Eating nothing but candy is a damned fool thing to do and comes with a slew of issues, up to and including malnutrition. And we're damn sure that if you overeat, obesity is in your future. But this hasn't stopped many in the health community, and quite a few others, proclaiming that candy is bad for you, regardless of how little you may consume.

Part of this is due to the pure luxury of candy. Nutritionally, most candies provide nothing outside of sugar and fat (if your candy of choice is chocolate). That's it. No vitamins, no minerals (unless directly added by the manufacturer), nothing. And as one can get sugar and fat in other food products that provide far more to our diet, candy, in the end, is little more than empty calories. As it provides nothing of substance or sustenance, it becomes an easy enemy of the moral brigade, regardless of whether these moralists are advocating a healthier lifestyle or an ethical one. Such admonishment and advocation show up in the strangest of packages. As Wendy Woloson notes in her book *Refined Tastes,* an article written in *The Friend* in the 1830s states that candy consumption by children of the lower class would lead to "intemperance, gluttony, and debauchery," all because, the article implies, the poor have little control over their destinies and the ability to refuse temptation. Candy shops were to be avoided because they were "hot beds of disease" and "filled with putrid rottenness."

With all of that bad publicity floating about, some true, but most not, a group of confectioners decided the best course of action was to get together and create an organization to help promote candy and defend the industry from claims both false and malicious. In 1884, representatives of dozens of American candy manufacturing firms got together and formed the National Confectioners Association, a trade association still in existence today. Their goals, written as a mission statement of sorts, were "to advance the standard of confectionery in all practicable ways, and absolutely to prevent hurtful adulterations; to promote the common business interests of its members, and to establish and maintain more intimate relations between them; and to take united action upon all matters affecting the welfare of the trade at large." Apparently there was enough of a problem with the quality of confectionery that the trade association felt as if standards had to be set.

By the 1899 convention in Buffalo, New York, the concerns

had changed from the quality of the product to that of confessing that something needed to be done to "hold up prices" while at the same time providing no evidence or path that would make it look like the National Confectioners Association would or could look like a trust seeking to set prices. The goal of NCA members was now clear: How could they find ways to make more money?

It's interesting to look at the NCA's mission statement today to see how it has changed. At the bottom of its website, found at www.candyusa.com, the mission statement reads as follows: "The National Confectioners Association fosters industry growth by advancing and promoting the interests of the confectionery industry and its consumers." While a lot has been removed from the initial goals, one small phrase had been added. The NCA now promotes "the interest of . . . its consumers." It's important to note that the interest of the consumer was not, at least initially, at the forefront of the minds of the trade association's creators.

So how did this desire to "hold up prices" manifest itself? In 1916, a circular was sent to many of the U.S. candy manufacturers and retailers by the executive committee of the NCA. It stated:

> At the last annual convention of the National Confectioners Association by resolution, the second Saturday in October of each year was designated as "Candy Day" with the purpose in view of bringing about nationwide displays and sales of candy by retailers on that date each year.

The plan to hold up prices? Increase demand. What better way to increase demand than to follow the path laid before them by the trade associations of other commodities, which had created success with "Coffee Day" and "Apple Day"? Their goal, spelled plainly in the *Confectioners and Baker's Gazette,* the trade paper of the time, was this: "If 'Candy Day' accomplishes no other purpose than that of demonstrating that it pays to interest the public occasionally in the industry the celebration will more than fulfill its purpose."

It had taken the industry a mere thirty-two years to realize that the consumer, at some level, mattered to the success of any given confectionery business. As for just how important the consumer was, and how truthfully to interact with them, that was the gray area.

Alas, Candy Day did not take off the way that the NCA had hoped, having to be canceled in 1917 and 1918 because of World War I. And there was little effort to push the idea nationally in 1919. By 1920, there was a small movement afoot to revive the day on a national level, but by then the NCA had moved on to other business: the holiday that was gaining popularity— Halloween.

But candy and Halloween would have to wait a full generation before becoming fully integrated. Some regional confectioners organized local holidays, such as Sweetest Day, a holiday found in the Great Lakes region of the United States, ostensibly designed to encourage us to remember friends, relatives, and other loved ones. In some areas the poor, the infirm, and the orphaned were also added to this list. On the third Saturday of October, one was to purchase candy and hand it off as a gift to someone apparently in need of a sugar boost. The legend states that it was Herbert Birch Kingston, a philanthropist and candy company employee from Cleveland, who "wanted to bring happiness into the lives of orphans, shut-ins and others who were forgotten. With the help of friends, he began to distribute candy and small gifts to the underprivileged."

It was also, quite likely, just a piece of cynical marketing. The dates are too close between Candy Day and Sweetest Day to be a coincidence. Additionally, evidence has not been found that puts Mr. Kingston in the confectionery industry. However, there is a 1920 census form that lists a Herbert Birch Kingston from Cuyahoga County in Ohio as an advertiser. As coincidence would have it, it would be with a regional advertiser that a candy maker could choose to promote Candy Day. Perhaps Candy Day could have been marketed as the " 'Sweetest Day' in the year" in order for it to gain traction and cement its popularity.

Not so coincidentally, this is exactly the ad that is seen in a variety of pharmaceutical trade publications in 1921, including *Northwest Druggist* and *The Midland Druggist and Pharmaceutical Review*, publications found in Minnesota and Ohio, respectively. In fact, in the October 1921 issue of *The Midland Druggist* we see the real force behind Sweetest Day. E. G Winger, head of publicity for the Northern Ohio Druggists Association, who helped promote Sweetest Day, was given accolades for his work in making the day a success:

> Large paid space was used by the candy manufacturers and distributors and the publicity committees made good use of the reading pages to put the case to the people. Slogans were used as inch ads all over the papers, such as "Don't forget the Kiddies today," "The Sweetest day in the year," and so on for "mother, sweetheart, and all."
>
> Thousands of boxes of candy were given away in Cleveland to the people in the institutions and hospitals, to the newsies, the poor, etc., making it a gala charity day as well as a good business proposition in sales to those who were able to pay for their sweets.

Mr. Kingston was nowhere to be found.

Regardless of its origins, Sweetest Day did take off in some regions of the United States, so much so that the NCA eventually saw fit to try to institute the holiday, if not nationally, then regionally. As late as 1937, the NCA instituted Sweetest Day in New York City, citing the success in Cleveland in drumming up candy sales as its reason for trying to establish this holiday in the Big Apple.

So what happened to Sweetest Day? Why isn't it at the top of everyone's calendar? Because eventually the NCA would integrate Sweetest Day with Halloween.

Halloween festivals predate Sweetest Day by many centuries in western Europe. There were two such festivals of Roman origin: Feralia, a festival when the Romans commemorated the passing of the dead; and the Day of Pomona, a day in the autumn where they celebrated the harvests of the fruits. The Romans brought these traditions into ancient Britain, and they were assimilated into the local traditions, eventually evolving into Samhain, the Celtic harvest festival.

Meanwhile, All Saints' Day was instituted by the Catholic Church; in 835 it was decreed to be held on November 1. All Saints' Day also goes by the name All Hallows Day, the day when all saints were to be remembered and celebrated for their holiness.

Now there were two celebrations in Gaelic regions at roughly the same time. Samhain was celebrated at the end of October, followed immediately by All Hallows Day. It wasn't long until Samhain came to be celebrated on All Hallows Eve.

Immigrants to America from Scotland in the eighteenth century and Ireland in the nineteenth brought their harvest festival along with them. It wasn't as popular in some areas of the country as it was in others, because it was perceived as a holiday of immigrants. These immigrants used the festival to celebrate and support their communities. By the end of the nineteenth century, Halloween was celebrated nearly exclusively as a community event, with harvest dances, costume dress-up, and people going door to door asking for food and money to either augment the community feast or help out the families whose harvest hadn't been as bountiful as others. This last activity is the foundation for trick or treating, yet it was still a long way from going door to door with the expectation of candy.

In fact, we don't see the idea of trick or treating, meaning "give me a treat or I'm going to egg your house back to the Paleolithic era," until the late 1920s. It was an idea that seems to have started in the western region of the United States or Canada and moved slowly east. The basic premise was simple: knock on a door, extort the person who answers the door, and then get a few cents, a cookie, or a popcorn ball.

 ### *Kate's Candy Bag*

POPCORN BALL

I admit that I like and respect popcorn balls, and have no problem in calling it a candy. But when compared to the bright and shiny brands of candy, the popcorn ball often falls short of meeting many a child's expectations.

The wisdom that comes with growing up makes me realize today that popcorn balls have far more intrinsic value than anything made by Mars or Hershey. When someone takes the time and care to make a confection, my palate finds that those candies taste a little extra special.

Candy Exchange Rate:
2 popcorn balls = 1 York Peppermint Pattie

Somehow, somewhere, Sweetest Day and Halloween combined. The history of this is, sadly, not specific. But the circumstantial evidence is there. As trick or treating took off in the 1930s and 1940s, those who had candy left over from Sweetest Day could respond quickly by handing out leftover candy.

But you can be sure that the members of the NCA had their eyes on this holiday. As early as 1922, V. L. Price, the man who helped initiate Candy Day, stated the following at the NCA convention:

> Have you any doubt, if manufacturers would create special "Hallowe'en Candies" and retailers in large numbers would feature special displays and sales on Hallowe'en, but that it would greatly increase candy sales on that day, and in doing it, would eventually make Hallowe'en a candy season.

By the 1950s, the two holidays had been fully merged, and popular media from magazines to television shows talked about trick or treating on Halloween. The treat of choice? Candy. By the time that the holiday special *It's the Great Pumpkin, Charlie Brown* was shown in 1966, the idea of trick-or-treating for candy and primarily candy was fully ensconced in the American psyche.

I looked at the bags of candy that filled the aisle. In front of me was the National Confectioners Association's dream fulfilled. According to their data, the Halloween season represents 23 percent of annual candy sales, and Halloween week is by far the greatest sales week of the year. Both statistics represent the largest share of any selling season. The candy companies of America love Halloween.

I reflected upon my own experiences with the great day. It was this holiday that gave me my sweet tooth, and I have nothing but, if you'll pardon the expression, the sweetest affection for those memories.

Kate's Candy Bag

SNICKERS BAR

This was the gold standard for candy for me when I was a child, and it still holds sway over me to this day. I look upon Snickers bars the same way I look upon comic books, hard rock, and puppy love. All these items have been stepping-stones to bigger and, arguably, better things in art, music, and relationships. Yet I still find myself drawn to these items of my youth.

So when foodies stake their claims to their favorite chocolates, I still feel the urge to proclaim "And don't forget the classic Snickers bar, with its nougat, caramel, and salted peanuts, all coated with a sweet milk chocolate." It may not be a plantation-sourced all-natural, fair-trade chocolate, but it still pulls at my heart.

Candy Exchange Rate:
1 Snickers bar = 3 York Peppermint Patties

But I stood there, in the aisle of the drugstore in Hershey, two days before Labor Day, looking at candy meant for Halloween, and I couldn't help but think that these memories were the result of some grand manipulation, some marketing scheme meant to leverage the youthful desire for sweetness into profit.

Again, did it matter? Did it matter how I arrived at those sweet memories? Did it matter that the dozen or so nights that I spent trick or treating, along with thousands, if not millions, of other children and teenagers, was due to the concerted effort of the National Confectioners Association?

I picked up a Snickers bar. This was the ultimate candy bar back when I was ten years old, and it still holds sway over me today. I love everything about the candy bar, from the salted peanuts and caramel within to the carefully marketed wrapper, with the deep cocoa brown coloring, emblazoned with the royal blue of the Snickers logo.

It didn't matter. It didn't matter any more than the festive atmosphere so carefully engineered at Disney World.

I paid for the Snickers bar and walked back to my car. It didn't bring back the innocence of my youth. But it still made me smile. Sometimes that's the best we can ask for out of life.

Chapter 19

What Is "Good" Candy?

● ● ● ● ● ● ● ● ● ● ●

As I flew home to Seattle, I had time to reflect on the realization that I had had in the candy aisle of the Hershey Rite-Aid. I had been approaching this quest all wrong. Candy as a juvenile endeavor was culturally based, instilled in me by my youthful enjoyment of a holiday that had been coopted by a trade association. And while this doesn't diminish the joy I felt back then, this knowledge did affect my perception of the holiday today. From here on out, I would never again experience the sheer joy of Halloween as I had as a child. The only way I could get close to that feeling as an adult would be to dress up in costume, go door to door, and have people hand me twenty-dollar bills. Yeah. This wasn't going to happen any time soon.

I wonder whether other people were as stunned when they hit adulthood as I was. After a childhood during which my greatest concern was whether to buy the grape Bubble Yum or the original flavor, being confronted by puberty, college tuition, credit reports, and self-awareness was akin to being repeatedly smacked in the face with a stick labeled RESPONSIBILITIES. The Mardi Gras aspect of Halloween was gone, replaced by time clocks and due dates. My premise had been proved correct: adulthood is when one has the means to buy every candy in the shop but no longer has the desire to do so.

It's a bit more nuanced than that, but not much. Somewhere along the line, here in the United States, sugar became a must-have craving and a health nut's shorthand for all that is wrong, nutritionally, with our nation's approach to health. Our candy industry has been one of the industries affected by this perspective. In 1997, each American gobbled up or savored more than 27 pounds a year. By 2004, that number had dropped to 24.7 pounds. Admitting you liked candy was the equivalent of telling a vegan that you liked veal.

Yet somewhere along the line, there evolved a new world of chocolate, one deemed acceptable by adults, one in which words such as "ganache" and "coveture" were common, and loud obnoxious commercials were avoided at all costs. This was a world where eating high-end confection had become socially acceptable.

I arrived in Seattle, a city that, in the election year of 2008, became the perfect representation of this new world. When candidate Barack Obama was asked what his favorite snack was, he told the reporter at *The New York Times* that he enjoyed handmade milk chocolates from Seattle's own Fran's Chocolates, especially the milk chocolate salted caramels. The fact is, these chocolates run near $12 for seven pieces. This isn't a sudden shift in America's palate. Sales of high-end chocolates have risen every year since 2000, and places that sell $10 bars of salted caramels are popping up all across the country.

This "trend" is one that has been one hundred years in the making and finds its origins in Belgium of all places.

While England and the United States were learning to sell confections to children, and finding big money in it, the rest of Europe had found a different model, one in which the value of the candy wasn't dependent on the fact that it was readily available. Rather, the value was in the skill and talent of the confectioner. And in the late 1800s, in the somewhat new country of Belgium, confectionery was a serious business. Chocolatiers there searched for ways to outdo one another by making better, rather than cheaper, chocolate.

When one looks at history, it isn't all that surprising that the Belgians got into the chocolate business. King Leopold II, the ruler of Belgium, looked to hop on the colonization bandwagon. The area of the world where Belgium planted itself was the Congo in Africa. And one of the primary exports of the Congo? Cocoa beans.

Near the end of the Gilded Age, a Belgian chocolatier by the name of Jean Neuhaus found a way to make chocolate into small, thin, delicate, hollow shells into which various other confections and syrups could be piped or poured. While the Cadburys and Hersheys of the world worked on bars of chocolate, the Belgians went the other way, looking to create bite-sized works of art. These candies were called "pralines," after the candying technique of coating one confection or sweet around another.

During the 1920s, the popularity of these chocolate pralines took off, and various candy and confection companies in Europe and North America followed suit. The names would be recognizable to anyone with a sweet tooth: Neuhaus, Cote d'Or, Leonidas, and Godiva all came onto the scene during this era.

Godiva is the brand that most Americans would recognize. Starting off as a Neuhaus imitator in 1926, Godiva found its success in marketing its chocolates as the ultimate expression of sophistication. In 1958, it opened its first shop outside of Belgium in Paris, and by 1966 it was selling high-end chocolate pralines in upper-class neighborhoods throughout the United States. Godiva's popularity was so great that the company was eventually purchased by the Campbell Soup Company.

Established confectioners "borrowed" from the Belgian approach to chocolate—Thorton's in the United Kingdom and Russell Stover in the United States. Suddenly, these candies ceased to be a juvenile predilection, but became an adult statement of sophistication. Sure, one could have M&M's or a Hershey bar. But consumers got the sense that if they really wanted to have a sophisticated palate, then a box of chocolates with an assortment of flavors, all marketed as "upscale" (to one degree or another) was the only way to go. Candy was now for children. Confectionery was for adults.

This divide intrigues me on an intellectual level because, conceptually, there's precious little difference between a bite-sized 3 Musketeers bar and a chocolate from Godiva with malted nougat in the center. Yet one costs far more than the other. The difference, we are told, stems from differences in ingredients and in technique. Each of these differences must be looked at on a company-by-company basis. Some of these companies would prefer this didn't happen, hoping that their consumers are entirely swayed by marketing.

When it comes to technique, one merely has to look at the logistics of the company to consider whether each piece of candy is made by man or machine. The larger the company, the less likely it is that the candy is made on site or with equipment that is not automated. Making confectionery can be quite a skill, and a talented artisanal confectioner would have to be paid higher than the $10 an hour or so that a person behind the counter at your local franchise of most worldwide brands is making. A simple conversation with any such counter help verifies this almost immediately.

Smaller stores are more likely to do so, and most proprietors

Kate's Candy Bag

WHITMAN'S SAMPLER

Whitman's may be the most unhygienic candy marketed today. This isn't the fault of the company, which very likely ensures the highest quality candy made in the cleanest of conditions. No, lack of hygiene ensues when the chocolate gets into a family with five children, each with a different favorite chocolate, and each with no desire to read the reference card that determines the difference between a milk chocolate–covered peanut butter crunch or a chocolate-covered cherry. The result? A box of candy with bites taken out of several pieces—evidence of some child's quest for a toffee chip.

Candy Exchange Rate:
Whitman's Sampler = 3 York Peppermint Patties

are quite happy to boast about the candy being made in the back room.

So the question for many of these brands comes down to the quality of the chocolate. It is from this point that the chocolate world takes a weird and wild turn.

Trying to determine quality in any product is an exercise in obsession. Yes, taste is subjective, but quality is not. Regardless of the product, there are brands that are better than others. The trick is determining the characteristics of the product that separate the good from the bad, and the great from the good. But who gets to set the criteria on which items will be judged?

Oftentimes, we find in our consumer-driven society that those criteria are set by those who happen to make or sell those products. This, to me, sounds like a conflict of interest, but such is the state of our world.

This is what happened in the world of chocolate when French chocolatiers Valrhona, Bonnet, and others went about reimaging chocolate into an exclusive gourmet food, one that could only truly be enjoyed by sophisticates. The result, whether intentional or not, was the creation of a division of chocolate eaters, with the Hersheys and Cadburys of the worlds on one side and higher-end, more expensive chocolate on the other. The criteria used to differentiate one type of chocolate over the other came down to the following. Good chocolate was healthy; bad chocolate was not. Good chocolate was pure; bad chocolate was not. Good chocolate could be traced back to its plantation of origin; bad chocolate could not.

When it came to health claims, milk chocolate was already fighting a losing battle. Sugar, one of the primary ingredients of chocolate, was already known to be a problem ingredient when consumed in excess. Milk fat wasn't much better. The higher-end chocolates tended to push dark chocolate, made with no milk (and thus no milk fat). They could then make their dubious health claims, which were true, even if only slightly.

Soon, though, the concept of "purity" came into the picture. Now the high-end chocolate companies began competing against one another. Dark chocolate bars around the world began putting the percentage of chocolate mass on their labels. Dark chocolate percentages run from 50 percent to 85 percent in many instances, while milk chocolate only runs between 30 percent and 40 percent. Although percent was only supposed to indicate the amount of chocolate—supposedly providing a more intense chocolate taste to the consumer—consumers began using these figures as a means to compare quality. A dark chocolate bar that boasted an 85 percent chocolate mass meant that it was only 15 percent sugar or fat. Milk chocolate, with its chocolate mass of around 35 percent, meant that 65 percent was filled with sugar or fat. Therefore, the 85 percent dark chocolate bar was 50 percent more pure than the milk chocolate bar.

Of course, this interpretation was complete and utter nonsense. For one thing, sugar and milk fat play a distinct role in chocolate, including everything from stabilizing the solid bar to taking the edge off the bitterness of the chocolate mass—which, without sugar, would be very bitter indeed.

This hasn't stopped the makers of high-end chocolates from labeling their chocolates this way, and to this day, we see consumers interpreting that chocolate mass percentage as an indication of chocolate purity (which is true) and equating it to quality (which is not true). There can be, and are, poorly made "high-end" chocolate bars out there, and well-made, truly delicious milk chocolate bars.

Makers of high-end chocolate differentiate their product from the mass-produced product via the cocoa's point of origin, oftentimes identifying the plantation on which it was grown, and in some cases the field in which it was raised. Debates currently rage on the differences between Venezuelan and Ecuadorian cocoa. A quick look at the available high-end chocolate bars will show which countries are considered particularly high-end, including such areas of the world as South America, Madagascar, and Java. One area of the chocolate-growing world that is considered poorer in quality is West Africa, a region that, perhaps not coincidentally, is the same area of the world where the chocolate corporations get their chocolate.

The idea of this comes from the philosophy of *terroir*, a term coined in viniculture that has made its way into the vernacular of many other commodities. The idea is simple—the characteristics of any agrarian product are the result of the region in which it is grown. This idea, by itself, is a little controversial, as it does not account for the techniques used to raise the product. Many argue that those techniques are just as important as the region, if not more so. Alas, there is no quick-speak marketing term for growing techniques that result in a better-tasting product, so it's simply easier to imply that any cocoa grown in Venezuela is of better quality than any cocoa grown in the Ivory Coast.

Viniculture, itself an industry prone to the marketing of sophistication and classism, lends several terms to the "high-end" chocolate industry. These chocolates are said to have "perfumes" and "bouquets" rather than "aromas," they are sourced to grand cru or premier cru regions, and many brands sell cocoa "reserves," all with the intent of distancing their chocolate from a simple, one-dollar Nestlé bar.

Here's the thing: while I don't doubt that there are people out there who have the palate to discern the difference between a dark chocolate bar with 70 percent chocolate mass sourced from Madagascar, and one with 75 percent chocolate mass sourced from Ecuador, I posit that most people can't. They would rather have a good chocolate bar than a bad one, but beyond that, they simply don't have the time or the inclination to develop their palate to the level of sensitivity where they can discern which fermentation technique was used. But consumers don't want to appear like idiots either, and when the chocolate professionals tell them that a Hershey bar tastes like spoiled chocolate, they believe it, and then spend an excessive amount of money on their chocolate to demonstrate to their friends that they have a sophisticated chocolate palate. There are chocolatiers out there willing to take advantage of these people.

This sort of marketing peaked in 2004, when a chocolate company out of Texas by the name of Nōka Chocolate began marketing itself as a high-end chocolate company, selling its wares at an amount that equated to $2,000 a pound. Its cachet improved when it was pimped by the likes of Neiman Marcus and Dean & DeLuca and then landed sponsorships for the Golden Globe and Emmy Awards.

The problem, as a blogger at dallasfood.org figured out in 2006, was that Nōka wasn't doing anything all that special with its chocolate. That is to say, Nōka were buying bulk chocolate (called couveture) from one company, melting it down, and re-packing it as its own. This is what most chocolatiers do. However, it should be noted that the chocolate they were purchasing likely came from Chocolat Bonnat, a French chocolate manu-facturer that prices its high-end, single-origin chocolate any-where between $12 and $18 a pound.

This isn't to say that every chocolate maker is telling lies, or that chocolatiers will rob you blind if you aren't careful. But as with any product, there are people who wish to make high-quality products, and then there are people who will gladly take advantage of the ignorant.

So how does one avoid being taken advantage of by those in the chocolate world who lack scruples? As difficult as this is to advise, one simply has to take the time to sample many, many different chocolates in order to get a handle on one's likes and dislikes, and then find the companies that have the products that meet one's taste.

Here's what you do if you want to learn how to taste choco-late. Use your senses, take a moment to contemplate what your senses are experiencing, and then note what works for you and what doesn't. Oh, and don't compare milk chocolate to dark chocolate, and don't compare either of them to white chocolate, which isn't really chocolate, but rather a confection of sugar, cocoa butter, and milk solids.

That's it, really. It is *that* simple. When you look at a bar of chocolate, does it have a fine white film upon it? That shouldn't be there, and you should note it. Did the bite of your dark chocolate have a complementary berry taste hanging around on the finish? That's a positive characteristic, and you should note it. Did your milk chocolate bar smell of cardboard? Another negative. Note it.

Some of these negative characteristics are a result of poor shipping, handling, or stocking, and it is to one's benefit not to jump to conclusions after one sampling of a piece of chocolate. So, oh darn, you may want to search out a second serving purchased at another location.

The point here is to use your own senses, and not those of others, to tell you what you like or dislike. Hershey's is famous for having a somewhat sour aftertaste, yet millions of people keep buying the candy bars. There is something that draws people to them, perhaps its tradition, or perhaps it's a simple matter of taste. Regardless, a conclusion that is based on informed opinions is all that's needed to defend one's choices in candy. Nothing more.

And if you're worried about how "sophisticated" you may or may not be, remember the core definition of the word itself— sophistication is having a refined knowledge of the ways of the world cultivated especially through wide experience. Repeating somebody else's words when discussing food is not sophistication— it's parroting. And it is far less fun than actually going out and sampling the many delicious chocolates available to us.

There are many chocolatiers out there who thrive on this end of the chocolate world, and these are the companies that are a joy to visit. These are the companies that will try to steer you to the chocolates that represent the positive side of the business. These are the companies that are more likely to acknowledge that there is a negative side to the chocolate world. Theo's Chocolate, located in my home town of Seattle, is one of these good guys.

Theo's makes its own chocolate. It buys cocoa beans, cleans

them, roasts them, mills them, and makes chocolate with them. There are only a dozen or so companies in the United States that make chocolate. Everyone else? They buy their chocolate from somewhere or someone else and use that to make their truffles or chocolate-covered salted caramels.

While this makes Theo's unique, it isn't this fact that makes the company *better*. What makes Theo's better, arguably, is its attention to detail, and the intellectual rigor it has taken to determine what makes a candy bar "good."

Tara and I walked into Theo's flagship location in the Seattle neighborhood of Fremont, and looked around the showroom. Our intent was to take a tour of the factory and then spend a respectable amount of money on chocolate. This had been my modus operandi for Cadbury and Hershey, and I saw no reason to alter this approach. We paid our entrance fee for the tour, and I realized immediately that this tour would be different from the others. The reason? Our ticket in was a blue hairnet that the woman behind the counter gave to us along with our receipt. Unlike at Cadbury and Hershey, I was going to be in the room where they actually made and packaged the chocolate.

Also unlike Cadbury and Hershey, Theo's had no desire to shove as many people as it could through the tour in any given day. The tour was capped at 520 people *per week*, and with this limitation, one needed a reservation weeks in advance in order to get into the back rooms.

But, again, that isn't a fact that makes it better than other chocolate companies.

When the call was made for those who were going on the tour, a collection of about one dozen or so blue-hairnetted consumers wandered to the back of the store, where a similarly hairnetted young woman took charge of the group. With a disposition that could make clinically depressed people break into a smile, she laid out some of the tour ground rules (don't cross the marked line, keep your hairnet on, eat as much chocolate as we can provide you), she guided us into a back room filled with two dozen fold-out chairs. We sat down, and she proceeded with a fifteen-minute presentation.

The guide was energetic in her description of the discovery of chocolate and how the cocoa bean is made ready for chocolate makers such as Theo's. With no more than a few laminated photographs and some well-timed samples of chocolate that were shared around the room, Theo's Chocolate was able to convey more information about the chocolate in and of itself within that fifteen minutes than Hershey and Cadbury had been able to do in the hours I had spent at their respective locations. It didn't take long to understand that Hershey and Cadbury were more keen on selling *the idea* of Hershey and Cadbury, while Theo's was keen on selling chocolate.

The guide brought up Theo's commitment to fair trade, an idea in which the basic premise is to provide higher wages than are typically paid to producers as well as helping producers develop knowledge, skills, and resources to improve their lives. Or to put it another way, to ensure that everyone along the supply chain of any given commodity gets paid a living wage.

One would think that this should not be an issue in today's economy, especially when it comes to cocoa's role in the candy industry and especially considering the history that sugar has brought to the candy industry. But here at the beginning of the twenty-first century, there are not just reports of low wages being paid to the growers of cocoa, but in some instances throughout the world there is slavery, including that of children.

The worst of the child slavery appears to be occurring in the West African nation of Ivory Coast, which supplies the world with around 40 percent of the global output of cocoa beans. As Carol Off details in her 2006 book *Bitter Chocolate*, the Ivory Coast's leadership in the cocoa trade comes at a tragic cost. There are reports of child trafficking from the neighboring nation of Mali into the Ivory Coast and onto the plantations, where they are worked for twelve to fourteen hours every day for little to no pay, depending upon the plantation.

The problem is bigger than most people realize. According to a report written by the Payson Center for International Development and Technology Transfer of Tulane University, a total of 820,000 children worked in cocoa-related activities in the Ivory Coast during a twelve-month period between 2008 and 2009. These activities included everything from weeding and clearing grounds to applying pesticides and spreading fertilizer.

The charges of child trafficking and enforced servitude did not go unnoticed by the U.S. Congress. In 2001, Senator Tom Harkin and Representative Eliot Engel drafted the Harkin-Engel Protocol, also known as the Cocoa Protocol, the intent of which was to create an international agreement aimed at ending child labor in the production of cocoa. It was signed by eight members of what is now the Chocolate Council of the National Confectioners Association, consisting of representatives from Hershey, Mars, Nestlé, and several other chocolate manufacturers. The protocol has now sunsetted without realizing its goals. The final report states unequivocally that the chocolate industry's funding of various initiatives has "not been sufficient," it has "not enforced industry-wide standards" in regard to the issue of child labor in West Africa, and the competitive environment in which the chocolate industry operates "may make it impossible to effectively self-regulate." The report then asks the question that no one in the chocolate world has been able to answer: Is the chocolate industry able to self-regulate in the absence of enforceable, legal repercussions?

And as the Ivory Coast finds itself in the midst of a civil war, the problem of child labor and slavery has been made even more difficult. Suffice it to say, the issue is just as relevant today as it was in 2001.

In order to address this issue, Theo's has signed up with an independent auditing agency that verifies every aspect of chocolate production from bean to bar to point of sale. By going a different route, Theo's has been able to accomplish in five years what Mars, Archer Daniels Midland, and others who had signed the Harkin-Engel Protocol could not do in ten.

The tour guide continued her presentation. "In order to be defined as milk chocolate by the FDA, you only need three things—cocoa butter, milk, and not less than 10 percent by weight of chocolate liquor. Here at Theo, our minimum requirement for milk chocolate is no less than 45 percent chocolate liquor. At many other companies, our milk chocolate bar could be defined as dark chocolate."

The section in the FDA that spells out the definition of milk chocolate is the Code for Federal Regulations Title 21, Volume 2, Section 163.130. In 2007, a number of American chocolate industry groups lobbied the FDA for a change to the definition of chocolate. This change would have allowed cocoa butter to be replaced with vegetable oil and would have saved these mass-producing candy companies 70 percent in costs with regard to their ingredients.

The backlash from consumers was immense, with Hershey particularly feeling the brunt of this public relations disaster. When the FDA took requests for comments from the public, Web sites went up across the Internet, directing consumers to the FDA comment page. The FDA rejected the alteration to the standards, and the requirement for "cacao fat" (as it is defined in the Code for Federal Regulations) remains. However, this hasn't stopped Hershey from changing its ingredients. Mr. Goodbar used to be a milk chocolate bar with peanuts. Today, you'll find that the ingredient list includes sugar, peanuts, vegetable oil (cocoa butter, palm, shea, sunflower and/or safflower oil), chocolate, and nonfat milk taking up the majority of the ingredients. The bar no longer makes any claim of being milk chocolate.

And it's not just Hershey. Cadbury has been adding a percentage of vegetable fat to its chocolate for at least a generation. As far back as 1973, when Britain joined the European community and started to take advantage of the trade benefits, there has been a debate on what constitutes chocolate. To many continental Europeans, British chocolate with its vegetable fat was seen as less than authentic. Spain and Italy were taken to court when they restricted sales of British-made chocolate because of its vegetable fat content; they lost their case in 2003. Here we are, 500 years after Columbus accidentally ran into the cocoa bean, and 130 years after the invention of milk chocolate, and we cannot decide on a singular definition of what chocolate actually is.

I frowned, as my mind elaborated on that thought. Here we are in the twenty-first century, and we can't even ensure that children are not used in the cultivation of the cocoa bean.

Tara nudged me out of my thoughts and showed me a bowl of chocolate pieces to be sampled. This one, apparently, contained coconut. I gladly picked up a piece and placed it in my mouth, letting my body temperature melt the chocolate and coat my tongue. The taste was clean and, well, chocolatey. The coconut paired nicely with the chocolate, and a feeling of simple pleasure emanated from the taste. My body loved the taste, but my head was still considering the bitter images created by greed and profit.

As we stood up to tour the manufacturing areas, I thought a bit about where I was and how far I had veered from the original intent of this exploration of candy. As the guide talked about the destoner, my head was wrapped in thoughts about whether we need or desire sweets and what that difference means. As we were shown the bean roaster, I was considering the place of sugar and chocolate in our own culture here in the United States. As the guide pointed out the mills, I was contemplating the infantilization of candy, how this affects our perception of confections, and how it creates a dissonance between the ideal of confection that is created in our head versus the cold, stark reality of these commodities.

It wasn't long before I was handed another sample (a chocolate-enrobed marshmallow), which I mindlessly consumed and enjoyed. But I was still deep in contemplation. The lot of us were then guided into the room where Theo's chocolates are packaged. Tara and I headed back up to the showroom.

I looked about the showroom, and I noticed something peculiar. Of the twenty-five customers in the room, only four were children. And out of the adults, it appeared as if not a one was below the age of thirty. Granted, considering the thousands of customers who cross the threshold of Theo's each year, a sample size of twenty-five is rather poor.

I examined the room, wanting to look for more detail.

What I noticed was a room that was made for adults, filled with products that were made for adults. Finding a candy bar made with fig, fennel, and almond, or another one flavored with herbs and spices to make it taste akin to chai tea, made me realize that these were candies made for people like me.

"Huh," I said at this revelation.

For someone who had the intent of recreating that moment in my youth when candy was nearly the sole purpose of my life, this seemed an odd place to try fulfill that fantasy. This was a place designed for people who no longer wanted to indulge in sweets on an everyday basis. This was a place established so that when that moment of indulgence did arrive, one could do so and presume some measure of quality, some measure of goodness (as nebulous as those words may be). There were no clowns, no wacky names such as Curly Wurly or Marshmallow Peeps, no animatronic cows.

I looked at a clear piece of evidence that proved this. Before me were Theo bars that had been approved for sale by noted British primatologist and anthropologist Jane Goodall.

This is what it came down to. My childhood had Willy Wonka, a fictional character who wore colorful outfits and hung out with oompaloompas. My adulthood has Jane Goodall, who was a Dame Commander of the Order of the British Empire and hung out with chimpanzees.

A question popped into my mind. Is this what I was looking for? Did I want to reacquaint myself with my childhood innocence by purchasing single-origin chocolate at a place with soft track lighting and an eye for ethical production techniques?

I thought about this, as well as my recent trip and where it had taken me. There was Keynsham Factory, outside of Bristol, where the town's tie to chocolate history had been sold from beneath them. There was Hershey, where the company was looking for ways to extract itself from the high wages and high costs of chocolate production. Then there was the history of plunder, slavery, misapplication of candies as medicine, and the continuing subtext of class status throughout candy's history. None of these are childish topics.

But there were times when I felt as close to that innocent bliss I had been looking for as I have ever been. It didn't come from the eating or purchasing of candy, but the end result was the same. It came from the joy of experiencing the wanderlust associated with travel. And what is wanderlust but the feeling of bliss when experiencing the joy of the unknown? Isn't that what candy was to us when we were younger?

I scanned the room again and gave a begrudging smile. Sure, there were serious concerns that Theo was trying to address and, yes, even market. To some extent, the customers here were cognizant of this. But the smiles on their faces said something else. Sure, their logical, rational, adult minds were likely justifying their purchases as being part of an answer to several difficult questions. But emotionally? Emotionally the people milling about the several display cases were here because they wanted chocolate. Their "oooos" and "aaahhhs" when they pointed to a

 Kate's Candy Bag

THEO'S BIG DADDY MARSHMALLOW

Theo's goes out of its way to court the adult palate. There is nothing wrong with this, and its chai tea and coconut curry chocolates are quite good. As I write the names of these chocolates, my body is inclined to leave what I am doing and head for my local grocery store to seek these chocolates out.

However, they have one candy that brings out the child in me. That is their Big Daddy Marshmallow. It's little more than a marshmallow placed on a graham cracker and enrobed in chocolate. But it's made by someone who gives a damn. The marshmallow has a hint of caramel flavoring, and the chocolate is of the high-grade quality that Theo's is known for. The result? The candy bar I had searched the world for, and found almost in my own backyard.

Candy Exchange Rate:
1 Big Daddy Marshmallow = 4 York Peppermint Patties

caramel, their expressions of orgasmic bliss when tasting a sample of chocolate, belied their real desire. They wanted to satisfy some inner piece of themselves, much like I was trying to do. For one second, maybe two, the problems of the world, let alone the problems with the history of candy, mattered not at all. In that one instance, all that mattered was candy. The fact that Theo had taken the responsibility to address the very adult issues surrounding its products gave us more license to enjoy.

A realization hit. This was privilege, plain and simple. I felt no guilt in acknowledging this. Just a basic, simple understanding. For the first time since leaving for my journey, I felt calm. I felt not the innocence of childhood, but the rational understanding of where I stood in the world as an adult. We live in a world where bad stuff has happened, is happening now, and will happen in the future. Candy gives us an all too brief respite from that. Finding a candy company that works to ensure that this "bad stuff" isn't going to occur in its circle of influence is both a symbol of this privilege and an evolution of it.

Maybe that's all we can ask for. Innocence lost rarely can return, and the years of joy that the ignorance of childhood brings is a luxury that we, as adults, cannot afford. The best we can do is purchase a piece of candy, pop it into our mouth, and hope that somewhere in the minutes of consumption, we can find that one second where nothing else matters except the self and that joy that a sugar fix can bring.

I turned to Tara. "Let's get out of here. I think I found what I was looking for."

Acknowledgments

Let's face it, the Acknowledgments section of any given book is its oddest part. The section provides no information relevant to the subject or themes within. It can also come across as a bit sappy or sentimental. And every time I write one, I can't help but think of the overwrought acceptance speeches we hear at any given awards ceremony.

That said, there are a handful of people in my life you need to be aware of. For without their help and expertise, you would have either a far different book or no book at all. My thanks go out to Jon Malysiak, who helped set the book up. To Cybele May, whose hard work and dedication to candy inspires me every time I read her work. To David Lebovitz, who schlepped me around candy stores when it was 95 degrees out and I was bitching about my sprained ankle. To Dawn McGinty, who did the impossible by making Boston even better. To Andrea Winchester, who rode shotgun with me in Italy and gleefully participated (and initiated) deep, philosophical conversations on confection's place in the world.

To Stephanie Geels, who cleaned up my messes here in Seattle, and Daniela Rapp at St. Martin's Press in New York, who has kept me on the straight and narrow. Both of these women teach me something new every time we work together.

And finally, to Tara Chen, who plays the most valuable role in my life by giving me a home to come back to.

Bibliography

"Advertising News and Notes; Action on City Ad Plan Delayed,"
New York Times, September 25, 1937; www.nytimes.com.

Ayto, John. *The Diner's Dictionary: Food and Drink from A to Z.*
Oxford: Routledge, 1993.

Banyer, Henry. *Pharmacopoeia Pauperum, Or, the Hospital Dispensatory: Containing the Medicines Used in the Hospitals of London,
by the Direction of Dr. Coatsworth, Dr. Mead, Dr. Cade, Dr.
Wadsworth, Dr. Hales, &c. : with Suitable Instructions for Their
Common Use.* London: T. Warner, 1718; books.google.com.

Beach, Frederick C., and George E. Rines. *The Encyclopedia
Americana: A Universal Reference Library Comprising the Arts and
Sciences, Literature, History, Biography, Geography, Commerce,
Etc., of the World.* New York: Scientific American, 1903.

Benjamin, Sandra. *Sicily: Three Thousand Years of Human History.*
Hanover, NH: Steerforth Press, 2006.

Benzoni, Girolamo, and W. H. Smyth. *History of the New World:
Shewing His Travels in America from A.D. 1541 to 1556, with Some*

Particulars of the Island of Canary. Cambridge: Cambridge University Press, 2010.

Broekel, Ray. *The Great American Candy Bar Book.* Boston: Houghton Mifflin, 1982.

Brookes, R. *The General Dispensatory: Containing a Translation of the Pharmacopœias of the Royal Colleges of Physicians of London and Edinburgh.* London: J. Newbery, and W. Owen, 1753.

Bulletin of the North Carolina State Board of Health. Wilmington, NC: Secretary of the Board, 1888.

Capatti, Alberto, Massimo Montanari, and Áine O'Healy. *Italian Cuisine: A Cultural History. Arts and Traditions of the Table.* New York: Columbia University Press, 2003.

Carter, Susan, and Richard Sutch. " "Fixing the Facts: Editing of the 1880 U.S. Census of Occupations with Implications for Long-Term Labor Force Trends and the Sociology of Official Statistics." *Historical Methods* 29 (1996): 5–24.

A Century of Sugar Refining in the United States, 1816–1916. New York: De Vinne Press, 1916.

Chen, Joanne. *The Taste of Sweet: Our Complicated Love Affair with Our Favorite Treats.* New York: Crown Publishers, 2008.

Chipman, Leigh. *The World of Pharmacy and Pharmacists in Mamlūk Cairo.* Leiden: Brill, 2010.

Cidella, Julie L., and Heike C. Alberts. "Constructing Quality: The Multinational Histories of Chocolate." *Geoforum* 37, no. 6 (2006): 999–1007.

Coe, Sophie D., and Michael D. Coe. *The True History of Chocolate.* New York: Thames and Hudson, 2007.

Colquhoun, Kate. *Taste: The History of Britain Through Its Cooking.* New York: Bloomsbury, 2007.

Confectioners' and Bakers' Gazette, July 10, 1916, p. 16; and September 10, 1920, p. 20; catalog.hathitrust.org.

Craig, Lee A. *To Sow One Acre More: Childbearing and Farm Productivity in the Antebellum North.* Baltimore, MD: Johns Hopkins University Press, 1993.

Crane, Eva. *A Book of Honey.* New York: Scribner, 1980.

Davidson, Alan. *The Oxford Companion to Food.* Oxford: Oxford University Press, 1999.

D'Antonio, Michael. *Hershey: Milton S. Hershey's Extraordinary Life of Wealth, Empire, and Utopian Dreams.* New York: Simon & Schuster, 2006.

Day, Ivan. "The Art of Confectionery," in *The Pleasures of the Table,* Peter Brown and Ivan Day, eds. York, UK: York Civic Trust, 1997.

Defoe, Daniel. "The Complete English Tradesman," *Burt Franklin Research & Source Works Series* 445. New York: B. Franklin, 1970.

Depew, Chauncey M. *1795–1895. One Hundred Years of American Commerce: A History of the First Century of American Commerce by 100 Americans, Edited by Chauncey M. Depew.* New York: D. O. Haynes, 1895; books.google.com.

Deprez, Esmé E. "What Are the World's Most Popular Candies?" *Business Week,* June 24, 2009; businessweek.com.

Dickie, John. *Delizia! The Epic History of the Italians and Their Food.* New York: Free Press, 2008.

Doutre-Roussel, Chloé. *The Chocolate Connoisseur: For Everyone with a Passion for Chocolate.* New York: Jeremy P. Tarcher/ Penguin, 2006.

Dufour, Philippe S., Antonio Colmenero de Ledesma, and John Chamberlayne. *The Manner of Making of Coffee, Tea, and Chocolate: As It Is Used in Most Parts of Europe, Asia, Africa, and America, with Their Vertues.* London: William Crook, 1685.

"E.G. Winger Helps Stage Cleveland Sweetest Day Activities," *Midland Druggist and Pharmaceutical Review,* 55, no. 10 (1921).

Eigeland, Tor. "Arabs, Almonds, Sugar and Toledo," *Saudi Aramco World,* May-June 1996; www.saudiaramcoworld.com/issue/199603/arabs.almonds.sugar.and.toledo.htm.

Elliott, John Huxtable. *Empires of the Atlantic World: Britain and Spain in America, 1492–1830.* New Haven, CT: Yale University Press, 2006.

Farmer, Fannie M. *The Boston Cooking-School Cook Book.* Boston: Little, Brown, 1914.

Fritze, Ronald H. *New Worlds: The Great Voyages of Discovery, 1400–1600.* Stroud: Sutton, 2002.

Forbes, R. J. *Studies in Ancient Technology*, vol. 5. Leiden: Brill, 1966.

Fussell, G. E., and Hugh Platt. *Delightes for Ladies.* London: Lockwood, 1948.

Galloway, J. H. *The Sugar Cane Industry: An Historical Geography from Its Origins to 1914. Cambridge Studies in Historical Geography*, vol. 12. Cambridge: Cambridge University Press, 1989.

Glasse, Hannah, and Karen Hess. *The Art of Cookery Made Plain and Easy: Excelling Any Thing of the Kind Ever Yet Published.* Bedford, MA: Applewood Books, 1997.

Goldin, Claudia, and Kenneth Sokoloff. "Women, Children, and Industrialization in the Early Republic: Evidence from the Manufacturing Censuses." *Journal of Economic History* 42, no. 4 (1982): 741–774.

Gray, Samuel Frederick. *A Supplement to the Pharmacopoeia; Being a Treatise on Pharmacology in General, Including Not Only the Drugs and Compounds Which Are Used by Practitioners of Medicine, but Also Those Which Are Sold by Chemists, Druggists, and Herbalists, for Other Purposes. Together with a Collection of the Most Useful Medical Formulae, an Explanation of the Contractions Used by Physicians and Druggists, the Medical Arrangement of the Articles of the London Pharmacopoeia, with Their Doses at One View, a Similar List of the Indigenous Plants of the British Islands Which Are Capable of Being Used in Medicine.* London: Underwood, 1821; books.google.com.

Grivetti, Louis, and Howard-Yana Shapiro. *Chocolate: History, Culture, and Heritage.* Hoboken, NJ: Wiley, 2009.

Ibn Sayyār al-Warrāq, al-Muẓaffar ibn Naṣr, Nawal Nasrallah, Sahban Ahmad Muruwwa, and Kaj Öhrnberg. *Annals of the Caliph's Kitchen: Ibn Sayyar Al-Warraq's Tenth-Century Baghdadi Cookbook: English Translation with Introduction and Glossary.* Leyden: Brill, 2007.

Jackson, Peter. "How Did Quakers Conquer the British Sweet Shop?" BBC, April 4, 2010; news.bbc.co.uk/go/pr/fr/-/2/hi/uk_news/magazine/8467833.stm.

James, R. *Pharmacopoeia Universalis, Or, a New Universal English Dispensatory: With a Copious Index.* London: J. Hodges and J. Wood, 1747.

Jarrin, W. A. *The Italian Confectioner, Or, Complete Economy of Desserts: According to the Most Modern and Approved Practice.* London: Routledge, Warne, and Routledge, 1861.

The Journal of Mental Science, vol. 33. London: Association of Medical Officers of Asylums and Hospitals for the Insane, 1887. books.google.comc.

Kawash, Samira. "How Candy and Halloween Became Best Friends." *Atlantic* 21 (Oct 2010); www.theatlantic.com/life/archive/2010/10/how-candy-and-hallowcen-became-best-friends/64895/.

Kawash, Samira. "October's Original Candy Holiday? 'Candy Day.'" *Atlantic* 26 (Oct 2010); www.theatlantic.com/life/archive/2010/10/octobers-original-candy-holiday-candy-day/65125/.

Kiple, Kenneth F., and Kriemhild Coneè Ornelas. *The Cambridge World History of Food.* Cambridge, UK: Cambridge University Press, 2000.

Krondl, Michael. *The Taste of Conquest: The Rise and Fall of the Three Great Cities of Spice.* New York: Ballantine Books, 2007.

Lawall, Charles H. "Pharmaceutical Ethics." *American Journal of Pharmacy.* Philadelphia: Philadelphia College of Pharmacy and Science, 1922. Vol. 94, 172–191.

Lehmann, Gilly. *The British Housewife: Cookery Books, Cooking and Society in Eighteenth-Century Britain*. Totnes, UK: Prospect, 2003.

Levey, Martin. *Early Arabic Pharmacology: An Introduction Based on Ancient and Medieval Sources*. Leiden: Brill, 1973.

Levey, Martin, and Noury Al-Khaledy. *The Medical Formulary of Al-Samarqandi and the Relation of Early Arabic Simples to Those Found in the Indigenous Medicine of the Near East and India*. Philadelphia: University of Pennsylvania Press, 1967.

Levin, David. "Tour the Tongue," *Nova*. June 1, 2009; http://www.pbs.org/wgbh/nova/body/tongue-taste.html.

Lewis, William. *The New Dispensatory: Containing, I. The Elements of Pharmacy. II. The Materia Medica, III. The Preparations and Compositions of the New London and Edinburgh Pharmacopoeias*. London: Nourse, 1785.

Love, Ann, Jane Drake, and Claudia Dávila. *Sweet! The Delicious Story of Candy*. Toronto: Tundra Books, 2007.

Macinnis, Peter. *Bittersweet: The Story of Sugar*. St. Leonards, NSW: Allen & Unwin, 2002.

Mason, Laura. *Sweets and Sweet Shops*. Princes Risborough: Shire, UK, 1999.

Mason, Laura. *Sugar-Plums and Sherbet: The Prehistory of Sweets*. Totnes, UK: Prospect, 2004.

McDaniel, Ruel. "Four Tons of Candy Each Year," *Bulletin of Pharmacy* 36, no. 4 (1922): 161; http://books.google.com.

McGee, Harold. *On Food and Cooking: The Science and Lore of the Kitchen*. New York: Scribner, 2004.

McNeill, F. M. *The Scots Kitchen: Its Traditions and Lore, with Old-Time Recipes*. London: Blackie & Son, 1929.

Mercier, Jacques. *The Temptation of Chocolate*. Brussels, Belgium: Éditions Racine, 2008.

Mintz, Sidney W. *Sweetness and Power: The Place of Sugar in Modern History*. New York: Penguin Books, 1986.

Moss, Sarah, and Alexander Badenoch. *Chocolate: A Global History.* London: Reaktion Books, 2009.

Off, Carol. *Bitter Chocolate: The Dark Side of the World's Most Seductive Sweet.* New York: New Press, 2008.

Official Descriptive and Illustrated Catalogue of the Great Exhibition of the Works of Industry of All Nations, 1851. London: Spicer Bros, 1851; http://books.google.com.

Oversight of Public and Private Initiatives to Eliminate the Worst Forms of Child Labor in the Cocoa Sector in Cote D'Ivoire and Ghana. Payson Center for International Development at Tulane University, March 31, 2011; www.childlabor-payson.org/.

Oxford Symposium on Food & Cookery. *Spicing Up the Palate.* London: Prospect, 1992.

Paavilainen, Helena M. *Medieval Pharmacotherapy, Continuity and Change: Case Studies from Ibn Sīnā and Some of His Late Medieval Commentators.* Leiden: Brill, 2009.

The Penny Cyclopædia of the Society for the Diffusion of Useful Knowledge. London: Charles Knight, 1837.

Peters, Hermann. *Pictorial History of Ancient Pharmacy; With Sketches of Early Medical Practice.* Chicago: Engelhard, 1889.

R. G. *The Accomplish'd Female Instructor: Or, a Very Useful Companion for Ladies, Gentlewomen, and Others. In Two Parts.* London: James Knapton, 1704.

Richardson, Tim. *Sweets: A History of Candy.* New York: Bloomsbury, 2003.

Rines, George Edwin, and Frederick Converse Beach. *The Encyclopedia Americana. A Universal Reference Library Comprising the Arts and Sciences . . . Commerce, Etc., of the World.* New York: Scientific American, 1905.

Rodinson, Maxime, and A. J. Arberry. *Medieval Arab Cookery.* Devon, England: Prospect Books, 2001.

Ruscelli, Girolamo, and William Ward. *The Third and Last Part of the the Secretes of the Reuerend Maister Alexis of Piemont By Him*

Collected Out of Diuers Excellent Authors, with a Necessary Table in the Ende, Conteyning All the Matters Treated of in This Present Worke. Englished by William Ward. Imprinted at London: By Thomas Dawson, for Iohn Wyght, 1578.

"Six Druggists Discuss Candy," *Bulletin of Pharmacy* 24 (1910): 418–422.

Skuse, E. *Skuse's Complete Confectioner: A Practical Guide.* London: Kegan Paul, 2004.

Stolls, Eddy. "The Expansion of the Sugar Market in Western Europe," in *Tropical Babylons: Sugar and the Making of the Atlantic World, 1450–1680,* Stuart B. Schwartz, ed. Chapel Hill: University of North Carolina Press, 2004.

Tannahill, Reay. *Food in History.* New York: Stein and Day, 1973.

Untermeyer, Louis. *A Century of Candymaking.* Boston: Barta Press, 1947.

Wagner, Gillian. *The Chocolate Conscience.* London: Chatto & Windus, 1987.

Washington, Martha, and Karen Hess. *Martha Washington's Booke of Cookery and Booke of Sweetmeats.* New York: Columbia University Press, 1995.

Wilson, C. Anne. *Food and Drink in Britain: From the Stone Age to the 19th Century.* Chicago: Academy Chicago Publishers, 1991.

Wright, Clifford A. *Cucina Paradiso: The Heavenly Food of Sicily.* New York: Simon & Schuster, 1992.

Woloson, Wendy A. *Refined Tastes: Sugar, Confectionery, and Consumers in Nineteenth-Century America.* Baltimore: Johns Hopkins University Press, 2002.

Index